Did Nostradamus Foresee Hitler?

Quatrain II-24 eerily predicts Hitler's rise to power. It is among Nostradamus' most well-known and accurate prophecies.

> Beasts ferocious from hunger will swim across rivers:
> the greater part of the field will be against Hister.
> The great one will cause him to be dragged into an
> iron cage, when the child of Germany will observe
> nothing.

> *Bêtes farouches de faim fleuves tranner:*
> *Plus part du champ encontre Hister sera,*
> *En cage de fer le grand fera trainer,*
> *Quand rien enfant de Germain observera.*

This is one of the Seer's most amazing predictions because it identifies its twentieth century subject by name. "Hister" is, of course, Hitler with one letter changed, a common anagrammer's ploy in the 1500s. The Nazi "beasts," hungry for conquest, crossed most of Europe's rivers in their sweep across the continent. The meaning of the "iron cage" has been missed. It merely refers to the fact that Hitler was jailed during the administration of President Ebert ("the great one"). The majority of the field of European nations did oppose Hitler, who certainly observed no law or convention of decency.

Rating: 10

This is a real dazzler because of the name designation. Ister was an ancient name for the Danube, but the context indicates a person. Then, too, Hitler was born almost within sight of the Danube.

About the Author

More of a generalist than a specialist, R. W. Welch has engaged in a variety of enterprises. He was a radio newsman and talk show host in the Seattle area in the 1950s and '60s. He then served eighteen years as manager of governmental affairs and public affairs for a telecommunications company and became involved in local politics in the 1970s. A lifelong "history junkie," Mr. Welch was disappointed by the generally lackluster analyses found in other books on Nostradamus, and decided he could probably do better himself.

To Write to the Author

If you wish to contact the author or would like more information about this book, please write to the author in care of Llewellyn Worldwide, and we will forward your request. Both the author and publisher appreciate hearing from you. Llewellyn Worldwide cannot guarantee that every letter written to the author can be answered, but all will be forwarded. Please write to:

R. W. Welch
℅ Llewellyn Worldwide
P.O. Box 64383, 1-56718-816-7
St. Paul, MN 55164-0383, U.S.A.

Please enclose a self-addressed, stamped envelope for reply, or $1.00 to cover costs. If outside the U.S.A., enclose international postal reply coupon.

Many of Llewellyn's authors have websites with additional information and resources. For more information, please visit our website at
http://www.llewellyn.com

COMET

OF

NOSTRADAMUS

August 2004–

IMPACT!

R. W. Welch

2001
Llewellyn Worldwide
St. Paul, Minnesota 55164-0383

Comet of Nostradamus © 2000 by R. W. Welch. All rights reserved. No part of this book may be used or reproduced in any manner whatsoever, including Internet usage, without permission in writing from Llewellyn Publications except in the case of brief quotations embodied in critical articles and reviews.

FIRST EDITION
Second printing, 2001

Cover design: Anne-Marie Garrison
Cover illustration: Mark Mille/Mason Illustration
Map illustrations: Carrie Westfall
Editing and book design: Christine Snow

Library of Congress Cataloging-in-Publication Data

Welch, R. W., 1929–
    Comet of Nostradamus : August 2004–Impact! / R. W. Welch.– 1st ed.
      p. cm.
    Includes bibliographical references and index.
    ISBN 1-56718-816-7
    1. Nostradamus, 1503-1566. Prophâties. 2. Comets–Collisions with
Earth–Miscellanea. 3. Mediterranean Region–Miscellanea. 4. Prophecies
(Occultism) I. Title.

BF1815.N8 A269 2001
133.3–dc21   00-042325

Llewellyn Worldwide does not participate in, endorse, or have any authority or responsibility concerning private business transactions between our authors and the public.
    All mail addressed to the author is forwarded but the publisher cannot, unless specifically instructed by the author, give out an address or phone number.

Llewellyn Publications
A Division of Llewellyn Worldwide, Ltd.
P.O. Box 64383, Dept. 1-56718-816-7
St. Paul, MN 55164-0383
www.llewellyn.com

Printed in the United States of America

Contents

Author's Note

Since they were composed in the sixteenth century, Nostradamus' verses are not always easy reading for those familiar with modern French. Aside from the changes time has wrought to the language, the Seer had a habit of throwing in Latin and Greek words at random, not to mention dialectical French. He coined words whenever so inclined and, of course, made frequent use of anagrams. Beyond these quirks, Nostradamus' punctuation was wildly erratic, apparently following no particular rule or pattern. Over the years, most of these eccentricities have been overcome by translators, but there are still a number of words and phrases that remain uncertain. The quatrains were first published in France in 1555.

The interpretation of the Nostradamus prophecies hinges not only on a firm grasp of history but also on a cryptographic knack for the intricate symbolism and word games favored by the Seer. Of the many commentators on Nostradamus perhaps only one, Anatole Le Pelletier, fully commanded both of these aspects. But Le Pelletier wrote his *Les Oracles de Michel de Nostredame* in the 1860s and so was unable to relate the Seer's prophecies to the most eventful century in human history—the twentieth. To a substantial extent, all the subsequent books on Nostradamus have been efforts to update Le Pelletier—with mixed results. The degree to which this book may approach the standard established by the premier Nostradamus interpreter is for the reader to decide.

While applying the quatrains to historic events since 1555 is task enough, the great challenge to any commentator is, of course, to ascertain what they may portend for our own future. This we attempt in the first and second chapters of this work, which contain the Future Quatrains. Events to come will themselves be the judge of these efforts.

PROLOGUE

Incident at Salon

In the far south of France, in the year 1564, an arranged meeting took place between young Prince Henry of the little kingdom of Navarre and a bearded sage named Michel de Nostredame. Michel's steel-gray eyes fixed on the eleven-year-old for a long, suspenseful time whereupon several onlookers heard an improbable prophecy: The lad was destined to be king of all France.

Twenty-five chaotic years later, a fatally stabbed Henry III of France used his last breath to name Henry of Navarre as his successor. Still, France was then a mere rump kingdom, fragmented by religious warfare. It was only after a long campaign of many battles and diplomatic maneuvers that Navarre finally entered Paris as the acknowledged King of France, Henry IV, in 1594.

The prophecy in this story is no mere anecdote. It is thoroughly documented history.[1]

---

1. Pierre L'Estoile, *Memoires pour servir a l'historie de France*, 1718, Vol. II, p. 2.

INTRODUCTION

Except perhaps one or two biblical figures, there is no seer who can rank with Nostradamus, the sixteenth-century French physician whose major work was the *Centuries*.

While his style is willfully abstruse and many of his predictions remain undeciphered, many others have proved to be stunningly accurate. It is almost beyond argument that Nostradamus foresaw the French Revolution and the rise of Napoleon. The evidence is almost as strong that he perceived World War II four hundred years before it happened, as well as its major protagonists, notably Hitler and Mussolini. More recent events, too, such as the Persian Gulf War, even the Reagan and Clinton administrations, seem to have fallen with the ken of this seer extraordinaire.

As we start a new millennium, we cannot help but wonder what this medieval master might have glimpsed of our own near future. That is the question considered in the first section of this book. We discover that Nostradamus saw the years following 2000 as some of the most portentous in history, fraught with disruptions both cosmic and mundane, most of them missed by current commentators and analysts.

There are psychics and there are psychics, some far more gifted and more authentic than others. The weight given to Nostradamus' predictions for our times hinges on how accurate he has been in the past. So, in the second half of this opus I try to answer the question: "What percentage of Nostradamus' prophecies qualify as psychic hits?"

Despite his successes, there are those who insist that Nostradamus was but a clever guesser abetted by uncommonly good luck and vague phraseology. Such skepticism is understandable.

Aside from some predictions that are virtually unintelligible, there are others that seem at least partly erroneous unless they have been misinterpreted or misapplied.

Most serious students of Nostradamus allow that he must have had a certain degree of clairvoyance, but there remains a great deal of dispute on how much. Edgar Leoni, one of the most thorough researchers, displays a generally skeptical approach. Yet Le Pelletier and Erika Cheetham, no mean analysts either, are convinced that the seer had myriad authentic insights into the future. Few hold that Nostradamus was infallible.

The French mystic put his predictions into 942 rhymed verses called quatrains, arranged in groups of 100 (hence, the term "centuries") except that the seventh "century" has only forty-two quatrains. Over time, a little more than 20 percent of these quatrains have come to have widely accepted interpretations. That percentage scarcely qualifies as dazzling but, in reality, it very much understates the case.

To anyone with a fair grasp of history who is willing to do the research, it soon becomes clear that Nostradamus' batting average is much higher than .200. In fact, he is more like a .375 hitter with a startling number of home runs. Many perfectly correct quatrains have been overlooked or misapplied. It was with some surprise that I discovered at least 353 of the quatrains in the *Centuries* are clear hits, a figure that is far beyond the conceivable reach of ordinary foresight, or luck, or any combination thereof. The case is virtually self-evident, but it is made all the more obvious by comparing the fifty-eight forged "sixtains" (ca. 1605), which imitate the style of the *Centuries* (ca. 1555), but which do not remotely approach the quatrains in predictive accuracy. The same holds for the twenty-five dubious "late quatrains" that mysteriously surfaced between 1589 and 1605.

———————

The thought that it is possible for certain rare individuals to receive glimpses of things to come causes us great difficulty. It seems to imply that the future is predetermined and that free will is therefore an illusion. To most of us such an idea is inherently abhorrent; we instinctively rebel against it. Few of us find much appeal in the notion that we could be mere automatons in some prescripted cosmic play—and we do not really believe it.

There are not a lot of ways out of this dilemma. The simplest is that time is not quite the inescapable envelope we think it is and that a few gifted ones are sometimes capable of a kind of psychic time travel. Thus, free will still functions but the prophet perceives the end product of all willed choices before the choices are actually made.

My own preferred explication is that a true seer somehow tunes into the Universal Mind, which comprehends all events, circumstances, trends, and human motivations and, therefore, is able to anticipate the future to a considerable degree—and may itself influence that future in subtle, largely indiscernible ways without actually dictating it. In this concept, the flow of events can be seen as a fusion of human and divine wills. It thus slays the dragon of determinism while retaining an element of divine guidance.

Another hypothesis, favored by some, supposes that there may be multiple possible futures, any one of which might be tuned in by some gifted psychic, and occasionally one picks up on a future that actually comes to pass.

It may well be that a complete solution to the problem of prophecy is beyond the scope of human rationality. Whatever the explanation, there is substantial evidence that a tiny number of exceptional souls, such as Nostradamus, Isaiah, and Jeremiah, have possessed an odd intuitive sense of things to come though none has attained flawless accuracy.

An obvious question confronts the reader of Nostradamus: Why is his style so enigmatic? We would hardly be surprised if whatever emanations he perceived were unclear, but it is plain that the Seer goes out of his way to obfuscate his meaning. Some possible motives are readily apparent. First, many of his predictions had unpleasant implications for the nobility of his day. Second, the Inquisition suspected Nostradamus was flirting with witchcraft, so there seemed some safety in obscurity. Third, there is a kind of Heisenberg effect[1] in prophecy: By predicting the future one may effect it—a daunting prospect. On balance, circumstances favored a cautious approach.

Do not discount, either, that the formulation of ingenious riddles was one of the modish diversions of the sixteenth century. These intellectual games were in fact viewed as a measure of the cleverness of a man-of-letters.

In this work I have opted for strict translation of the original French even though the result may at times be somewhat awkward in English. Free translations of Nostradamus have too often devolved into fanciful interpretations as commentators stretched the quatrains to fit inapplicable events or situations. I have also tried to avoid the unwarranted flights of metaphorical speculation that have marred most previous analyses of the *Centuries*. The quatrains are remarkable enough in themselves without resorting to such special effects.

The objective here is not to stray off course in the direction of excessive credulity or excessive skepticism, but rather to present the quatrains for what they are: intriguing evidence that we do not yet know all there is to know about the innate powers of the mind.

---

1. Physicist Werner Heisenberg, known for his Uncertainty Principle, postulated that it is impossible to conduct observations of certain sub-atomic events without affecting those events.

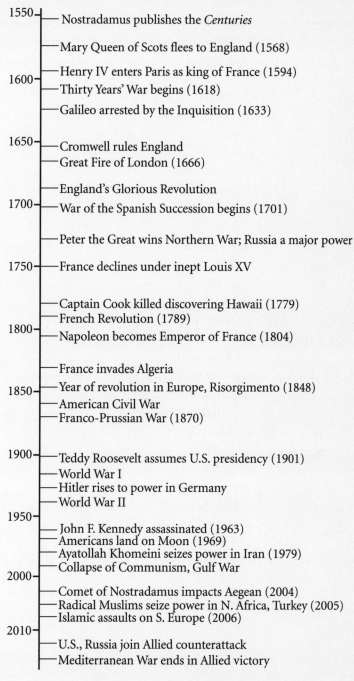

1550 — Nostradamus publishes the *Centuries*

— Mary Queen of Scots flees to England (1568)

— Henry IV enters Paris as king of France (1594)
1600 —
— Thirty Years' War begins (1618)

— Galileo arrested by the Inquisition (1633)

1650 —
— Cromwell rules England
— Great Fire of London (1666)

— England's Glorious Revolution
1700 —
— War of the Spanish Succession begins (1701)

— Peter the Great wins Northern War; Russia a major power

1750 —— France declines under inept Louis XV

— Captain Cook killed discovering Hawaii (1779)
— French Revolution (1789)
1800 —
— Napoleon becomes Emperor of France (1804)

— France invades Algeria
1850 —— Year of revolution in Europe, Risorgimento (1848)
— American Civil War
— Franco-Prussian War (1870)

1900 —— Teddy Roosevelt assumes U.S. presidency (1901)
— World War I
— Hitler rises to power in Germany
— World War II
1950 —
— John F. Kennedy assassinated (1963)
— Americans land on Moon (1969)
— Ayatollah Khomeini seizes power in Iran (1979)
— Collapse of Communism, Gulf War
2000 —
— Comet of Nostradamus impacts Aegean (2004)
— Radical Muslims seize power in N. Africa, Turkey (2005)
— Islamic assaults on S. Europe (2006)
2010 —
— U.S., Russia join Allied counterattack
— Mediterranean War ends in Allied victory

Timeline of Major Events predicted by Nostradamus

Chapter 1

THE COMET OF NOSTRADAMUS

Attempts to divine the meanings of Nostradamian quatrains before their fulfillment have not been notably successful. It has been done. For example, Le Pelletier clearly saw that Quatrain VIII-43 foretold the shattering fall of Napoleon III (see page 240). But the cryptic nature of most of the verses makes them easy to misinterpret. It is also true that prophetic pronouncements usually come clear only when we have reached a certain vantage point in time, when they can be seen to fit into a contemporary context. It is for the most part fruitless to try to decipher any quatrain that is set more than a few years into the future.

Even this short horizon can be tricky, as seen in the case of the dated Quatrain X-72:

The year 1999, seventh month, from heaven will come
a great King of terror: to bring back to life the great
King of Angolmois. Before and after Mars to reign by
good luck.

L'an mil neuf cent nonante neuf sept mois,
Du ciel viendra un grand Roi d'effrayeur:
Ressusciter le grand Roi d'Angolmois,
Avant aprés Mars regner par bonheur.

The verse was widely seen as a presage of an atomic missile strike, or a cataclysmic meteor collision with Earth in July 1999. This was most likely a failure on the part of the commentators and not the Seer.

The verse may easily refer to the birth of a future terrorist/tyrant since all souls, after all, originate in heaven. Nostradamus could have used the phrase "from heaven will come" simply to connote that this individual is to be an instrument of destiny, a figure in divine design. "Angolmois" may be an anagram for Mongols (as most think), or it could mean the French city of Angouleme. So this grim king might be either a new Genghis Khan or a new Charles IX, a scion of the house of Angouleme, who presided over the infamous St. Bartholomew's Day massacre of 1572. It will be some decades, then, before the accuracy of this quatrain can be determined.

Too much ominous significance was placed on Quatrain X-72 for an understandable reason: The date was so close to the year 2000. Though the end of the millennium held a natural fascination for people, it had no real portent in itself, i.e., it was just a round number, nothing more.

But those who saw the "king of terror" as an incoming bolide were not without some justification. The Jovian impact of the Shoemaker-Levy comet in 1994 alerted humanity to the danger, which has always been there, that comets pose to Earth. To anyone familiar with the *Centuries*, the crashing of comet fragments into Jupiter was like the ringing of a distant bell. Not only do many quatrains concern comets but several are remarkably specific when closely considered. They tell of a comet that will hurl itself into our planet and, further, they give the trajectory and the point of impact and the time: the middle of the year 2004 according to all the astrological signs.

The comet of Nostradamus will enter our atmosphere at a low angle near 48 degrees north. Its coma, or perhaps falling fragments, will scorch southern France and central Italy before the nucleus of the comet explodes just off the Aegean coast of Greece. The size of this space missile is uncertain, but it will be bigger than the Tunguska comet[1] that exploded over Siberia in 1908, flattening a thousand square kilometers of forest. The Tunguska comet did not alter the weather but, according to the quatrains, the comet of Nostradamus will, at least in the northern hemisphere. Dust and debris from the comet's explosion will linger in the atmosphere for many months, filtering out sunlight and ruining many crops.

But the impact of the comet does not end there. Its effects so weaken Greece that the country poses an easy target for Islamic radicals who, aided by Iran, seize control of Turkey. Aggression against Greece triggers a spreading war that ultimately engulfs most of the countries of the Mediterranean and beyond. This great conflict is well described by Nostradamus and is detailed in chapter 2 of this book, "The War Years."

First, a look at the quatrains dealing specifically with the comet of Nostradamus.

Future Quatrain I-46: The Comet Over France

> Very near Auch, Lectoure, and Mirande great fire will
> fall from the sky for three nights. A most stupendous
> and astonishing event will occur. Very soon afterwards
> the earth will tremble.

> *Tout aupres d'Aux, de Lectore et Mirande*
> *Grand feu de ciel en trois nuits tombera:*
> *Cause aviendra bien stupende et mirande:*
> *Bien peu après la terre tremblera.*

---

1. Some scientists favor the theory that the Tunguska event was actually a meteorite. But the distinction between comets and meteors has become increasingly fuzzy.

Here the Seer advises of the approach of a great comet. It will pass low over southern France, raining debris on the Earth below for three nights. But the nucleus of the comet is headed for the Aegean area after flashing directly over Rome (as seen in later quatrains). Though the comet's coma will inflict damage on France, much worse is to befall the Greeks. The trembling of the earth obviously refers to the impact of the comet's head, which will be the energy equivalent to hundreds or thousands of nuclear bombs.

Future Quatrain II-3: Impact in the Aegean

> Because of the solar heat on the sea of Euboea the fishes
> half cooked. The inhabitants will come to cut them
> when Rhodes and Genoa will fail them the biscuit.

> *Pour la chaleur solaire sus la mer*
> *De Negrepont les poissons demi cuits:*
> *Les habitants les viendront entamer*
> *Quand Rhod. et Gennes leur faudra le biscuit.*

The solar heat is often interpreted as a nuclear blast but the inhabitants would hardly eat radioactive fish. The only other feasible source for this extreme heat would be a comet or meteor striking off the shores of the Greek island of Euboea.[2] Various quatrains point to a comet. Damage from shockwaves, tidal waves, and debris would, of course, be horrendous. The Euboeans evidently have to eat the fish when disaster relief expected from Rhodes and Genoa fails to arrive on time.

---

2. Meteors are essentially space rocks. The solid nucleus of a comet is less dense but vastly larger, up to 100 kilometers in diameter. A collision of either one with the Earth means a colossal explosion and enormous heat.

Future Quatrain II-41: The Pope Flees

The great star will burn for seven days; the swarm will cause two suns to appear. The big mastiff will howl all night when the great pontiff will change country.

La grande étoile par sept jours brûlera,
Nuée fera deux soleils apparoir:
Le gros mâtin toute nuit hurlera
Quand grand pontife changera de terroir.

The comet of Nostradamus ("great star") will light up the skies for a week before it strikes Earth. To avoid the approaching calamity, the pope will flee the Vatican. Concern for the pope's safety would be well justified because a straight line drawn from southern France, where the comet's effects are first noted (Quatrain I-46, page 3), to the Aegean, goes right over Rome. Equally striking is the Seer's use of the word "swarm," because that is just what a comet is: a swarm of matter. As it nears the Earth, the comet will be comparable in brightness to the sun. The "big mastiff" could have some abstract meaning, but it might also be straightforward, i.e., this pope will own a large pet guard dog.

Future Quatrain II-43: The Earth and Peace Shattered

During the appearance of the bearded star the three great princes will be made enemies (i.e., of France). Struck from the sky, peace and earth quaking. Po, Tiber overflowing; serpent placed on the shore.

Durant l'etoile chevelue apparente,
Les trois grands princes seront faits ennemies:
Frappés du ciel, paix terre tremulente,
Pau, Tymbre undans, serent sur le bord mis.

There is a strong link in the quatrains between the advent of Nostradamus' comet ("bearded star") and war in the Mediterranean. The comet's effects on Italy and Greece weaken them so that they are vulnerable to attack. The serpent on the shore is the prophet's figure for a

Muslim invasion of Italy, a theme of several quatrains in this chapter and the next. All the chronological indicators for the war point to early in the new millennium (as in Future Quatrain II-46, below). The "three great princes" are three leaders (specified in chapter 2) who lead resurgent Islam against southern Europe. This verse and others predict the comet will affect the weather, provoking heavy rains and flooding rivers.

Future Quatrain II-46: More Trouble Ahead

> After great trouble for humanity, a greater one is
> prepared. The Great Mover renews the centuries: rain,
> blood, milk, famine, steel, and plague. In the heavens
> a long spark running.

> *Apres grand trouble humain, plus grand s'apprete*
> *Le grand moteur les siecles renouvele:*
> *Pluie, sang, lait, famine, fer et peste,*
> *Au ciel vu feu, courant longue etincelle.*

This is a key verse that provides the first definitive clue on the arrival time of Nostradamus' comet. The "long spark running" is obviously a comet and the renewal of "the centuries" can only mean the start of a new millennium. In other words, the time frame is within a few years of 2001, the first year of the impending new millennium. The twentieth century with its two world wars and the Cold War certainly qualifies as a time of "great trouble for humanity." But the coming of the comet heralds still another wave of misfortune, not only the blast impact of the comet itself, but a new burst of armed conflict in its wake. (The Seer often used the combination of blood and milk as a symbol of calamity.)

Future Quatrain II-81: Fire and Flood

Through fire from the sky the city almost burned.
The Urn threatens Deucalion again: Sardinia vexed
by the Punic foist after Libra will leave her Phaeton.

Par feu du ciel la cité presque aduste:
L'Urne menace encore Deucalion:
Vexée Sardaigne par la Punique fuste,
Après que Libra lairra son Phaeton.

Deucalion being a Greek survivor of a great flood, it is apparent from this verse that the comet of Nostradamus ("fire from the sky") will strike in the sea off Greece causing horrific tidal waves and flooding. The "city almost burned" is most likely Athens itself, which the comet will only narrowly miss. The second part of the verse again foresees a Mediterranean war on the heels of the comet with a North African fleet ("Punic foist") attacking Sardinia. The attack will be in late October after the sun sign Libra. ("Phaeton" is merely poesy for the sun.)

Future Quatrain II-96: Fire and War

A burning torch will be seen in the sky at night near
the end and the beginning of the Rhône: Famine,
sword; relief provided too late. Persia turns to invade
Macedonia (northern Greece).

Flambeau ardent au ciel soir sera vu
Pres de la fin et principe du Rosne:
Famine, glaive: tard le secours pourvu,
La Perse tourne envahir Macedoine.

The passage of Nostradamus' comet over southern France just before its impact in the Aegean is seen by Frenchmen from one end of the Rhône River to the other. Once more the comet is tied to military action in the Mediterranean area with Persia (Iran) specifically identified as one of the Islamic aggressors. An Iranian assault on Greece clearly implies that the fundamentalist Muslims have by this time taken over Turkey and allied it with Iran—an event predicted in other verses. The relief that comes too late ties in nicely with Future Quatrain II-3, page 4.

Future Quatrain IV-58: Italy's Tribulation

> To swallow the burning sun in the throat, the
> Etruscan land washed by human blood. The chief, pail
> of water, to lead his son away. Captive lady conducted
> into Turkish land.

> *Soleil ardent dans le gosier coller,*
> *De sang humain arroser terre Etrusque:*
> *Chef seille d'eau, mener son fils filer,*
> *Captive dame conduite en terre Turque.*

This verse is often scoffed at by critics of Nostradamus as making absolutely no sense, but it is really not that difficult. The first line describes the passage of Nostradamus' comet over central Italy ("Etruscan land"). The air will be so hot that it burns peoples' throats as they breathe. Most likely, crops will be scorched. The rest of the verse concerns the subsequent invasion of Italy by Muslim forces. An Italian leader, using a "pail of water," rescues his son from the fires of the invasion. However, an Italian woman of some distinction is captured by the invaders and held in Turkey.

Future Quatrain V-32: Impending Destruction

> Where all is good, the Sun all beneficial and the Moon
> is abundant, its ruin approaches. From the sky it
> advances to change your fortune. In the same country
> as the seventh rock.

Où tout bon est, tout bien Soleil et Lune
Est abondant, sa ruine s'approche:
Du ciel s'avance varier ta fortune,
En meme etat que la septieme roche.

The verse opens with an excellent description of sunny Greece as the great comet nears the Earth and the Aegean area. Obviously, this intruder from space will seriously alter the fortunes of the Greek nation, causing intense heat and extensive blast damage and the flooding of shorelines. The "seventh rock" reinforces the fact that Nostradamus is talking about Greece here. He is referring to the Seven Ionian Isles, the smallest of which, Paxos, is indeed not much more than a limestone rock.

Future Quatrain V-90: Woe to the Isles of Greece

In the Cyclades, in Perinthus and Larissa, in Sparta
and the entire Peloponnesus: very great famine,
plague through false dust. Nine months will it last and
throughout the Chersonese (Gallopoli Peninsula).

Dans les cyclades, en perinthe et larisse,
Dedans Sparte tout le Pelopnnesse:
Si grande famine, peste par faux connisse,
Neuf mois tiendra et tout le chersonese.

This is a particularly intriguing quatrain since comets are made up in part of carbon dust ("false dust"). Upon the explosion of Nostradamus' comet, most of Greece and European Turkey ("Perinthus," "Chersonese") will be covered with this "false dust," which will ruin crops that are also damaged by the comet's heat, contributing to the severe food shortages. The comet's effect on food production lingers for nine full months. The verse indicates that disease will follow in the wake of the famine, as it often does.

Future Quatrain V-98: First Effects

> At the forty-eighth climacteric degree, at the end of
> Cancer, very great dryness: Fish in the sea, river and
> lake cooked hectic. Bearn, Bigorre in danger through
> fire from the sky.

> *A quarente-huit degré climacterique,*
> *A fin de Cancer si grande secheresse:*
> *Poisson en mer, fleuv, lac cuit hectique,*
> *Bearn, Bigorre par feu ciel en detresse.*

At first this verse seems mildly at variance with others specifying that Nostradamus' comet approaches circa the forty-fifth parallel (south France) and strikes during Leo, the sign following Cancer. But it is clear from the trajectory of the comet that it does not hit Earth directly, but is captured by its gravity, circling our planet before impact. On its first pass, around July 22, the white hot comet grazes and scorches the Earth at latitude 48 degrees north. Since a coastal area (*mer*) is indicated, one of only four areas would be involved: Newfoundland, Brittany, Sakhalin, or western Washington State. On its final approach, the comet damages the south of France (which event is calculated in advance by astronomers).

Future Quatrain VI-5: A Rain of Terror

> Very great famine through pestiferous wave, through
> long rain the length of the arctic pole. "Samarobryn"
> one hundred leagues from the hemisphere, they will
> live without law exempt from politics.

> *Si grande famine par onde pestifere,*
> *Par pluie longue le long du pole arctique:*
> *Samarobryn cent lieues de l'hemisphere,*
> *Vivront sans loi exempt de politique.*

The dust cloud from the explosion of Nostradamus' comet will have grievous effects throughout the Northern Hemisphere ("the length of the arctic pole"). The burst spews vast areas with carbon dust, precipitating heavy carbon-laden rains and attendant crop failures. The second half of the verse is fascinating since it seems to describe a space station—the only thing that would be located a hundred leagues (ca. 300 miles) from the hemisphere. "Samarobryn" is some sort of coded designation, maybe an acronym. This space vehicle—no doubt Russo-American[3]—is in orbit when the comet hits. The occupants, of course, would be insulated from earthly politics.

Future Quatrain VI-6: Something Wicked in the Sky

> There will appear towards the North not far from
> Cancer, the bearded star: Susa, Siena, Boeotia, Ertria.
> The great one of Rome will die, the night over.
>
> *Apparaitra vers le Septentrion*
> *Non loin de Cancer l'etoile chevelue*
> *Suze, Sienne, Boece, Eretrion,*
> *Mourra de Rome grand, la nuit disparue.*

The comet of Nostradamus will first be spotted near the constellation Cancer, or just before the advent of the astrological sign of Cancer, which begins on June 22. The latter interpretation fits with Future Quatrain V-98, page 10, but either or both might be correct. The locales mentioned are in northern Italy and Greece, all of them on the final approach path of the comet. The "great one of Rome" is probably not the pope since he leaves the city as the comet approaches (Future Quatrain II-41, page 5). Evidently, the Italian president or the prime minister refuses to flee the capital and is killed—probably in a fire caused by the passing comet, though falling debris is also a possibility.

---

3. Such a space venture is actually under construction as of this writing, orbiting near the very altitude predicted here.

Future Quatrain VI-97: A Fiery Neapolitan Sky

At forty-five degrees the sky will burn. Fire to
approach the great new city: In an instant a great scattered flame will leap up, when one will want to get
evidence from the Normans.

Cinq et quarante degrés ciel brulera,
Feu approcher de la grande cité neuve:
Instant grande flamme eparse sautera,
Quand on voudra des Normans faire preuve.

Like a number of other verses, this one recounts the passage of
Nostradamus' comet over southern France at about 45 degrees north.
In the quatrains, the new city is usually Naples, originally Neapolis
(literally, "new city"), located close to the comet's path. It is not clear
whether Naples is badly damaged. The great leaping flame is simply
the explosion of the comet on impact or just before impact as in the
1908 Siberian comet blast. The last line is obscure from our present
vantage, but it may be that French (Norman) astronomers will be the
first to calculate where the comet will strike. A Greek president would
want their data turned over to his scientists, posthaste.

Future Quatrain VIII-2: A Chronological Marker

Condom and Auch and around Mirande, I see fire
from the sky encompassing them. Sun and Mars conjoined in Leo, then lightning at Marmande: great hail,
wall falls into the Garonne.

Condon et Aux et autour de Mirande,
Je vois du ciel feu qui les environne:
So Mars conjoint au Lion, puis Marmande
Foudre, grande grele, mur tombe dans Garonne.

The quatrain reiterates that the comet's coma will envelop towns in
southern France but adds a key astrological parameter. The sun and
Mars conjoin in Leo in August of the years 2000, 2002, and 2004, all

close enough to the dawn of the new millennium (2001) to fit the parameter of Future Quatrain II-46, page 6. (The conjunction does not occur again until 2015.) Of these three possible years, Future Quatrain III-3, below, clearly isolates the one that marks the comet's arrival.

Here, the hail falling in August points to severe climatic disruptions fostered by the comet, including heavy rains that flood the Garonne, collapsing a wall at Marmande.

Future Quatrain III-3: An Arrow to 2004

> Mars and Mercury, and the silver (moon) joined
> together, towards the midi (south France) extreme
> dryness. In the bed of Asia one will say the earth
> trembles; Corinth, and Ephesus then in perplexity.

> *Mars et Mercure, et l'argent joint ensemble,*
> *Vers le midi extreme siccité:*
> *Au fond d'Asie on dira terre tremble,*
> *Corinthe, Ephese lors en perplexité.*

As already seen, the comet of Nostradamus strikes home in the Aegean between Corinth and Ephesus. The dryness refers to the heat effect of the comet as it passes over southern France. The trembling of the earth hints at more than just the explosion of the comet; its impact evidently triggers an earthquake, likely in quake-prone Turkey. Most significant though, the astronomical alignment in this verse occurs in only one of the three years prescribed by Future Quatrain VIII-2, page 12—about August 19, 2004. This then is the designated year of the cataclysm.

Future Quatrain VIII-16: Tidal Wave!

> At the place where Jason had his ship built, there will
> be a flood so great and so sudden that one will have
> no place to fall upon. The waves to mount Olympian
> "Fesula."

Au lieu que HIESON fait sa nef fabriquer,
Si grand déluge sera et si subite,
Qu'on n'aura lieu ni terre s'attaquer,
L'onde monter Fesulan Olympique.

The Greek legendary hero, Jason, had his ship built just north of the island of Euboea at Iolcus on the Gulf of Vólos, the very area where Nostradamus says the millennial comet will impact. So the verse is forecasting that a colossal tidal wave will be generated by the comet's explosion, flooding the nearby plain. *Fesulan* is evidently modern-day Farsala, which is a full twenty miles inland from the gulf, so the magnitude of the destructive wave will be far greater than any in recorded history. The verse leaves little question that this comet will be many times the size of the one that hit Siberia in 1908.

Future Quatrain IX-91: A Plague from Above

The horrible plague will fall upon Perinthus and Nicopolis, the Peninsula and Macedonia. It will devastate Thessaly and Amphipolis. An unknown evil, and from Anthony a refusal.

L'horrible peste Perynte et Nicopolle,
Le Chersonese tiendra et Marceloyne:
La Thessalie vastera l'Amphipolle
Mal inconnu, et le refus d'Anthoine.

The locales are all Grecian except Perinthus (*Eski Eregli* in Turkish), very near Greece in European Turkey. The plague that falls upon these places is the debris and carbon dust from the exploding millennial comet. The event is termed an "unknown evil" because nothing like it has been experienced before. The reference to Anthony is not yet discernable to us. Most likely, it involves a west European official who fails to respond to a Greek plea connected with the comet or the subsequent Mediterranean War (perhaps England's Prime Minister Tony Blair?).

Chapter 2

THE WAR YEARS

E ven more grievous than the physical impact of Nostradamus' comet is the fact that it unleashes the
dogs of war in the Mediterranean. The havoc spread
by the comet in Greece is seen by the radicalized
Arabs, Turks, and Iranians as literally a heaven-sent
opportunity to "liberate" the Muslim minorities of the
Balkans and acquire territory. The notion of "holy
war" for Allah is basic to fundamentalist Islam.

The move against Greece triggers a response from
Italy that in turn is assaulted by the Islamic powers.
Spain and France and finally Russia come into the
conflict and the battle begins to turn against the Muslim bloc.

The United States is involved but does not take the
leading role in the struggle, evidently because the
nation is torn by severe internal strife at the time
(Future Quatrain X-81, page 32).

The war plot line prophesied by Nostradamus is remarkably coherent and, in light of today's Middle East situation, completely logical. The geopolitics and the predicted military moves on all sides make perfect sense five centuries after the quatrains were composed.

For the most part, the Mediterranean War verses are offered in their numerical order even though this is not necessarily chronological. However, the last twelve verses clearly apply to the late climactic stages of the war and are presented separately.

Some verses concerning the Mediterranean War seem more likely than others from our present vantage point, so each is given a probability rating—a rough estimate of feasibility. Bear in mind that Nostradamus did not regard all future events as immutably fixed even if some are very nearly so. That he subscribed to the notion of a free will factor is evinced by some predictions that take the form of warnings: Avoid A or B will surely follow.

If the Seer did not perceive a frozen future he must have known that some of his prophecies would not come true—another reason, perhaps, why the quatrains tend toward obscurity. More importantly though, if there is this malleability then consideration of the Nostradamus auguries could help us to avoid some of the very negative events that he forecasts.

Future Quatrain I-40: Madness in Istanbul

> The false trumpet concealing madness will bear Byzantium (Istanbul) a change of laws: From Egypt one will go forth one who wants withdrawal of edicts altering monies and standards.

> *La trompe fausses dissimulant folie*
> *Fera Bisance un changement de loi:*
> *Ira d'Egypte qui veut que l'on delie*
> *Edit changeant monnaies et alois.*

This and a number of other quatrains forecast a revolutionary change in Turkey, almost certainly a militant Muslim coup. The "false trumpet" and "madness" are very apt terms for Islamic fundamentalism.

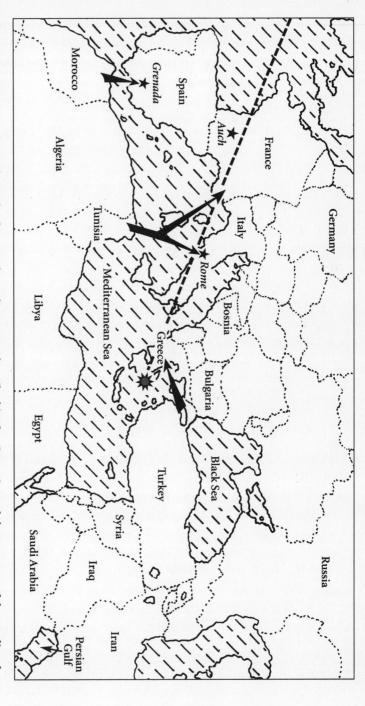

Figure 2.1: This map shows the path of Nostradamus' comet as described in the *Centuries* and the progress of the predicted Mediterranean War. The low trajectory (dotted line) suggests that the comet will be captured by Earth's gravity and will circle the planet one or more times before impact. The arrows show the direction of the main Islamic military thrusts against southern Europe.

Apparently, the moderate Egyptian government will be justifiably alarmed by the developments in Turkey and will send a representative to admonish the Turks against revolutionary excesses, both economic and social.

Probability rating: 60%
Bordering as it does on Iran and having a large Shiite population, Turkey is vulnerable to fundamentalist influences. Actually, fatal rioting erupted between moderate and radical Turk Muslim factions in March of 1995, and fundamentalists now constitute the largest political party in the country.

Future Quatrain II-30: A New Hannibal

> One whom the infernal gods of Hannibal will cause to
> be reborn, terror of mankind: never more horror nor
> worse days in the past than will come to the Romans
> through Babel.

> *Un qui les dieux d'Annibal infernaux*
> *Fera renaitre, effrayeur des humains*
> *Once plus d'horror ni plus pire journaux*
> *Qu'avint viendra par Babel aux Romains.*

This verse jibes with others that forecast a resurgence of militant Islam. "Babel" (present-day Iraq) is a classic anti-Christian symbol representing the conglomerate of Islamic nations that will combine to war against Euro-Mediterranean lands as forecast in Future Quatrains III-64, V-27, VIII-78, and others. The reference to the Carthaginian conqueror, Hannibal, implies that a militarist ruler from North Africa—Algeria, Tunis, or Libya—will be involved in the Muslim coalition and will lead an attack on Rome itself when Italy is involved in the conflict. Whether the assault will be a raid or a full-scale invasion is not clear, but the havoc and destruction will be extensive.

Probability rating: 40%

Such a stroke would be an audacious one, even for a radical Muslim, but it is by no means out of the question, especially if Italy is severely disrupted by the millennial comet.

Future Quatrain III-60: A Takeover in Turkey

> Throughout all Asia (Minor) great proscription, even
> in Mysia, Lycia, and Pamphilia. Blood will be shed
> because of the absolution of an evil young king filled
> with felony.

> *Par toute Asia grande proscription,*
> *Même en Mysie, Lysie, et Pamphilie.*
> *Sang versera par absolution*
> *D'un jeune noir rempli de félonie.*

Since the cities named are all in Asia Minor, the term "Asia" is being used in the classical sense, that is, modern Turkey. "Great proscription" is a hallmark of fundamentalist Islamic regimes, as is bloodshed, so the thrust of the verse surely concerns a militant Islamic coup in Turkey. The leader of this movement will be comparatively young and will have been pardoned from some previous offense ("absolution") before seizing power.

Probability rating: 60%

One of the strongest motifs in the *Centuries* deals with a resurgence of militant Islam, which we are beginning to see today. It may be that the comet itself is what triggers the radical takeover in Turkey, because the fundamentalists see the comet as a portent of Allah's displeasure with the secular government. Or perhaps the government fails to deal effectively with the impact of the comet on Turkey's western shores.

Future Quatrain III-64: A Fleet Sails Against Islam

> The chief of Persia (Iran) will engage great Olchades
> (Spain). The trireme fleet against the Mahometan
> people from Parthia and Media, and the Cyclades
> pillaged: long rest at the great Ionian port.

> *Le chef de Perse remplira grande Olchades,*
> *Classe trireme contre gens Mahometiques*
> *De Parthe, et Mede: et pillar les Cyclades:*
> *Repos longtemps au grand port Ionique.*

This verse introduces the theme of a fundamentalist Muslim attack on Greece, no doubt from a radicalized Turkey, and also indicates Spanish involvement in the conflict (see Future Quatrain V-55, page 25). The leader of the Islamic alliance will be Iran ("Parthia and Media") significantly, the main extremist Islamic power of the present day. The Muslim thrust provokes a naval response from the West and an armada sails east to Aegean waters. The Greek Cyclades Islands are to be the scene of major battles, after which the Western fleet pauses to regroup and refit at an Ionian Sea port.

Probability rating: 50%
This is an arresting prophecy since it has only moved into the realm of feasibility since the advent of the Khomeini revolution in Iran. The verse ties in with Future Quatrain III-90, below.

Future Quatrain III-90: A Persian Tiger

> The great Satyr and Tiger of Hyrcania presents a gift to
> those of the Ocean: A fleet's chief will set out from Car-
> mania, one who will take land at the Tyrren Phocaean.

> *Le grand Satyre et Tigre de Hyrcanie*
> *Don presenté à ceux de l'Ocean:*
> *Un chef de classe ira de Carmanie,*
> *Qui prendra terre au Tyrren Phocean.*

There is more detail here on the predicted war of resurgent Islam against Greece. A fierce leader from northern Iran ("Hyrcania") will build up the Iranian navy ("gift to those of the ocean"). Then, an Iranian fleet will sail from the Persian Gulf ("Carmania") through Suez to the Mediterranean—probably to assist the Turkish assault on Greece. This fleet anchors just north of Izmir at the town of Foca, which was founded by Genoans (Tyrrenians) near the site of the ancient Aegean city of Phocaea.

Probability rating: 60%

It is already obvious that Iran is intent on becoming a major power. Its naval build-up is actually already underway and a fleet moving into the Mediterranean via the Suez is easily feasible. (Note that there was no Suez Canal when this verse was written.)

Future Quatrain III-94: A Prophecy on the Prophecies

> For five hundred years more one will keep count of
> him who was the ornament of his time: Then sudden-
> ly great light will he give, he who for this century will
> render them very satisfied.

> *De cinq cents ans plus compte l'on tiendra*
> *Celui qu'etait l'ornement de son temps:*
> *Puis à un coup grande clarté donra*
> *Qui par ce siecle les rendra trés contents.*

Almost without question the Seer is talking about himself in this quatrain. He is saying that while his own century will be satisfied with his works, his greatest fame will come five centuries later, i.e., in the twenty-first century. He may have been right. Nostradamus has never been more popular than he is now, and his reputation should continue to grow, if and as more of his prophecies are fulfilled. The Seer could also be referring to some spectacularly successful prediction or predictions that come true in the twenty-first century or to some interpretation of his works that result in a great burst of recognition.

Probability rating: 65%
Based on the Seer's previous track record, it seems more likely than not that his repute will continue to grow with time.

Future Quatrain IV-59: A Light at Geneva

> Two beset in burning fervor by thirst for two cups
> (already) quenched; the strong point honed, and an
> old visionary will show to the Genevans the track
> of Nira.

> *Deux assieges en ardente ferveur:*
> *De soif eteints pour deux pleines tasses,*
> *Le fort lime, et vieillard reveur,*
> *Aux Geneuois de 'Nira' montra trace.*

A subtle but not insoluble verse that contains the striking anagram "Nira," which could stand for both Iran and Iraq (with the allowable change of one letter). Both nations—the two beset by thirst—are evidently intended. The "two cups already quenched" likely represent the glory days of both countries long ago when they were major players on the world stage—days which both thirst to revive. As we have already seen, Nostradamus predicts just such an attempt to recapture the past via a resurgence of Islamic power. The quatrain sees an elder statesman warning of the Islamic expansion plan, evidently at one of the many international conferences held at Geneva.

Probability rating: 55%
There is nothing very unlikely about this scenario. It suggests that Iran and Iraq will bury the hatchet to further the cause of Islamic expansion. Such a development is also indicated in Future Quatrain II-30, page 18.

Future Quatrain V-25: Targets East and West

The Arab Prince of Mars, Sun, and Venus in Leo, the rule of the Church will succumb by sea: Out of Persia (Iran) very nearly a million men; the true serpent will invade Byzantium and Egypt.

Le Prince Arabe Mars, Sol, Venus, Lion,
Regne d'Eglise par mer succombera:
Devers la Perse bien près d'un million,
Bisance, Egypte ver. serp. invadera.

Like Future Quatrain II-30 (page 18), this verse forecasts a successful seaborne assault, led by an Arab warrior prince, on Rome, the site of "the rule of the Church." The astronomical alignment in line one occurs in both 2006 and 2007. Meanwhile, Iranian troops headed by the "true serpent" occupy Egypt after assisting militant Islamics in their takeover of Turkey. A notable aspect here is that Israel is not mentioned even though the Seer foresaw its reestablishment (Quatrain III-97, page 137). It may be that the Muslims shrewdly avoid (or just postpone) an attack on Israel in hopes of keeping the United States out of the fray—a tactic that turns out to be only partially successful according to Future Quatrain VIII-9, page 28.

Probability rating: 40%
An intriguing aside to this verse: In 1909, Pope Pius X had a terrifying vision of just such an attack on Rome, which forces a future pope to flee the city.

Future Quatrain V-27: Persians and Turks

Through fire and arms not far from the Black Sea, he will come from Persia to occupy Trebizond (Turkey): Pharos, Mytilene to tremble; the Sun joyful, the Adriatic Sea covered with Arab blood.

Par feu et armes non loin de la marnegro
Viendra de Perse occuper Trebisonde:
Trembler Pharos, Methelin, Sol alegro,
De sang Arabe d'Adrie couvert onde.

This verse describes Iranian (Persian) participation in a militant fundamentalist takeover of Turkey. The scenario is clear; a radical Islamic leader arises in Turkey (see Future Quatrain III-60, page 19), aiming to seize the government, and is aided by an armed Iranian intrusion into Turkey. Pharos (Egypt) and Mytilene (Greece) are understandably much alarmed. And, as seen in Future Quatrains VIII-78, page 29, and III-64, page 20, an attack on Greece does follow. The mention of a sea battle on the Adriatic strongly suggests that Muslim Albania is involved in the assault on Greece and/or that Italy intervenes on the side of the Greeks. The Islamic navy is defeated, evidently in the summer ("sun joyful").

Probability rating: 50%

In light of history, current trends, and the presence of very large Shiite minorities in both Turkey and Albania, this prediction is perfectly feasible and as likely as not to materialize.

Future Quatrain V-54: Iran Strikes North and West

From beyond the Black Sea and great Tartary, there will be a King who will come to see Gaul. He will transpierce Alania and Armenia, and within Byzantium he will leave his bloody rod.

Du Pont Euxine, et la grande Tartarie,
Un Roi sera qui viendra voir la Gaule,
Transpercera Alane et l'Armenie,
Et dedans Bisance lairra sanglante gaule.

This prediction expands on Future Quatrain V-27, above. The Iranian leader who intrudes into Turkey ("Byzantium") will at the same time push the Iranian frontier north to the Caucasus Mountains, overrunning Armenia. The Alani are the present-day Ossetes who live high in the Caucasus range. This Persian potentate will also visit France, no doubt in a diplomatic effort to neutralize the French in the predicted Graeco-Turkish war.

Probability rating: 45%

The probability of this one coming to pass is clearly comparable to that of Future Quatrain V-27 though additional factors are involved.

Future Quatrain V-55: A Mighty Arab

> In the country of Arabia Felix (Yeman) there will be
> born one powerful in the law of Mahomet: To vex
> Spain, to conquer Grenada, and further by sea against
> the Ligurian people.

> *De la Felice Arabie contrade,*
> *Naitra puissant de loi Mahometique:*
> *Vexer l'Espagne, conquester la Grenade,*
> *Et plus par mer à la gent Ligustique.*

The subject here is doubtless the great leader of the Arabs in the predicted Mediterranean War. Though born in the Yemani region, he will evidently command Islam's west Mediterranean campaign, landing in southern Spain and taking Grenada (see Future Quatrain VI-80, page 26). It seems he will also lead a strike at the northwest Italian coast (Liguria). This verse may well be connected with the mahdi quatrain, Future Quatrain X-75, page 31.

Probability rating: 40%

The assault on Liguria may be only a raid since the locale would be strategically risky for a full-scale Muslim invasion attempt. The conquest of Granada, though, is confirmed by Future Quatrain VIII-51, which tells of a Turkish general pushing farther yet:

> The Byzantine making an oblation after having taken
> Cordoba to himself again: His road long, rest, wine
> vines lopped, on the sea passing prey taken by the Pil-
> lar (Gibraltar).

Future Quatrain VI-54: A Coup in Morocco

At daybreak at the second crowing of the cock, those
of Tunis, of Fez, and of Bougie, by the Arabs the King
of Morocco captured, the year sixteen hundred and
seven of the Liturgy.

Au point du jour au second chant du coq
Ceux de Tunes, de Fez, et de Bugie,
Par les Arabes captif le Roi Maroq,
L'an mil six cent et sept, de Liturgie.

   The verse almost certainly depicts another fundamentalist Muslim
takeover, this one in Morocco, with the help of Tunis and Algeria
("Bougie")—both of which will have fallen earlier before the militant
Islamic tide. The date here has befuddled analysts, but it probably
refers back to the implementation of the Nicene Creed, the basic liturgical statement of Christian belief. The origin of the creed is murky,
but it seems to have emerged as a liturgical standard not long after the
Council of Constantinople in A.D. 381. Hence, the Seer is talking about
a time around the year 2000.

Probability rating: 60%

A fundamentalist coup in Algeria—which very nearly happened in the
early '90s—would effectively doom the present moderate regime in
Morocco.

Future Quatrain VI-80: A Strike at Spain

From Fez the realm will reach those of Europe, their
city ablaze and the blade will cut. The great one of
Asia by land and sea with a great troop, so that blues
and perses will pursue the cross to death.

De Fez le regne parviendra à ceux d'Europe,
Feu leur cité, et lame tranchera:
Le grand d'Asie terre et mer à grande troupe,
Que bleus, pers, croix à mort dechassera.

After the militant Muslims take over Morocco ("Fez") as foretold in Future Quatrain VI-54, page 26, they will launch an attack on Grenada in southern Spain (see Future Quatrain V-55, page 25). It seems that the city of Grenada will suffer heavy damage. Meanwhile, the Middle Eastern Islamic armies will be attacking at the other (Asian) end of the Mediterranean. *Bleus* can mean military recruits, suggesting the rapid enlargement of the Islamic armies. "Perses" may be a play on "Persians" even though perse is a shade of deep blue.

Probability rating: 40%

Such an invasion of Spain would require a highly coordinated assault by land, sea, and air forces, now perhaps beyond the capability of the Islamic powers. But given Arab financial resources, the necessary build-up would not take long.

Future Quatrain VII-6: The Sack of the Italian Coast

> Naples, Palermo, and all Sicily through Barbarian
> hand will be uninhabited: Corsica, Salerno, and the
> Isle of Sardinia, famine, plague, war, end of evils
> remote.

> *Naples, Palerme, et toute la Sicille,*
> *Par main Barbare sera inhabitée:*
> *Corsique, Salerne et de Sardeigne l'Ile,*
> *Faim, peste, guerre fin de maux intentée.*

Nothing mysterious about this verse: It clearly portrays a series of Islamic ("Barbarian") assaults on the western Italian coast. As such, it lines up with the quatrains forecasting a raid by the Muslims on Rome. The most likely scenario is that North African forces will seize Sicily and Sardinia and use the isles as bases to launch a series of damaging attacks against the coastal cities of Italy, and later against Corsica and the southern coast of France as well.

Probability rating: 40%

The verse covers the same ground as the more general Quatrain II-4, which reads:

> From Monaco to near Sicily the entire coast will remain
> desolated: There will remain there no suburb, city, or
> town not pillaged and robbed by the Barbarians.

Future Quatrain VIII-9: The Americans Arrive

> While the Eagle (United States) and the Cock (France)
> are united at Savona, the Sea, Levant, and Hungary:
> The army at Naples, Palermo, the March of Ancona,
> Rome, Venice—a dreadful outcry because of Barbary
> (North Africa).

> *Pendant que l'Aigle et le Coq à Saunoe*
> *Seront unis, Mer, Levant et Ongrie:*
> *L'armee à Naples, Palerne, Marque d'Ancone,*
> *Rome, Venise par Barbe horrible cri.*

An American expeditionary force—none too soon—lands at Savona, teaming with French units to assist the Italians who are being pressed by North African invaders on several fronts: Naples, Palermo, Ancona, Rome, and Venice. Their build-up complete, the Yanks and the French move to the relief of Venice, then push into Croatia (part of Hungary in Nostradamus' time) to battle the Bosnian Muslims. (See Future Quatrain IX-28, page 40). The next move seems to be a joint seaborne strike at the Levant. While American troops may well be key in turning the tide in the Mediterranean War, various quatrains put the French more in the forefront of the conflict.

Probability rating: 40%

The United State's response in the Mediterranean War appears somewhat tardy, which might reflect a lack of military preparedness or, alternately, political turmoil in the country at the time (see Future Quatrain X-81, page 32).

Future Quatrain VIII-78: Northern Greece Invaded

A soldier of fortune with twisted tongue will come to
pillage the sanctuary of the gods: To the heretics he will
open the gate, thus stirring up the Church militant.

Un Bragamas avec la langue torte,
Viendra des dieux le sanctuaire:
Aux heretiques il ouvrira la porte,
En suscitant l'Eglise militaire.

The "sanctuary of the gods" is plainly Greece, in particular Mount
Olympus, legendary home of the Hellenic deities. So the quatrain
describes a military adventurer—most likely a Turk—who overruns
Greek Macedonia at least as far as Mount Olympus. The "heretics"
would be the Muslims. The verse, then, fits neatly with the Seer's theme
of a radical Islamic invasion of Greece that stirs up the Christian states
of the Mediterranean, ultimately bringing them into the war.

Probability rating: 55%

The "soldier of fortune" is perhaps the same as the felonious young
leader who engineers the militant Muslim takeover of Turkey depicted in Future Quatrain III-60, page 19.

Future Quatrain VIII-96: An Arab-Israeli Settlement

The barren synagogue without any fruit will be
admitted among the infidels: the daughter of the persecuted of Babylon miserable and sad, her wings
clipped.

La synagogue sterile sans nul fruit
Sera recue entre les infideles:
De Babylon la fille du poursuit
Misere et triste lui tranchera les ailes.

The "daughter of the persecuted of Babylon" is Israel. The verse
indicates that at some point Israel will be pressured into an accord with

the Arabs, which will make most Jews unhappy. Most likely, in exchange for formal recognition ("admitted") and boundary guarantees, the Israelis will give up some land to the Arabs (Golan Heights perhaps) and grant autonomy to much of the West Bank. The reference to the synagogue as barren very likely alludes to the barren fig tree of Mark II: 12-14, which is widely interpreted as a figure of Judaism.

Probability rating: 70%

The pact between Israel and the Palestine Liberation Organization in mid-1993 plainly illustrates that matters in the Middle East are moving in the direction forecasted by the Seer.

Future Quatrain IX-60: The Muslim State in Bosnia

> Conflict, Barbarian in the black headdress, blood
> shed; Dalmatia to tremble: Great Ishmael will set up
> his promontory: Ranes to tremble, Portuguese aid.

> *Conflit Barbare en la Cornette noire,*
> *Sang epandu, trebler la Dalmatie:*
> *Grand Ismaël mettra son promontoire,*
> *Ranes trembler secours Lusitanie.*

This timely verse deals with the emergence of a full-fledged Islamic state in Bosnia, already half accomplished. The Yugoslav peace treaty of 1995 carved out an autonomous Muslim region comprising about half of Bosnia. This quatrain and others (e.g., Future Quatrain IX-28, page 40) indicate that the Bosnian Muslims will side with the Islamic bloc during the Mediterranean War and will launch a drive on Dalmatia. This new Muslim state is termed "Ishmael's promontory," because Ishmael was the traditional ancestor of the Arabs (equated with the Muslims by the Seer). At about this same time, Iran ("Ranes") will be hit by a major earthquake, and neutral Portugal will send humanitarian aid.

Probability rating: 65%

There can be no doubt that the outbreak of the Mediterranean War would fracture the tenuous coexistence of the Christian and Muslim Serbs in Bosnia. A renewal of war between the two factions would necessitate an Islamic conquest of Dalmatia to provide a maritime supply link to other members of the Muslim bloc.

Future Quatrain X-75: The Advent of a Mahdi?

> Long awaited he will never return in Europe; he will appear in Asia: One of the league issued from the great Hermes, he will grow over all the kings of the East.

> *Tant attendu ne reviendra jamais,*
> *Dedans l'Europe en Asie apparaitra:*
> *Un de la ligue issu du grand Hermes,*
> *Et sur tous Rois des Orients croitra.*

The Mahdi is a long-prophesied great Muslim leader who is supposed to lead Islam to a new golden age of triumphant glory. The quatrain suggests that one will arise in Asia who will be widely accepted by Muslims as the Mahdi. Since Hermes was a "messenger of the Gods," a prophet is indicated, but a false one since Hermes was a trickster and not of the true faith (Christianity). Likely this new imam will exercise great influence over other "Eastern" leaders and will be a major player in the prophesied Mediterranean War. He may be the same individual described in Future Quatrain V-55, page 25.

Probability rating: 65%

With the rise of fundamentalist Islam, the times are ripe for the appearance of a mahdi. More than likely, someone will seize the opportunity. (In Nostradamus' era, with large Muslim populations in the Balkans, it would not have seemed unlikely for the Mahdi to appear in Europe.)

Future Quatrain X-81: Firefight on the Capitol Mall

> A treasure placed in a temple by Hesperian (Ameri-
> can) citizens, therein withdrawn to a secluded place.
> The avid ones to cut the links, the temple retaken, rav-
> ished, appalling prey in the midst of this.

> *Mis tresor temple citadins Hesperiques,*
> *Dans icelui retiré en secret lieu:*
> *Le temple ouvrir les liens fameliques,*
> *Repris, ravis, proie horrible au milieu.*

This is an unsettling quatrain presaging armed conflict on the Washington, D.C., capitol grounds. The treasure is probably the United States Constitution, the single most revered document on the planet, housed in the National Archives rotunda ("temple"). Evidently, a militia group tries to seize the Constitution for either symbolic or bargaining purposes.

The outcome is unclear but the quatrain suggests heavy casualties—even the destruction of the Constitution itself—in the melee. The cutting of the links (line three) may mean the cutting of locks or fences but also indicates a separatist group. There is no chronological clue but the recent emergence of militia organizations (see Quatrain VI-94, page 222) points to the near future.

Probability rating: 50%

Since alleged subversion of the Constitution is the great complaint of paramilitary groups, a fulfillment seems easily feasible. Two other verses that appear to be tied to this one are analyzed next: the coupled quatrain, X-82, and II-65, page 33.

Future Quatrain X-82: The Tide of the Battle

> Cries, weeping, tears will come with knives. Seeming
> to flee, they will deliver a final attack. High platforms
> set up around the parks; the living pushed back and
> quickly killed.

> *Cris, pleurs, larmes viendront avec couteaux,*
> *Semblant fuir, donneront dernier assaut,*
> *L'entour parcs planter profonds plateaux,*
> *Vifs repousses et meutis de prinsaut.*

This coupled verse describes the action predicted in the preceding quatrain, X-81. The "high platforms" suggest that rumors of a possible attack cause the government to set up elevated sentry platforms in the Mall (by the Capitol). The sentries are attacked with knives, but the last line is delphic. Which side is pushed back and killed? Either the Seer went blank on the outcome or it is indeterminate, teetering on a razor's edge.

Probability rating: 50%

This one may be tied to Future Quatrain II-65:

> The sloping park, great calamity to be done as to Hesperia (America) and Insubria (Italy). Fire in the ship (of state), plague and captivity, Mercury in Sagittarius, Saturn will fade.

The civil strife in the United States evidently hinders American assistance to Italy in the face of the Islamic onslaught.

Future Quatrain I-73: France in the Fray

> France because of negligence assailed at five places;
> Tunis, Algiers stirred up by Persians (Iran): Leon,
> Seville, Barcelona having failed, there will be no fleet
> for the Venetians (Italians).

> *France à cinq parts par neglect assaillie,*
> *Tunis, Argiels emus par Persiens:*
> *Leon, Seville, Barcelone faillie,*
> *N'aura la classe par les Venitiens.*

Line two snaps the reader to attention because Iran even today is actively backing fundamentalist Muslim movements in North Africa. In the future Mediterranean War, it seems France will be surprised by

Muslim military strikes that will hit Corsica (Future Quatrain VII-6, page 27) and probably the four main ports of southern France—Marseilles, Nice, Toulon, and Sete. A likely scenario is that the Islamic powers get advance word on French plans to enter the war so they launch pre-emptive strikes. Meanwhile, the Spanish will show up late with naval assistance for Italy, which is under attack by North African forces (see Future Quatrain VII-6).

Probability rating: 55%

Since line two is already being fulfilled, the rest of the quatrain has to be given fair prospects. This verse is amplified by Quatrain III-82:

> Frejus, Antibes, towns around Nice, will be thoroughly devastated by land and sea: Locusts on land and sea, the wind propitious, captured, dead, bound, pillaged without law of war.

Future Quatrain I-74: A Turkish Defeat

> After tarrying they will venture into Epirus: The great relief will come towards Antioch. The black crimped-haired king will strive strongly for the Empire: Bronzebeard will roast him on a spit.

> *Apres sejourné vagueront en Epire:*
> *Le grand secours viendra vers Antioche,*
> *Le noir poil crepe tendra fort à l'Empire:*
> *Barbe d'airain le rotira en broche.*

Since the scene of the action here is the Greek-Turkish theatre, the verse predicts a Western victory over the Turks who will be led by one with black, crimped hair. After their assault on eastern Greece, the Turks will pause before moving into Epirus (northwest Greece). At about this time, though, the West launches a counterstrike at the Tarsus-Antioch region of Turkey. (See Future Quatrain VI-85, page 40.) The success of this attack, evidently led by a blondish Frenchman, collapses the Turkish drive on Greece ("great relief"). The Turk leader is strategically "roasted."

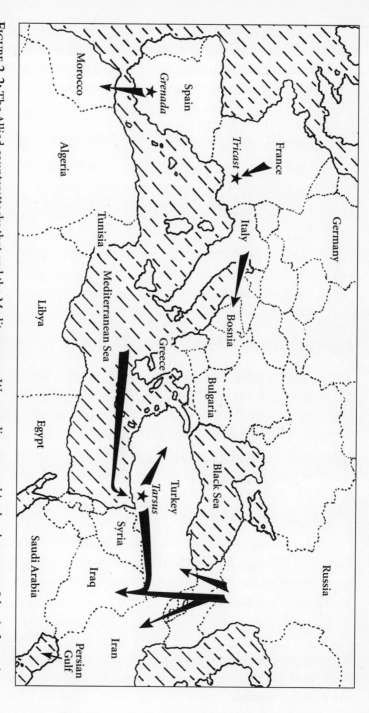

FIGURE 2-2: The Allied counterattacks that end the Mediterranean War are diagrammed in the above map. Islamic forces in the south of France are crushed at Tricast while the Spanish repulse the invasion of Grenada and invade Morocco. A Franco-American force overwhelms Muslim Bosnia. Then the French and Spanish team to strike at southern Turkey as the Russians enter the war with thrusts at east Turkey, Iran, and Iraq. The following quatrains detail these actions.

Probability rating: 45%

The scenario is highly plausible in the context of the predicted Mediterranean War. "Bronzebeard" is evidently the same French leader who is the subject of Future Quatrain V-74, page 39.

Future Quatrain II-62: The End of Saddam Hussein

> "Mabus" then will soon perish. There will come of
> people and beasts a horrible rout: Then suddenly one
> will see vengeance. Century, hand, thirst, hunger
> when the comet will run.

> *Mabus puis tôt alors mourra, viendra*
> *De gens et bêtes une horrible défaite:*
> *Puis tout à coup la vengeance on verra,*
> *Cent, main, soif, faim quand courra la comète.*

A highly intriguing quatrain because "Mabus" is a good anagram for "Saddam" (with the permissible change—actually just a reversal—of one letter.) Apparently, Saddam Hussein will still be in power during the Mediterranean War and an active player in the Muslim alliance. This verse foretells his compete defeat and destruction at the hands of the Allies. The following quatrain (Future Quatrain III-31, page 37) provides the details of the military action. There are two chronological clues: "Century," of course, suggests a new century; "the comet," as we have seen, can be expected early in the dawning millennium.

Probability rating: 50%

The odds seem to favor a continuation of Saddam's regime until the time of the Mediterranean War. There can be little doubt that he would be one of the major Islamic protagonists and a prime target of the Allies' counterattack.

Future Quatrain III-31: The Russians Come In

> On the fields of Media, of Arabia, and of Armenia two
> great armies will assemble thrice: The host near the
> bank of the Araxes, they will fall in the land of the
> great Suleiman (Turkey).

> *Aux champs de Mede, d'Arabe et d'Armenie*
> *Deux grandes copies trois fois s'assembleront:*
> *Près du rivage d'Araxes la mesnie,*
> *Du grand Soliman en terre tomberont.*

The geography here strongly implies that at some point the Russians will enter the future Mediterranean War on the side of the West. The Russian forces will engage the Iranians ("Media"), the Arabs (Iraq?), and the Turks. The Araxes runs out of eastern Turkey to form the border between Iran and Armenia. The implication here is that the Turks and Iranians will be defeated near this river by Russian forces, which will then move south to invade Iraq, the nearest Arab state. In all probability, Russian entry would be a mortal blow to the Islamic coalition, heralding an end to the war.

Probability rating: 45%
The scenario here presents a highly feasible climax to the Mediterranean War. While the Bible (Ezekiel) seems to predict a Russian intrusion into the Near East and the Holy Land in the last days, Nostradamus is not necessarily talking about the same event. (However, see chapter 4, "Commentary on the Future.")

Future Quatrain III-93: Top Gun to the Front

> In Avignon the chief of the whole empire will make a
> stop for the sake of distressed Paris: Tricastins will
> hold the anger of Hannibal: Lyons will be poorly con-
> soled by the change.

Dans Auignaon tout le chef de l'empire
Fera arret pour Paris desolé:
Tricast tiendra l'Annibalique ire:
Lyon par change sera mal consolé.

The Islamic landings on the southern French coast will cause such great distress in Paris that the French president will go to Avignon to take personal command of the situation. Those of Lyon, on the invasion path, will be skeptical of this move; nonetheless, the advancing "Hannibal," the same Muslim leader who raids Rome (Future Quatrain II-30, page 18), will be stopped near St. Paul-Trois-Chateau (Tricast), just north of Avignon.

Probability rating: 35%
The verse comports with Quatrain III-99, which predicts a major Muslim defeat east of Avignon:

> On the grassy fields of Alleins and Vernegues of the
> Leberon range near the Durance, the conflict will be
> very sharp for both armies. Mesopotamia [i.e., Baby-
> lon] will fail in France.

Future Quatrain V-16: The Allies Strike Back

> The Sabean tear no longer of great value. Turning
> human flesh to ashes though death, at the isle of
> Pharos disrupted by the Crusaders when a harsh
> specter will appear at Rhodes.

A son haut prix plus la larme sabee,
D'humaine chair par mort en cendre mettre,
A l'ile Pharos par Croissars perturbee,
Alors qu'à Rhodes paraitra dur espectre.

Pharos was an ancient islet off Alexandria so the verse foresees an attack on the coast of Egypt by the western Allies ("Crusaders"). Clearly, Egypt is to become part of the radical Muslim coalition (predicted in Future Quatrain V-25, page 23). The phrase "human flesh to ashes" points to the use of modern weaponry such as napalm, incendiary bombs, and perhaps nuclear devices. The "Sabean tear" is frankincense, which is no longer Arabia's most valuable product. Oil, of course, is now the great Arab resource. The mysterious "specter" at Rhodes in the Aegean is simply the specter of militant Islam.

Probability rating: 45%

Allied seizure of its key port of Alexandria would virtually put Egypt out of the war. But "disrupted" is more suggestive of a bombardment than a full-scale invasion. An Islamic fleet may be the main target.

Future Quatrain V-74: The Nemesis of Islam

> Of Trojan blood will be born a Germanic heart who
> will rise to very high power: He will drive out the for-
> eign Arabic people, returning the Church to its pris-
> tine preeminence.

> *De sang Troyen naitre coeur Germanique*
> *Qui deviendra en si haute puissance:*
> *Hors chassera gent étrange Arabique,*
> *Tournant l'Eglise en pristine preeminence.*

This is simply a description of the leader who will defeat militant Islam and drive it back out of Italy, Greece, and the Riviera. He will evidently be French but with some Germanic ancestry; the French aristocracy fancied itself as being descendants of the Trojans while many of the northern French have Germanic blood from the days of the Frankish invasions. As a result of this leader's efforts, the Christian Church and its people will emerge triumphant again in the Mediterranean.

Probability rating: 40%

Quatrain V-80 seems to be a continuation of this one:

> Ogmios (the Celtic Hercules) will approach great Byzantium (Turkey); the Barbaric League (Muslim coalition) will be driven out: Of the two laws the heathen one will give way, Barbarian and Frank in perpetual strife."

Future Quatrain VI-85: The French Counterattack

The great city of Tarsus will be destroyed by the Gauls,
all of the Turban captives: Help by sea from the great
one of Portugal, first of summer, St. Urban's Day.

La grande cité de Tharse par Gaulois
Sera detruite, captifs tous à Turban:
Secours par mer du grand Portugalois,
Premier d'eté le jour du sacre Urban.

This quatrain accords with Future Quatrain V-74, page 39, which indicates it will be a French leader who repels the future militant Muslim expansion. Accordingly, the French will join Italy and Greece in the struggle against the Islamic coalition and a French army will land on the south coast of Turkey and take Tarsus, inflicting heavy damage and capturing many prisoners. It will be a summertime campaign, though "St. Urban's Day" is no help because there were several St. Urbans. The Portuguese will aid the French in some way, perhaps with supplies, ships, or military intelligence.

Probability rating: 40%

The failure of Iran's mission to keep France neutral (Future Quatrain V-54, page 24) proves to be a decisive factor in the war.

Future Quatrain IX-28: Retribution in the Balkans

Allied fleet from the port of Marseille, in the port of
Venice to march to the Pannonias: To depart at the
gulf and bay of Illyria (Dalmatia). Destruction to
Sicily, cannon shots for the Ligurians.

Voile Symacle port Massiliolique,
Dans Venise port marcher aux Pannons:
Partir du gouffre et sinus Illirique,
Vast à Socille, Ligurs coups de canons.

This is an exceptionally fascinating quatrain because the Muslim state emerging in old Yugoslavia (predicted in Future Quatrain IX-60, page 30) lies in the ancient territories of Pannonia and Illyria. The implication here is that this future Islamic nation will actively support the radical Muslim coalition, thereby triggering a punitive attack by the Western allies. An Allied task force[1] will rendezvous with Italian forces at Venice, then land troops on the Dalmatian coast to attack Bosnia. Muslim ships will try to divert the Allied fleet by shelling the northwest Italian coast while battles continue in Sicily.

Probability rating: 40%

There is an uncanny aura about this verse, almost as if the Seer had in front of him a map of Europe for the year 2000. It may relate to Quatrain V-13:

> With great fury the Roman Belgian King will want to vex the barbarian with his phalanx: Gnashing fury, he will chase the North Africans from Pannonia to the pillars of Hercules.

Future Quatrain X-86: Victory in Sight

> Like a griffin will come the King of Europe, accompanied by those of Aquilon (Russia): He will lead a great troop of red ones and white ones, and they will go against the King of Babylon.

> *Comme un griffon viendra le Roi d'Europe,*
> *Accompagné de ceux d'Aquilon:*
> *De rouges et blancs conduira grande troupe,*
> *Et iront contre le Roi de Babylon.*

Tied with Future Quatrain III-31, page 37, this verse depicts the western Allies' counteroffensive against militant Islam. The "griffin,"

---

1. Apparently, Franco-American (see Future Quatrain VIII-9, page 28).

half eagle and half lion, was in myth an avenging beast, here representing combined air and ground forces. The "red ones" and "whites ones" are easily identified. White was the color of the Bourbons and the only Bourbon king still reigning is Spain's; so the "King of Europe" is the Spanish monarch. By dint of their revolutionary roots, the "red ones" are the Russians. Thus, a Spanish force, landing with the French in southern Turkey, will veer eastward to link up with the Russians and together drive into Iraq ("Babylon"). The French, as seen in Future Quatrain I-74, page 34, head northwest to collapse the rear of the Turkish forces in Greece.

Probability rating: 45%

What is striking here is that the Seer's scenario makes perfect strategic sense; it is just the way trained generals would conduct the final campaign. The griffin could also be seen as a joint figure of Bourbon royalty (the lion) and the double eagle of Russia.

Future Quatrain X-95: The Spanish Counteroffensive

> To the Spains will come a very powerful King, by land
> and sea subjugating the South: This will cause harm,
> lowering again the crescent, clipping the wings of
> those of Friday.

> *Dans les Espaignes viendra Roi trés-puissant,*
> *Par mer et terre subjuguant le Midi:*
> *Ce mal fera, rebaissant le croissant*
> *Baisser les ailes à ceux du Vendredi.*

It is noteworthy that Spain is one of the few countries that still has a king. The Spanish monarchy will strike back against the future Islamic intrusion, freeing Grenada and crossing the Mediterranean to invade Morocco (subjugating by sea). The campaign will apparently cause very heavy damage as it progresses (line three), but will ultimately crush militant Islam ("those of Friday") in northwest Africa.

Probability rating: 40%

This quatrain has been applied to Philip II who put down a Muslim revolt in southern Spain. But his weak stabs at the North African coast were utterly ineffectual, so it is likely that this is a future quatrain.

Future Quatrain X-96: Final Victory

> The Religion of the name of the seas will triumph
> against the sect of the son of Adaluncatif: The obsti-
> nate, lamented sect will be fearful of the two wounded
> by Aleph and Aleph.

> *Religion du nom des mers vaincra,*
> *Contre la secte fils Adaluncatif:*
> *Secte obstinee deploree craindra*
> *Des deux blesses par Aleph et Aleph.*

Nostradamus summarizes the Mediterranean War with a deviously crafted quatrain never fathomed. The first line may be seen as a play on the similarity between the Latin *ponti*, meaning "seas" (Fr. *mers*), and the French word *Pontife*. The religion of the Pontiff, of course, is Catholicism, the church of the major Western powers in the Mediterranean War. These will be victorious over the "son of Adaluncatif"— a coded term for Caliph of the Moon ("a de lune Calif"), i.e., a Muslim leader; so the "lamented sect" is Islam. Since "Aleph" is Semitic and since Arabic names very often start with "A," the two Alephs must be Arabic leaders who "wound" the Roman Catholic and Greek Orthodox churches ("the two wounded") in the Mediterranean War. Thereafter, though, Islam will be cowed by fear of these twin Christian societies.

With this declaration of ultimate triumph for the West, Nostradamus concludes his prophecy of the Mediterranean War. The finality of the verse leaves the impression that this is the concluding episode, at last, of the 1,400-year-old Christian-Muslim conflict.

Chapter 3

NOSTRADAMUS' GREATEST HITS

Nostradamus' crystal ball, even if not infallible, reflected the future remarkably well, as is evident from the number of quatrains already fulfilled. On the following pages are listed over 350 such quatrains, many of them previously unsolved or not properly recognized.

In other words, more than a third of the Seer's 942 predictions have already come to pass. How many more will be realized in the coming years can only be guessed, but a cumulative accuracy in the range of 50 percent seems easily within reach. Such an extraordinary success rate suggests we should give considerable attention to what has been forecast for our own times (verses outlined in the prior chapters).

Along with the fulfilled quatrains in this section, we offer a sort of impact rating on each verse—a rough measure of its overall impressiveness. Some prophecies are obviously more daring than others, and that much more striking if they come true. Some are highly detailed, others somewhat vague. Using a scale of ten, only quatrains rated over 7.5 are included here. Only a few predictions are given a perfect score—those forecasting unique events in detail with complete accuracy.

Quatrain I-3: Revolution Rocks France (1789)

> When the litter is overturned by the whirlwind, the
> faces will be covered by their cloaks. The republic will
> be vexed by new people; then whites and reds will
> judge in contrary ways.

> *Quand la litiere du tourbillon versee,*
> *Et seront faces de leurs manteaux couvers,*
> *La republique par gens nouveaux vexée,*
> *Lors blancs et rouges jugeront à l'envers.*

Nearly all commentators see this prophecy as a picture of the French Revolution, the "litter" (as a curtained portable chair) being the symbol of royalty. The cloak-covered faces are interpreted as those of the many aristocrats who fled France during the bloody revolt under whatever cover they could devise. The "reds" are, of course, the revolutionaries while white was the color of the royal Bourbon family. The word "republic" is significant since hardly any existed in Nostradamus' time.

Rating: 8.5

The quatrain's only weakness is that it lacks an unequivocal geographic indicator. In such cases, though, the Seer is almost always talking about France.

Quatrain I-4: Napoleon and the Papacy

> In the world there will be one monarch who will not
> long be in peace or alive: Then the fishing bark will be
> lost; it will be ruled to its greatest detriment.

> *Par l'univers sera fait un Monarque,*
> *Qu'en paix et vie ne sera longuement:*
> *Lors se perdra la piscature barque,*
> *Sera regie en plus grand detriment.*

Emperor Napoleon is without a doubt the subject of this quatrain. During his war-plagued reign, the emperor hijacked Pope Pius VII to France and held him prisoner, often imposing humiliating directives on the Church and its lands. In the quatrains, "the fishing bark" always means the papacy—the pope being "a fisher of men." Napoleon died at the relatively young age of fifty-one.

Rating: 9

Since the events of this prophecy would have seemed unlikely in Nostradamus' time, the prediction is an impressive one.

Quatrain I-8: Henry Saves the City of Light

> How many times will you be taken, solar city? The
> laws changeable, barbarian and vain, your evil
> approaches: You will be more tributary. The great
> Hadrie will recover your veins.

> *Combien de fois pris cité solaire*
> *Seras, changeeant les loix barbares et vaines:*
> *Ton mal s'approche: Plus seras tributaire,*
> *Le grand Hadrie recouvrira tes veines.*

The "solar city" is quite likely Paris, which Nostradamus considered the center of the universe. This quatrain warns of the impending French religious wars that erupted in 1562 and dragged on for over three decades—until the final victory of Henry IV ("great Hadrie").

During this era, the "laws" were simply royal edicts and the constantly changing treaties of accord between the warring parties, most of them exercises in futility ("vain"). Charles IX's directive for the St. Bartholomew's Day massacre was certainly "barbarian." While the Seize controlled Paris, the city was *tributaire* to the pope and the Spanish. France and Paris did recover marvelously under Henry IV.

Rating: 9.5

This multifaceted verse is correct in all its aspects and also includes the specific name "Hadrie" (the Seer's customary anagram for Henry). The validity of the quatrain is further enhanced by the fact that Nostradamus is known to have specifically foreseen Henry of Navarre's rise to the French throne (see the Prologue).

Quatrain I-9: The Ottoman Onslaught

> From the Orient will come the Punic heart, accompanied by the Libyan fleet, to vex the Adriatic and the heirs of Romulus (Italy); Malta trembling and the nearby isles empty.
>
> *De orient viendra le coeur Punique*
> *Fâsher Hadrie et les hoires Romulides,*
> *Accompagné de las classe Libyque,*
> *Trembler Melites et proches îles vides.*

The "Punic heart" can only mean the Ottoman Turks who in the Seer's time controlled the old Carthaginian (Punic) territories of North Africa. The Ottomans were a constant threat to Adriatic Italy and warred with Venice in the late sixteenth century. In 1565, aided by their North African vassals ("Libyan fleet"), the Turks besieged Malta for several months and were only repulsed after some of the fiercest fighting in the annals of warfare.

Rating: 9

This is a strong and specific quatrain with no significant drawbacks. The Libyan fleet was actually from Algeria, but in ancient times the term "Libya" was used to refer to all of North Africa.

Quatrain I-11: Italian Defeats in World War II

> The movement of sense, heart, feet, and hands will be
> in accord in Naples, Leon, and Sicily: Swords, fires,
> waters; then the noble Romans submerged, killed,
> dead because of a weak brain.

> *Le movement de sens, coeur, pieds et mains*
> *Seront d'accord. Naples, Leon, Sicile:*
> *Glaives, feux, eaux: puis aux nobles Romains,*
> *Plonges, tues, morts par cerveau debile.*

Though unsolved so far, this prophetic account of drownings and deaths in war neatly fits the crushing defeats inflicted on the Italian navy in World War II, as at Taranto. Naples and Sicily, obviously, represent Italy. The Spanish province of Leon is poetic synecdoche for Spain, which was ruled by Mussolini's fellow fascist, Franco. Hence, the reference to accord between the two nations. The "weak brain" probably refers to Mussolini whose many strategic blunders led his nation to disaster.

Rating: 8.5

There is very little to criticize in this quatrain—a neat, if not spectacular hit for Nostradamus.

Quatrain I-14: The French Revolution and the Guillotine

> From the enslaved people songs, chants, and requests
> for princes and lords captive in prisons. In the future
> such (requests) will be received as divine utterances
> by headless idiots.

> *De gent esclave chansons, chants et requetes,*
> *Captifs par Princes et Seigneurs aux prisons:*
> *A l'avenir par idiots sans tetes,*
> *Seront reçus par divines oraisons.*

This is one of the Seer's several prophecies dealing with the French Revolution. The quatrain pictures the chants and demands of the peasants while King Louis and his family were imprisoned. The "headless idiots" are the numerous revolutionary leaders who played to the voice of the mob but who later fell victim to the guillotine.

Rating: 8

Though the quatrain is a bit vague in some ways, the reference to headless idiots in connection with the revolution is striking.

Quatrain I-18: The French Lose North Africa

Because of Gallic discord and negligence a passage
will be opened to Mohammed: The land and sea of
Senoise soaked in blood; the Phocaean port (Marseilles) covered with ships and sails.

Par la discorde négligence Gauloise
Sera passage à Mahomet ouvert:
De sang trempé la terre et mer Senoise
Le port Phocen de voiles et nefs couvert.

This quatrain has long stumped commentators, partly because of the puzzling "Senoise" reference. There is no such land or sea, but the name may be merely a reversal of "quarrel itself" (*se* meaning "itself" in French, *noise* meaning "quarrel"). Hence, "the land and sea of Senoise (the quarrel itself) soaked in blood." The French were badly divided after World War II by the Islamic drive to free Algeria. After much fighting, the colony was let go and thousands of refugees poured into France through the port of Marseilles.

Rating: 9

Once Nostradamus' little Senoise trick is disposed of, the quatrain appears clear, specific, and accurate.

Quatrain I-20: France in World War II

> The cities of Tours, Orleans, Blois, Angers, Reims, and
> Nantes vexed through sudden change: Tents will be
> pitched by those of foreign tongues; streams (of
> men?), darts at Rennes, trembling of land and sea.

> *Tours, Orleans, Blois, Angers, Reims et Nantes,*
> *Cités vexées par subit changement:*
> *Par langues etranges seront tendues tentes,*
> *Fleuves, dards Renes terre et mer temblement.*

The only time all these French cities suffered full-scale occupation
by foreign troops was during World War II with the invasion of the
Nazis, so the time frame here is clear. The last line has puzzled commentators, but Rennes was the first major city captured by General
Patton's army after his famed Normandy breakthrough, an event
accompanied by horrific aerial bombardments. Hence, the darts that
shake the earth (last line).

Rating: 7.5
The substance of the prediction is correct, but the enigmatic use of
"streams" in line four distracts somewhat.

Quatrain I-23: Battle of St. Quentin (World War I)

> In the third month, the sun rising, the Boar and the
> Leopard on the field of Mars to fight: The tired Leop-
> ard raises its eye to the heavens, sees an eagle playing
> around the sun.

> *Au mois troisieme se levant le Soleil,*
> *Sanglier, Leopard, au champ Mars pour combattre:*
> *Leopard lassé au ciel etend son oeil,*
> *Un Aigle autour du Soleil voit s'ebattre.*

Attempts have been made to apply this prediction to the battle of
Waterloo, but that engagement was in June, not March. A better fit is

the battle of St. Quentin, one of the climactic struggles of World War I, which began at dawn, March 21, 1918. The British Lion (termed a leopard by the French) was badly mauled by the German "Boar," but the Brits just managed to prevent the Germans from driving them into the sea. The exhausted English were buoyed by the fact that America (the "eagle") was beginning to send sufficient troops to the western front to soon turn the tide.

Rating: 8

The quatrain is nicely poetic, but that very fact produces some loss of precision in the meaning.

Quatrain I-24: Napoleon in Italy

> At the new city, pensive as to condemnation, the bird
> of prey comes to offer itself to the heavens: After vic-
> tory, pardon to the captives: Cremona and Mantua
> will have suffered great evils.

> *A cité neuve pensif pour condamner,*
> *L'oiseau de proie au ciel se vient offrir:*
> *Après victorie à captifs pardonner,*
> *Cremone et Mantoue grands maux aura souffert.*

During his spectacular Italian campaign, young General Bonaparte (a "bird of prey," indeed) arrived at Villa Nova ("new city") worried about condemnation from the French Directory, which feared his rising popularity and with whom Napoleon was constantly squabbling. His relations with headquarters and the entire campaign were marked by the most audacious winning gambles ("offer to the heavens"), convincing Napoleon that he was "a man of destiny." After his victory at the siege of Mantua, Napoleon treated prisoners well.

Rating: 8.5

Cremona suffered much less than Mantua in the Corsican's Italian war; nonetheless, this is a remarkable prophecy.

Quatrain I-25: Pius XII and the Dead Sea Scrolls

Lost, found, hidden for so long a time; the pastor will
be honored as a demigod: Before the Moon finishes
its full period he will be dishonored by other winds.

Perdu, trouvé, cashé de si long siecle,
Sera pasteur demi Dieu honoré:
Ains que la Lune acheve son grand siecle,
Par autres vents sera deshonoré.

Sundry attempts to associate the French word *Pasteur* with Louis
Pasteur do not succeed because Pasteur was never dishonored by any
stretch of the imagination. The "pastor" in question is probably a
pope. The first line is the key since it appears to allude to the discovery of the Dead Sea Scrolls in 1947, the greatest biblical find ever, during the reign of Pius XII. Pius enjoyed enormous prestige due to his
great learning and piety but suffered much loss of stature when ques-
tions arose about his lack of response to the Nazi persecution of the
Jews. Pius' eclipse began within a cycle of the moon (18.6 years) after
World War II.

Rating: 8.5

This quatrain is entirely accurate, and though it seems somewhat
abstract, it is almost impossible to apply to any other historical setting.

Quatrain I-26: The Kennedy Assassinations

The great one falls of the lightning in the daytime;
Evil predicted by the bearer of demands: According to
the prediction another falls in the nighttime. Strife at
Reims, London, Tuscan plague.

Le grand du foudre tombe d'heure diurne,
Mal, et predit par porteur postulaire:
Suivant presage tombe de l'heure nocturene,
Conflit Reims, Londres, Etrusque pestifere.

Many consider this prophecy to foreshadow the deaths of John and Robert Kennedy, though the identity of the "bearer of demands" has been a problem. Likely, the line alludes to Soviet Premier Khrushchev who threatened President John F. Kennedy with war unless Russian demands were met in the Berlin and Cuban crises. The daytime and nighttime aspect of the deaths is on the mark, and the assassination of Robert Kennedy was predicted by some psychics. There was enough strife in governmental circles in France and Britain during this critical period. There was no "plague" in Tuscan, Italy, but there was disastrous flooding (1963).

Rating: 9

While the last line could have been better, the net effect of the quatrain is impressive.

Quatrain I-29: D-Day

> When the terrestrial and aquatic fish will be put upon
> the beach by a strong wave, its form strange, attrac-
> tive, and frightful, by sea the enemies (are) very soon
> at the walls.

> *Quand le poisson terrestre et aquatique*
> *Par forte vague au gravier sera mis,*
> *Sa forme étrange suave et horrifique,*
> *Par mer aux murs bien tôt les ennemis.*

This quatrain presents a graphic, poetic picture of the amphibious landing craft used in World War II. It illustrates that imagery was involved to some degree in Nostradamus' precognition, that it was not just a matter of astrological calculation. Since the German defenses on the coast of France were known as the Atlantic Wall, the last line indicates that the D-Day invasion of Normandy is the event that Nostradamus perceived.

Rating: 7.5

The one bothersome aspect of this quatrain is the use of the word "enemies," suggesting that Nostradamus perceived the Normandy invasion but not the nature of it, i.e., that it was actually an invasion by forces friendly to France. It could be that there is no French point of view here and that "enemies" simply designates the opponents of the Wall's defenders.

Quatrain I-30: The Captain Overstays His Welcome

> Through the stormy seas the strange ship will
> approach the unknown port. Afterwards, death and
> pilfering, notwithstanding the signals of the palm
> branch: Good advice given late.

> *La nef étrange par le tourment marin*
> *Abordera près de port inconnu,*
> *Nonobstant signes de rameau palmerin,*
> *Après mort, pille: bon avis tard venu.*

Though unsolved until now, this verse is a patent account of Captain James Cook's ill-fated landing in Hawaii in 1779. After exploring the stormy northwest American coast, Cook headed for the Hawaiian Islands and discovered the Big Island (Hawaii). His reception was friendly at first ("palm branch"), but later there were misunderstandings and incidents of pilfering on both sides. Though Cook sailed his ship away, it was driven back by bad weather, and soon after landing a fatal argument erupted over a stolen small boat. Cook and four of his men were killed as were a number of Hawaiians.

Rating: 9

No doubt someone on Cook's staff had some "good advice" for the headstrong captain during this unfortunate episode—evidently unheeded.

Quatrain I-31: World War II

> The wars in Gaul will last for many years, beyond the
> course of the monarch of Castulo (Spain): Unsettled
> victory will crown three great ones; the Eagle, Cock,
> Moon, Lion, Sun are marked (greatly affected).

> *Tant d'ans en Gaule les guerres dureront,*
> *Outre la course du Castulon monarque:*
> *Victoire incerte trois grands couronneront,*
> *Aigle, Cog, Lune, Lion, Soleil en marque.*

The line of the Spanish monarchy was broken in 1931 when King Alphonso was ousted. Eight years later World War II erupted and France was overrun. But the end of the war saw the triumph of "three great ones:" Roosevelt, Churchill, and Stalin. It was "an unsettled victory" because the Cold War immediately followed. The "Eagle, the Cock, and the Lion" are the United States, France, and Britain. The "Moon" would be China and the "Sun," Japan.

Rating: 8

An above-average prophecy, weakened slightly by the fact that the Spanish monarchy was reestablished in 1975.

Quatrain I-32: The Last Years of Bonaparte

> The great Empire will soon be transferred to a little
> place which will very soon come to grow: A very lowly
> place in a petty country in the middle of which he will
> come to lay down his scepter.

> *Le grand Empire sera tôt translaté*
> *En lieu petit qui bien tôt viendra croitre:*
> *Lieu bien infime d'exigue comté*
> *Ou au milieu viendra poser son sceptre.*

Napoleon's great empire shrank down to the tiny island of Elba after his defeat in 1814, but not for long. His domain came to grow when he escaped Elba and reestablished power in Paris. After Waterloo, the Corsican was once again confined to a petty island, St. Helena, where his "scepter" was permanently retired.

Rating: 7.5
The verse works well enough but is overly metaphorical. It is not really very clear whether the last two lines refer to Elba or St. Helena, though the latter seems more appropriate.

Quatrain I-33: The Siege of Antwerp

> Near a great bridge of a spacious plain, the great Lion
> with imperial forces will cause a felling outside the
> austere city. Because of fear the gates will be opened
> to him.

> *Près d'un grand pont de plaine spacieuse,*
> *Le grand Lion par forces Cesarees,*
> *Fera abattre hors cité rigoureuse,*
> *Par effroi portes lui seront reserées.*

Though previous commentators have had little luck decoding this quatrain, it applies strikingly to the brilliant Alexander Farnese and the siege of Antwerp in 1584. Farnese led King Philip's effort to quell the Protestant revolt in the Spanish Netherlands. Several lesser cities opened their gates and fell to him before he laid siege to the stronghold of Antwerp ("austere" because that is how the Netherland Protestants were regarded). Here on the coastal plain, Farnese organized a huge "bridge" of boats across the Scheldt River to cut Antwerp's line of supply. Finally, fearing famine, the city surrendered.

Rating: 9.5
This prediction is more detailed than most and is accurate in all aspects—a slam-dunk for the Seer.

Quatrain I-35: Death of Henri II of France

> The young lion will overcome the old one on the field
> of battle in single combat. He will put out his eyes in a
> cage of gold: two wounds in one, then he dies a cruel
> death.

> *Le lion jeune le vieux surmontera*
> *En champ bellique par singulier duel:*
> *Dans cage d'or les yeux lui crevera:*
> *Deux classes une, puis mourir, mort cruelle.*

This famous quatrain describes the death of Henri II in a joust with Count Montgomery only a few years after publication of Nostradamus' *Centuries*. The younger Montgomery's splintered lance pierced Henri's helmet, putting out an eye. Infection set in and after several pain-filled days, the king succumbed.

Rating: 9
The phrase "two wounds in one" necessitates counting the infection as the second wound. Still, the quatrain's overall impact can be measured by the fact that it made Nostradamus an instant celebrity.

Quatrain I-37: Pearl Harbor

> Shortly before the Sun sets, battle is given a great peo-
> ple in doubt: Ruined, the marine port makes no reply;
> bridge and sepulchre in two strange places.

> *Un peu devant que le Soleil s'esconse,*
> *Conflit donné grand peuple dubieux:*
> *Profliges, port marin ne fait reponse,*
> *Pont et sepulcre en deux estrange lieux.*

This is a clear quatrain that, oddly, has escaped solution. The rising sun was the emblem of Japan, but the attack on Pearl Harbor was a blunder that shortly caused that sun to set. The United States was ambivalent about the war until attacked, favoring the Allies but unwilling to get into the fray. The surprise attack on the harbor was so devastating that American forces could launch no counterstrike. The last line refers to the battleship *Arizona*, later converted into a unique monument and undersea tomb. The "bridge" is the ship's bridge, strangely under water.

Rating: 9.5

The prophecy is lucid, specific, and nearly flawless.

Quatrain I-38: Japan and the United States in World War II

> The Sun and the Eagle will (each) appear as victor.
> The vanquished reassured with a vain response: With
> hue and cry they will not cease arming. Revenge,
> because of death a timely peace achieved.

> *Le Sol et l'Aigle au victeur paraitront,*
> *Response vaine au vaincu l'on asseure:*
> *Par con ne cris harnois n'arreteront,*
> *Vindicte, paix par mort si acheve à l'heure.*

The rising "Sun" of Japan swept to a stunning series of victories in the early phases of World War II, only to be crushed later by the counterattacks of the American "Eagle." The "vain response" must refer to General Doolittle's brilliantly improvised raid on Tokyo in April of 1942, which did little damage but provided Americans with a colossal morale boost. America's frantic arms build-up is noted in the prediction. Because of the huge death toll inflicted by the atomic bomb, Japan surrendered much before it otherwise might have.

Rating: 8.5

A solid quatrain (following one on Pearl Harbor) that has somehow eluded solution.

Quatrain I-47: The League of Nations

> The sermons from the Lake of Geneva annoying,
> from days they will grow into weeks, then months,
> then years; then all will fail. The magistrates will
> damn their useless laws.

> *Du lac Leman les sermons facheront,*
> *Des jours seront reduits par des semaines,*
> *Puis mois, puis ans, puis tous defailliront,*
> *Les Magistrats damneront leur lois vaines.*

Geneva was the home of the spectacularly unsuccessful League of
Nations established in the wake of World War I. The conclave became
infamous for its endless debates and indecision while Hitler, Mussolini, and Japan pushed the world closer and closer to the catastrophe of
World War II. All three Axis powers ignored the League with impuni-
ty and it essentially collapsed in 1939.

Rating: 9

The quatrain has also been applied to Calvin's Geneva theocracy[2] that
ultimately failed but only after a long period of considerable success.
Most commentators prefer the League of Nations solution.

Quatrain I-49: Peter the Great's Northern War

> Very much before such intrigues (a reference to the
> preceding quatrain), those of the East by virtue of the
> Moon in the year 1700 will cause a great many to be
> carried off, almost subjugating the northern corner.

> *Beaucoup, beaucoup avant telles menees*
> *Ceux d'Orient par la vertu lunaire:*
> *L'an mil sept cent feront grands emmenees,*
> *Subjugant presque le coin Aquilonaire.*

---

2. Calvin ruled Geneva from 1541 until his death in 1564, rigidly enforcing his religious views.

A startling quatrain because it is dated and altogether correct. Previous commentators have missed the essence of it, most assuming "those of the East" to be the Turks instead of the Russians. Czar Peter's Northern War, which did in fact subjugate most lands in Russia's northwest corner, lasted from 1700 to 1721. The peace treaty gave Peter his long-sought window on the Baltic. He was able to mount his northern drive only by virtue of an advantageous peace treaty with the Turks—those of the (crescent) moon—in 1700.

Rating: 10
This is a very daring and successful quatrain that is factual as well as geographically and chronologically precise. It would be nitpicking not to give it full points.

Quatrain I-50: Franklin D. Roosevelt

> Of the aquatic triplicity there will be born one who
> will make Thursday his holiday: His fame, praise, rule,
> and power will grow; by land and sea a tempest in the
> Orient.

> *De l'aquatique triplicité naitra*
> *D'un qui fera le jeudi pour sa fete:*
> *Son bruit, los, regne, sa puissance croitra,*
> *Par terre et mer aux Orients tempete.*

It is surprising that such a clear quatrain has remained unsolved for so long. Franklin Roosevelt was born under the sign of Aquarius, one of the three water signs. He was the president who signed the legislation making Thanksgiving ("Thursday") an official national holiday (though it had long been celebrated). Roosevelt's fame and power probably exceeded any other president's. The last line of the prophecy plainly alludes to the tempest unleashed by Japan's December 1941 attacks in the Pacific, perhaps with double-meaning overtones about the kamikaze (meaning "divine wind") suicide attacks late in the war.

Rating: 10

This quatrain is specific, detailed, lucid, and flawless—an unqualified success.

Quatrain I-52: The Sultan Selim and Napoleon

> The two wicked ones conjoined in Scorpio, the Grand
> Seignior murdered in his hall: plague to the Church by
> the new King combined of low and northern Europe.

> *Les deux malins de Scorpion conjoints,*
> *Le grand Seigneur meurtri dans sa salle:*
> *Peste à l'Eglise par le nouveau Roi joint,*
> *L'Europe basse et Septentrionale.*

The "two wicked ones" are Saturn and Mars, both considered malevolent influences by astrologers. Dr. Christian Wollner[3] points out that this not-so-common conjunction occurred in 1807, the year Sultan Selim III (titled "Grand Seignior") was deposed, to be strangled in the seraglio the next year. At this time, Napoleon had spread his rule far into southern and northern Europe. Bonaparte, who made a puppet of the pope, was assuredly trouble to the Church.

Rating: 9

One could quibble that Nostradamus did not hit the exact year of the sultan's death, but overall the prophecy holds up well.

Quatrain I-53: Revolution in Europe

> Alas! One will see a great people tormented and the
> holy law in utter ruin: different laws throughout all
> Christendom, when a new mine of gold and silver is
> discovered.

---

3. Dr. Wollner worked out the astrological charts for numerous quatrains ca. 1926.

Las! qu'on verra grand peuple tourmenté
Et la loi sainte en totale ruine,
Par autres lois toute Chretienté,
Quand d'or, d'argent trouve nouvelle mine.

The standard interpretation, which goes back to Le Pelletier, is that the verse depicts the French Revolution of 1789 and the subsequent confiscation of Church properties, which provided the state with a new "mine" of gold and silver. This is good enough, but another application works equally well. The socialist and anticlerical revolutionary movement of 1848 spread chaos through several European countries, especially France, forcing many changes in the laws. About this time, huge new gold and silver strikes were made in California and Nevada (Sutter's Mill in 1846 and the fabled Comstock lode in 1859).

Rating: 8.5

The two interpretations seem to have about the same degree of merit. The second is less metaphorical, but devotees of Le Pelletier could argue that there was more "ruin" to holy laws in 1789 than in 1848.

Quatrain I-55: Communist Rule in Russia

Under the climate opposite to the Babylonian there
will be great effusion of blood. The unrighteous will
be on land and sea, in air and sky: sects, famine,
realms, plagues, confusion.

Sous l'opposite climat Babylonique,
Grand sera de sang effusion,
Que terre et mer, air, ciel sera inique:
Sectes, faim, regnes, pestes, confusion.

The reference to "the unrighteous" in the sky clearly places this quatrain in the twentieth century, the age of the airplane. The climate of Babylon being hot and dry, the opposite would be the cold, damp steppes of Russia. Also, Moscow is due north of Babylonia. The Communist rule of Russia, particularly under Stalin, was marked by some of the greatest bloodletting in human history. The quatrain's last line is a graphic description of life in the USSR during the decades of Red rule. (Curiously, I have not seen this interpretation elsewhere.)

Rating: 8
The prophecy has no real faults except that it might be considered too general in nature.

Quatrain I-57: Death of Louis XVI

Through great dissension the earth will tremble.
Accord broken, lifting the head to the sky: The bloody
mouth will swim in the blood; on the ground the face
anointed with milk and honey.

Par grand discord la terre tremblera,
Accord rompu dressant la tête au ciel:
Bouche sanglante dans le sang nagera,
Au sol la face ointe de lait et miel.

Almost from the time of the French Revolution this graphic quatrain has been recognized as a presage of Louis XVI's execution. Shortly before the king was guillotined, the French National Assembly negated the old social contract by abolishing royalty ("accord broken"). The phrase "lifting the head to the sky" refers to the executioner's practice of holding the severed head of the victim aloft for the witnesses to see. As part of his coronation, Louis was anointed with milk and honey.

Rating: 8.5
This is an admirably vivid prophecy, so descriptive that it leaves hardly any doubt about its subject.

Quatrain I-60: The Napoleonic Wars

> An Emperor will be born near Italy, one who will cost
> his empire a high price: They will say that from the
> sort of people who surround him he is to be found
> less a prince than butcher.

> *Un Empereur naitra près d'Italie,*
> *Qui a l'Empire sera vendu bien cher:*
> *Diront avec quels gens il se rallie*
> *Qu'on trouvera moins prince que boucher.*

Emperor Napoleon, perhaps understandably, is the subject of more quatrains than any other individual. He was born near Italy on the island of Corsica (where an Italian dialect is spoken). Bonaparte's endless wars and campaigns did in fact cost France a horrendous price. In cooperation with the glory-obsessed military men surrounding him, Napoleon nearly succeeded in sacrificing a whole generation of young Frenchmen to his dreams of an empire.

Rating: 8.5
The prediction is quite accurate as far as it goes, but the last two lines do not carry a lot of hard information.

Quatrain I-63: The Modern Post War World

> The scourges passed, the world shrinks. For a long
> time peace and populated lands: One will travel safely
> by air, land, sea, and wave; then wars stirred up anew.

> *Les Fleaux passés diminue le monde,*
> *Longtemps la paix terres inhabitées:*
> *Sur marchera par ciel, terre, mer et onde,*
> *Puis de nouveau les guerres suscitées.*

The striking allusion to air travel, which would have been incomprehensible in Nostradamus' time, clearly places this prediction in our era. The passing of scourges plainly refers to modern medicine's victories over the horrific plagues that were common in the Prophet's lifetime. The "long time peace" probably reflects the Seer's Eurocentric outlook. There has been no major war in Europe for more than half a century—an extraordinary length of time by historical standards.

Rating: 9

The "wars stirred up anew" conceivably could refer to the disruptions in Yugoslavia in the 1990s, but more likely the Seer had in mind the impending Mediterranean War destined to follow in the wake of the 2004 comet.

Quatrain I-64: World War I Battlefields

> They will think they have seen the sun at night when
> they will see the pig half-man: Noise, chant, battle,
> fighting in the sky perceived, and one will hear brute
> beasts talking.

> *De nuit Soleil penseront avoir vu*
> *Quand le pourceau demi-homme on verra:*
> *Bruit, chant, bataille, au ciel battre apercu,*
> *Et bêtes brutes à parler l'on orra.*

This vivid portrayal of a World War I battlefront demonstrates the element of imagery that must have been involved in Nostradamus' precognitions. Soldiers often wore gas masks that gave them a decidedly porcine appearance. The Seer perceived these "pig half-men" talking and shouting in unison as they charged the enemy. The first line depicts the brilliant aerial flares used to light up the nighttime no man's land. World War I was the first war in which airplanes engaged in combat over the battlefield.

Rating: 9

Though strongly poetic, the quatrain is also detailed enough to give it a high ranking. (A previously unsolved quatrain.)

Quatrain I-69: Italy's Reunification

> The great round mountain of seven stades, after
> peace, war, famine, flood, will roll far sinking great
> countries, even the ancient ones of great foundation.

> *La grande montagne ronde de sept stades,*
> *Après paix, guerre, faim, inondation,*
> *Roulera loin abimant grands contrades,*
> *Memes antqiues, et grande fondation.*

Though fulfilled over a century ago, this quatrain has escaped solution because of its arcane imagery. The "great round mountain" is certainly volcanic Vesuvius (which is seven stades high), used fittingly here as a figure of the eruption of revolutionary, nationalistic fervor that united Italy in the nineteenth century. Naples, in the shadow of Vesuvius, was one of the hotbeds of the Risorgimento, a movement which swept over all of Italy, sinking many old kingdoms, including the 1,000-year-old Papal States.

Rating: 8
While colorful and accurate, the quatrain's somewhat abstract quality leaves it a bit short of the ideal.

Quatrain I-70: Khomeini's Islamic Revolution

> Rain (of blood), famine, war in Persia not over; the
> too great faith will betray the monarch. Finished
> there, begun in Gaul (France): a secret sign for one to
> be moderate.

> *Pluie, faim, guerre en Perse non cessée,*
> *La foi tropo grande trahira le monarque,*
> *Par la finie en Gaule commencee:*
> *Secret augure pour à un etre parque.*

The meaning of this quatrain became evident only when the Ayatollah Khomeini, who engineered his Islamic revolt from France, returned to Iran ("Persia") in 1979 and seized control of the country in a few days of fighting. The "too great faith" alludes to fanatic Shiite Muslim resistance to the Shah's efforts at westernization. The last line applies to President Jimmy Carter's restrained policy in the ensuing United State's embassy hostage crisis, prompted perhaps by unpublicized diplomatic pressures from west European allies. Soon after, a long, bloody, and futile war broke out between Iran and Iraq.

Rating: 9

Outside of a slight vagueness in the last line, this is a highly impressive quatrain.

Quatrain I-76: Napoleon Bonaparte

> With a name so wild will he be brought forth that the
> three sisters will have the name for destiny: Then he
> will lead a great people by tongue and deed; more
> than any other he will have fame and renown.
>
> *D'un nom farouche tel proferé sera,*
> *Que les trois soeurs auront fato le nom:*
> *Puis grand peuple par langue et fait duira,*
> *Plus que nul autre aura bruit et renom.*

The object of this quatrain is immediately obvious because the "name so wild" can only be Napoleon, a name not only unusual but one that bears an eerie similarity to Apollyon, the Greek angel of destruction. The three sisters are the three Fates of Greek mythology. It is no exaggeration to say that Bonaparte's "fame and renown" exceeded that of any other personage of his time, perhaps of any time.

Rating: 9

The many strikingly accurate quatrains dealing with Napoleon are perhaps the strongest evidence there is that Nostradamus was indeed an authentic seer, somehow able to perceive certain aspects of the future.

Quatrain I-78: Marshall Pétain and Vichy France

It will be born of an old chief with dulled senses,
degenerating in knowledge and arms: The chief of
France dreaded by its sister; fields divided, granted to
the troops.

D'un chef vieillard naitra sens hebeté,
Degenerant par savoir et par armes:
Le chef de France par sa soeur redouté,
Champs divises, concedes aux gendarmes.

Most commentators think this quatrain must apply to one-time French hero Marshall Pétain though they have not been able to handle the word "sister" (*soeur*). Probably, Nostradamus is alluding to Vichy France itself as the sister of the true France. The people of Vichy France hated the aging Pétain and viewed him as a Nazi puppet though he had been one of France's most glorious leaders in World War I. During most of World War II, the fields of France were divided with the Nazis, occupying the northern portion of the country. The first line merely refers to the formation of Vichy France with Pétain as its head.

Rating: 9

The prediction is a little murkier than it should be but contains numerous accurate elements and no miscues.

Quatrain I-82: The Year of Revolt (1848)

When the columns of wood (trees) tremble greatly,
driven by the south wind, covered with red ochre: A
very great assembly will pour forth, Vienna and Austria will tremble.

Quand les colonnes de bois grand tremblee,
D'Auster conduite couverte de rubriche:
Tant videra dehors grande assemblee,
Trembler Vienne et le pays d'Austriche.

The first part of this ingenious verse pictures a revolutionary gale ("red ochre") sweeping up from the south to impact Austria. The Seer uses the wind metaphor because the disturbance begins in the characteristically windy month of March. In 1848, a revolutionary movement broke out in mid-March in Vienna when thousands took to the streets protesting against the imperial regime and demanding a constitution. The insurrection continued for months before it was forcibly put down by the Austrian army. The revolutionary spirit did come from the south where uprisings in Palermo and Naples had erupted in January and rapidly spread to northern Italy.

Rating: 9

Widespread resistance to the old order was fed by the election of the liberal, if somewhat naive, Pope Gregory XVI in 1846. This is a fine verse with a subtlety that accounts for the lack of an earlier solution.

Quatrain I-83: Italy vs. Greece (World War II)

> The strange nation will divide the spoils. Saturn in Mars, his aspect furious: horrible slaughter of the Tuscans and Latins; Greeks who will be ready to strike.

> *La gent étrange divisera butins,*
> *Saturne en Mars son regard furieux:*
> *Horrible strage aux Toscans et Latins,*
> *Grecs, qui seront à frapper curieux.*

In World War II, Mussolini launched a bumbling attempt to conquer Greece, suffering defeats and heavy losses until the German army intervened to decide the issue. After pulling Il Duce's "chestnuts from the fire," the Nazis ("the strange nation") dictated the terms of the final settlement, deciding who got what. The astrological reference is a very negative one; Nostradamus is merely noting the inauspicious prospects of the Italian invasion.

Rating: 8.5

This is a neat if not sensational hit for the Seer. The last line could be stronger.

Quatrain I-85: Murder of the Guise Brothers by King Henry (1588)

Because of the lady's reply, the King troubled: Ambassadors will take their lives in their hands. The great one doubly will imitate his brothers—two who will die through anger, hatred, and envy.

Par la response de dame, Roi troublé:
Ambassadeurs mepriseront leur vie:
Le grand ses freres contrefera doublé,
Par deux mourront ire, haine et envie.

This quatrain was resolved four centuries ago when two of the brothers Guise were killed on orders of the envious and spiteful King Henry III of France. The king's mother, Catherine de Médici, refused to countenance the murders, which became such a monumental scandal that the king was criticized—at some risk to themselves—by various envoys and deputies. The third Guise brother, the Duke of Mayenne, assumed the mantle of his dead brothers as head of the Catholic League.

Rating: 9

The prediction deals accurately with a fairly complex set of circumstances.

Quatrain I-86: The Flight of Mary, Queen of Scots

The great queen when she shall see herself vanquished will act with an excess of masculine courage: On horseback, she will pass over the river totally naked (vulnerable), pursued by the sword: It will mark an outrage to faith.

La grande Reine quand se verra vaincue,
Fera excés de masculin courage:
Sur cheval, fleuve passera toute nue,
Suite par fer: à foi fera outrage.

The consensus opinion applies this prediction to Mary Stuart who, when her army was defeated near Glasgow by the Protestant Scots in 1568, had to flee to England. It was a hard ninety-two-mile ride, traveling mostly at night with almost no food and no place to sleep save the cold ground. Crossing the Dee River, Mary's party destroyed the wooden bridge there to foil pursuers. Since Mary, like Nostradamus, was a devout Catholic, the Seer would understandably view the whole episode as an outrage to faith.

Rating: 9

Nostradamus could be accused of excessive poetic license with the word "naked," but he was, after all, looking for a rhyme. (Critics are wrong who say Mary crossed the river by ferry, not horseback. The ferry was across Solway Firth, a bay.)

Quatrain I-87: Volcanic Eruptions and Plate Tectonics

> The Earthshaker's fire from the center of the earth
> will cause trembling around the new city: Two great
> rocks will make war for a long time; then Arethusa
> will redden a new river.
>
> *Ennosigee feu du centre de terre*
> *Fera trembler autour de cité neuve:*
> *Deux grands rochers longtemps feront la guerre,*
> *Puis Arethuse rougira nouveau fleuve.*

A fascinating quatrain since it appears to show knowledge of twentieth-century geological science. The "new city" is Naples (Neapolis) near Mount Vesuvius. After centuries of relative quietude, Vesuvius erupted with particular violence in 1631 following days of sharp quakes. "Arethusa" is associated with Sicily, so a great lava flow from Mt. Etna is predicted. The ultimate fiery river from Etna reached Catania in 1669. But it is the line about the two great rocks making war that is most stunning. Only in the past few decades have we known that tectonic eruptions result from a collision of two massive crustal plates.

Rating: 8.5

Forecasting an eruption of Etna is safe enough since the volcano has an active history. Nonetheless, the third line of the quatrain is amazing.

Quatrain I-88: A Turn in Napoleon's Fortunes

The divine ill (God's wrath) will surprise the great
Prince shortly before he will have married a woman.
His support and credit will suddenly become slim;
counsel will perish for the shaven head.

Le divin mal surprendra le grand Prince
Un peu devant aura femme epousee,
Son appui et credit à un coup viendra mince,
Conseil mourra pour la tête rasee.

An intriguing prophecy in light of the common belief (in his time) that Napoleon's luck ran out when he left Josephine to marry Marie Louise of Austria. About the time of the divorce, things started going badly in Spain, and soon thereafter came the Russian disaster. Then some key advisors, such as Tallyrand, began to distance themselves from Bonaparte, who was called "the little crophead" (line four).

Rating: 8.5

The quatrain is general enough to apply to more than one case, but it surely fits Napoleon better than anyone else.

Quatrain I-89: The Long Wars

All those from Lerida (Spain) will be in the Moselle,
putting to death all those from the Loire and Seine
(the French). Marine relief will come near the high
wall when the Spaniards open every vein.

Tous ceux de Ilerde seront dedans Moselle,
Mettant à mort tous ceux de Loire et Seine;
Secours marin viendra près d'haute velle
Quand Espagnols ouvrira toute veine.

Though the events of this verse cover a goodly time span, they are contained within the Eighty Years' War for Dutch independence, which chronologically encompassed the related Thirty Years' War in central Europe. The Spanish began operating in the Moselle area early in the Thirty Years' War (1618–1648). In 1636, they launched an invasion of France from there and for a time threatened Paris itself. The rest of the quatrain clearly refers to the fabled rescue of the besieged city of Leyden (1574) when the Dutch opened their dikes to the flood so that their ships could sail to the walled city with supplies. As the last line indicates, the Spanish efforts to suppress the Dutch rebellion were bloody in the extreme.

Rating: 9

The only drawback to these entirely accurate predictions might be the extended time frame, so that the verse verges on being a split quatrain.

Quatrain I-91: The Cold War

> The Gods will make it appear to humans that they
> (the Gods) will be the authors of a great conflict.
> Sword and lance before the sky is seen serene, when
> there will be greater affliction towards the left hand.

> *Les Dieux feront aux humains apparence,*
> *Ce qu'ils seront auteurs de grand conflict:*
> *Avant ciel vu serein epee et lance,*
> *Que vers main gauche sera plus grand afflict.*

For four decades, there was a prevailing opinion that World War III between the free world and the Communist bloc would be inevitable, decreed by fate. The massive arms build-up on both sides is referred to as "sword and lance," weapons having forms suggestive of the menacing ballistic missiles. But suddenly the skies appear serene with the abrupt collapse of the Soviet superpower. The Cold War was costly to both sides, but ultimately it broke the back of Communism—the political left.

Rating: 8.5

This was a previously unsolved quatrain that is both poetic and accurate though quite subtle.

Quatrain I-92: The Palestinian Wars

> Under the U. N. peace will be proclaimed everywhere,
> but not long after pillage and rebellion. Because of a
> refusal town, land, and sea encroached upon, dead
> and captives one third of a million.

> *Sous un la paix partout sera clamée,*
> *Mais non longtemps pillé et rébellion,*
> *Par refus ville, terre et mer entamée,*
> *Mort et captifs le tiers d'un million.*

If *un* of line one (French version) is translated as the initials for the United Nations (U. N.), this becomes a fascinating verse. Following World War II, the United Nations was being hailed as the avenue to world peace. But when the United Nations okayed the partition of Palestine to create a Jewish state, the Arab "refusal" to recognize it led to "pillage and rebellion" as Arabs protested and battled against the new Israel. Beginning in 1946, a series of wars between the Jews and the Arabs punctuated Middle Eastern affairs. Many towns and much land changed hands ("encroached upon"). Reliable figures are hard to find regarding the number killed and captured in these wars, but a "third of a million" would not be much off the mark.

Rating: 8.5

Un (meaning "one") could, of course, be an individual, and the verse could still work, but the U. N. interpretation is so apropos it almost jumps off the page.

Quatrain I-93: Western Europe in World War I

> The land of Italy will tremble near the mountains.
> The Lion and the Cock not too well confederated;
> because of fear one will help the other. Only Castulo
> and the Celts moderate (neutral).

> *Terra Italique près des monts tremblera,*
> *Lion et Coq non trop confederes,*
> *En lieu de peur l'un l'autre s'aidera,*
> *Seul Castulon et Celtes, moderes.*

Warfare on the Italian front in World War I (featuring massive artillery barrages) was concentrated at the foot of the Alps. The English "Lion" came to the aid of France ("the Cock"), but there was substantial friction between the two about the conduct of the war throughout. "Castulo" is probably poetic synecdoche for Spain, one of the few nations that stayed neutral. The "Celts" here are apparently the Irish, then part of the United Kingdom, but so anglophobic and lukewarm on the war that Britain levied no troops from Ireland.

Rating: 7.5

An obvious weak point of the prophecy is that several of the smaller European nations (e.g., in Scandinavia) actually managed to maintain neutrality. Still, there is a good deal of merit in the quatrain.

Quatrain I-94: War and Death and Sultana

> At "Port Selin" the tyrant put to death, liberty
> nonetheless not recovered. The new Mars (war) by
> way of vengeance and remorse; the Lady honored
> through force of terror.

> *Au port Selin le tyran mis à mort*
> *La liberté non pourtant recouvree:*
> *Le nouveau Mars par vindicte et remort*
> *Dame par force de frayer honorée.*

The era of Kussem Sultana, one of the most colorful women in Turkish history, is the subject of this verse. She was the mother of the weak-minded Sultan Ibrahim I and was practically the ruler at Istanbul ("Port Selin") during his reign. He was murdered in a mutiny in 1648, but Sultana held power for another eight years, ruling through the terror of the Janissaries, whom she alone could control. Despite the death of Ibrahim, who had begun the conquest ("new Mars") of Venetian Crete, the island did not recover its liberty but eventually came entirely under the Turks. Sultana was finally strangled with the cords of her bed curtains in a palace coup.

Rating: 9

A vividly accurate quatrain right down to the "vengeance and remorse" of line three. Ibrahim invaded Crete because the Venetians had burned some of his ships, an action they must have soon regretted.

Quatrain I-96: Glasnost Galore

> He who will have charge of demolishing temples and
> sects, changed through fantasy: He will come to do
> more harm to rocks than to the living because of the
> din in his ears of a polished tongue.

> *Celui qu'aura la charge de detruire*
> *Temples et sectes, changes par fantaisie:*
> *Plus aux rochers qu'aux vivants viendra nuire*
> *Par langue ornee d'oreilles ressassie.*

The subject of this unsolved verse is former Soviet President Mikhail Gorbachev. As leader of the Communist Party, he might have been expected to sternly oppose religion and other freedoms, but he held the "fantasy" that Communism and democracy could thrive in Russia simultaneously. Obviously, he was wrong. The "polished tongue" is that of Ronald Reagan who developed an improbable rapport with Gorbachev and had significant influence on him. The quatrain's third line seems obscure but probably refers to the Soviets' unbridled industrialization policy—exploitation of all natural resources regardless of environmental impact—hence, the "harm to rocks," or more broadly, the earth.

Rating: 8.5
Gorbachev did, indeed, do little damage to his people ("the living"); in fact, he brought an end to the bloody Soviet intrusion into Afghanistan.

Quatrain I-98: The British Lose in Greece

> A chief who will have led a great number of people far
> from skies of their own, of language and customs
> strange: Five thousand finished in Crete and Thessaly;
> the chief fleeing in a marine barn (troop ship?).

> *Le chef qu'aura conduit peuple infini*
> *Loin de son ciel, de moeurs et langue étrange:*
> *Cinq mil en Crete et Thessalie fini,*
> *Le chef fuyant sauvé en marine grange.*

More than 30,000 British troops were sent to Greece early in World War II to aid the outmanned Greeks against the Axis invaders. The Allies attempted to make a stand in Thessaly but were beaten back, the Brits fleeing by ship to Crete—which the Germans soon conquered by means of an aerial invasion. The great majority of the British expeditionary force was taken prisoner in the campaign; several thousand were wounded, but the number of Brits actually killed in action was in the neighborhood of the Seer's "five thousand."

Rating: 8.5
The Seer seems to be straining for a rhyme with "marine barn," but the rest of the prediction works well.

Quatrain II-1: Wellington's Peninsular Campaign

Towards Aquitaine by the British Isles, by these themselves (the British) great incursions. Rains, frosts will make the soil uneven. Port Selyn will cause mighty invasions.

Vers Aquitaine par insuls Britanniques
De par eux-memes grandes incursions.
Pluies, gelées feront terroirs iniques,
Port Selyn fortes fera invasions.

Late in the Napoleonic wars, the famed British general Lord Wellington drove into southern France ("Aquitaine") via Iberia. The offensive proceeded despite adverse winter weather with both armies sometimes halted in their tracks by heavy downpours. "Port Selyn" (port of the moon) is Constantinople, then capital of Turkey. In Nostradamus' day, there was almost constant ebb-and-flow warfare between the Turks and the West until Napoleonic times when the Greek and Serb revolts signaled the beginning of the end for the Turkish Empire.

Rating: 8.5

This quatrain has some strong aspects even though the last line drifts away from the main thrust. The Turks reached their high tide at Vienna in 1683 where they were finally turned back by the Poles and Austrians.

Quatrain II-6: Hiroshima and Nagasaki

Near the ports and within two cities there will be two scourges the like of which was never seen. Famine within plague; people put out by the steel tip, crying to the great immortal God for relief.

Aupres des portes et dedans deux cités
Seront deux fléaux, et onc n'aperdu un tel,
Faim dedans peste, de fer hors gens boutés,
Crier secours au grand Dieu immortel.

This quatrain immediately calls to mind images of the only two cities ever hit by atomic bombs: Hiroshima and Nagasaki. Both suffered the ghastly "scourges," and both are port cities. Nostradamus likens the effects of radiation sickness to a combination of "famine within plague," a pretty fair comparison (certainly as good as any sixteenth-century mind could be expected to devise). The "steel tip" must allude to the pointed, metal nose of the bomb itself. There can be no question about the fulfillment of the last line.

Rating: 9

Altogether, this is a strikingly vivid and accurate portrayal with drawbacks only for the very literal-minded.

Quatrain II-8: Founding of the United States of America

> Temples consecrated in the original Roman manner,
> they will reject the underlying foundations, taking
> their premier and humane laws, chasing, though not
> entirely, the cult of the saints.
>
> *Temples sacres prime facon Romaine,*
> *Rejeteront les goffes fondements,*
> *Prenant leur lois premieres et humaines,*
> *Chassant, non tour, des saints les cultements.*

The Seer seems to view the United States, though not inaptly, as sort of a modern-day Roman Republic (see Quatrain IV-95, page 165). Most of America's great government buildings ("temples") are modeled after the Roman style. The founding fathers did in fact reject the traditional governmental bedrock of Church and monarchy, yet they hewed to traditional Christian values (line three) even while vigorously insisting on the separation of church and state (line four).

Rating: 8

Le Pelletier thought this one might describe the Feast of the Supreme Being[4] during the French Revolution—not entirely unreasonable—but that episode was vehemently anti-Christian. The last line, as well as the whole tone of the verse, conforms better with the early stages of the United States.

Quatrain II-9: Hitler's Third Reich

Nine years the thin one (or vegetarian) will hold the reign in peace; then he will fall into a very bloody thirst. Because of him a great people will die without faith and law, slain by one far more debonair.

Neuf ans le regne le maigre en paix tiendra,
Puis il cherra en soif si sanguinaire:
Pour lui grand peuple sans foi et loi mourra
Tué par un beaucoup plus deonnaire.

Though he was not named chancellor until later, Hitler became the dominant figure in German politics in 1930 when his fledgling Nazi Party won a stunning 107 seats in the September elections. The major industrialists quickly swung in behind him and exactly nine years later—September 1939—der Führer unleashed World War II in Europe. The Nazi regime, which certainly had no respect for either law or faith, was crushed as the "debonair" Franklin Roosevelt brought the full force of American power against the Third Reich. Hitler was in fact a vegetarian as Nostradamus implies.

Rating: 9

This is one of the Seer's most piercing prophecies though not entirely beyond debate since Hitler did not become chancellor until 1933.

---

4. Famous speech by Robespierre.

Quatrain II-11: Napoleon Makes It Big

The next son of the elder will attain very great height
as far as the realm of the privileged: Everyone will fear
his fierce glory but his children will be ejected from
the realm.

Le prochain fils de l'aisnier parviendra
Tant eleve jusqu'au regne des fors:
Son apre gloire un chacun la craindra,
Mais ses enfants de regne jetes hors.

Nostradamus, perhaps understandably, seems almost obsessed
with France's greatest soldier. This is one of more than a dozen quatrains dealing with Bonaparte who was a second son and, of course,
reached the greatest heights of glory and privilege. He was for more
than a decade the terror of Europe. But with the return of the Bourbon monarchy, Napoleon's children, who once seemed destined to
rule, were removed from power, literally proscribed.

Rating: 8

The prediction is certainly accurate enough but could have profited
from more detail.

Quatrain II-12: Stalin's War on Religion

Closed eyes opened by antique fantasy, the garb of the
monks will be put to naught. The grand monarch will
chastise their frenzy, ravishing the treasure in front of
the temples.

Yeux closes, ouverts d'antique fantaisie,
L'habit des seuls seront mis à neant:
Le grand monarque chatiera leur frenesie,
Ravir des temples le tresor par devant.

This quatrain is less obscure than previous commentators have supposed. At seventeen, a young seminarian named Joseph Stalin had his

eyes opened to the fantasy of utopian Communism, an idea with roots centuries old. Once in power, he did his best to put religion out of business, relentlessly suppressing the Church, confiscating its properties and historic treasures. Angry churchmen who ventured to resist Stalin's state of atheism soon found themselves in Siberia. Stalin was, of course, an absolute dictator, justifying the use of the term "monarch."

Rating: 9

A somewhat subtle prophecy in certain respects but altogether correct.

Quatrain II-15: The Curtain Falls on Fascist Italy

> Shortly before the monarch is assassinated, Castor and Pollux in the ship, bearded star: The public treasury emptied by land and sea—Pisa, Asti, Ferrara, Turin, under interdict.

> *Un peu devant monarque trucidé,*
> *Castor Pollux en nef, astre crinite:*
> *L'erain publique par terre et mer vidé,*
> *Pise, Ast, Ferrare, Turin terre interdite.*

The assassination of Mussolini after Italy's fall to the Allies in World War II is foreseen here. "Castor and Pollux" are the twin Anglo powers—Britain and the United States—invading by ship in 1943. Italy was by this time exhausted and bankrupted by its futile war effort (line three). The cities named are all in northern Italy, which found itself under Nazi rule ("interdict") in the wake of the Italian surrender. The "bearded star" is D'Arrest's comet, which passed by the Earth about the time of the Allied invasion.

Rating: 8.5

The slightly oblique second line has led commentators awry, but everything in this previously unsolved verse fits nicely. The interpretation is supported by the following coupled quatrain, II-16.

Quatrain II-16: The Allies Invade Italy (World War II)

Naples, Palermo, Sicily, Syracuse; new tyrants, celestial
lighting fires: Force from London, Belgium (Ghent
and Brussels) and Susa, great slaughter; triumph leads
to festivities.

Naples, Palerme, Sicile, Syracuses,
Nouveaux tryans, fulgures feux celestes:
Force de Londres, Gand, Bruxelles et Suses,
Grand hecatombe, triomphe faire festes.

In 1943, British and American forces launched their invasion of
Italy from Tunisia, site of the city of Susah, or Sousse. Most of the
American troops had earlier been based in southern England near
London. The allusion to Belgium appears curious at first, but some of
the British units had previously served in the defense of Belgium.
"Celestial lighting fires" suggests the allied bombings. The "new
tyrants" are the Fascists—or the Nazis who seized control of Italy after
the invasion. The Allied triumph prompted much celebration, even by
Italians, most of whom were fed up with Mussolini.

Rating: 8
While the Belgian reference seems unnecessary, the net merit of the
prediction is considerable.

Quatrain II-19: The Zionist Resettlement of Israel

Newcomers, a place built without defense, place occupied then uninhabitable: Meadows, houses, fields,
towns to take at pleasure; hunger, plague (of conflict?), war, extensive arable land.

Nouveaux venus, lieu bati sans defense,
Occuper place par lors inhabitable:
Près, maison, champs, villes prendre à plaisance,
Faim, peste, guerre, arpent long labourable.

Though ignored by previous commentators, this quatrain is actually an adept description of the return of the Jews to Palestine. The movement became substantial after World War I and gave momentum to the reestablishment of Israel in 1948. Arabs were essentially defenseless against the influx, Palestine being under the control of Britain which favored Zionism. Through irrigation the Israelis made much desert land habitable. Intermittent wars between Arabs and Jews produced many Palestinian refugees, some of whom suffered from hunger.

Rating: 9

An almost flawless quatrain, though we could wish for a geographic clue.

Quatrain II-22: The Greek-Turkish War (1920–22)

> The imprudent army of Europe will depart, collecting itself near the submerged isle: The accursed kind will bend the phalanx. At the navel of the world, a greater voice substituted.

> *Le camp Ascop d'Europe partia,*
> *S'adjoignant proche de l'ile submergée:*
> *D'Araon classe phalange pliera,*
> *Nombril du monde plus grande voix subrogée.*

The Greeks, in the wake of World War I, imprudently challenged the larger Turkish nation for territory on the coast of Asia Minor. In 1922, the Greek army ("phalanx") was routed near Symrna and fled to the Aegean island of Khíos. To Nostradamus, a devout Catholic Christian, the Muslim Turks were an "accursed kind." The "navel of the world" is Rome, and the last line of this previously unsolved quatrain points to the election of a greater pope—which actually occurred with the election of the highly regarded Pius XI in early 1922.

Rating: 9.5

Accurate, complex, and detailed, the prophecy is a remarkable one—though Nostradamus is once again groping for a rhyme with the pointless *submergée* in the second line.

Quatrain II-24: Hitler and the Nazis

> Beasts ferocious from hunger will swim across rivers:
> The greater part of the field will be against Hister. The
> great one will cause him to be dragged into an iron
> cage, when the child of Germany will observe nothing.

> *Bêtes farouches de faim fleuves tranner:*
> *Plus part du champ encontre Hister sera,*
> *En cage de fer le grand fera trainer,*
> *Quand rien enfant de Germain observera.*

    This is one of the Seer's most amazing predictions because it identifies his twentieth-century subject by name. "Hister" must be Hitler, with one letter changed, a common anagrammer's ploy in the 1500s. The Nazi "beasts," hungry for conquest, crossed most of Europe's rivers in their sweep across the continent. The meaning of the "iron cage" has been missed; it merely refers to the fact that Hitler was jailed during the administration of President Ebert ("the great one"). The majority of the field of European nations did oppose Hitler, who certainly observed no law or convention of decency.

Rating: 10

This is a real dazzler because of the name designation. Ister was an ancient name for the Danube, but the context indicates a person. Then, too, Hitler was born almost within sight of the Danube.

Quatrain II-28: The Wandering Ayatollah

> The penultimate of the surname of the Prophet will
> take the moon (Islam) for his light and repose: He
> will wander far because of a frantic head in delivering
> a great people from imposition.

> *Le pénultième du surnom du Prophète*
> *Prendra Diane pour son jour et repos:*
> *Loin vaguera par frénétique tête,*
> *En délivrant un grand peuple d'impos.*

The subject is clearly a Muslim leader and evidently the Ayatollah Khomeini since the first syllable of Khomeini sounds the same as the penultimate syllable of Mohammed (HUM with a guttural "H"). Khomeini certainly had a "frantic head" and wandered far—to France and back. For good or ill, he did deliver his Iranian countrymen from foreign influence; Iran had been something of an American client state. The verse is tied to the following one, II-29, which is also about the Ayatollah.

Rating: 9

Although this verse was previously unsolved, there are several quatrains centered on Khomeini, suggesting that his Iranian fundamentalist revolution will have strong historical repercussions.

Quatrain II-29: The Ayatollah Returns

> The Easterner will leave his seat to pass the Apennine
> mountains to see Gaul: He will transpierce the sky, the
> waters and the snow, and everyone will be struck with
> his rod.

> *L'Oriental sortira de son siege,*
> *Passer les monts Apennins voir la Gaule:*
> *Transpercera le ciel, les eaux et neige*
> *Et un chacun frappera de sa gaule.*

The Shah of Iran's nemesis, Ayatollah Khomeini, was for a time exiled to France ("Gaul"), a journey that took him across the Apennine mountains of Italy. Once again, Nostradamus forecasts air travel with the phrase "transpierce the sky." In 1979, Khomeini returned to Iran to seize power and imposed his rigid Muslim orthodoxy on the nation. Anyone who resisted his Islamic new order was harshly dealt with ("struck with his rod")—either killed or imprisoned and often beaten.

Rating: 9

There is specific geography in the quatrain, and the allusion to air travel makes it even more noteworthy.

Quatrain II-32: Trouble Brews in the Balkans

> Milk, frog's blood prepared in Dalmatia. Conflict
> given, plague near Treglia: A great cry will sound
> through all Slavonia; then a monster will be born near
> and within (the province or see of) Ravenna.

> *Lait, sang grenouilles escoudre en Dalmatie.*
> *Conflit donné, peste près de Balenne (Treglia):*
> *Cri sera grand par toute Esclavonie,*
> *Lors naitra monstre près et dedans Ravenne.*

This is one of the undecoded quatrains strangely enough, since it is quite specific chronologically and geographically. Mussolini ("the monster") was born very near Ravenna in 1883. The "plague" near Treglia refers to a major eruption of nearby Vesuvius in 1872. "Milk and frog's blood" is merely poesy for the witch's brew of trouble then bubbling in Dalmatia. Italians and Slavs were in constant strife with each other and their Austrian overlords. A "great cry" was arising among the subject Slavic peoples for independence from Austria-Hungary, a cry that led directly to World War I when the archduke Ferdinand was assassinated in neighboring Bosnia by Serbian Slavs. A witch's brew, indeed!

Rating: 10

Once understood, this is among the most dazzling quatrains. It shows deep insight into the Balkan situation 300 years after it was penned.

Quatrain II-38: The Hitler-Stalin Pact

> A great number will be condemned when the monarchs will be reconciled. But for one of them such a bad encumbrance will arise that they will hardly be joined together.

> *Des condamnes sera fait un grand nombre*
> *Quand les monarques seront conciliES:*
> *Mais a l'un d'eux viendra si mal encombre*
> *Que guere ensemble ne seront rallies.*

The 1939 pact between Hitler and Stalin, who were ideologically hostile, paved the way for their partitioning of Poland and was the death knell for millions of Polish Jews. The cynical agreement aroused an unprecedented uproar in Communist parties around the world, so much so that many thousands of members left the party—a serious "encumbrance" for Stalin. The Nazis and the Russians never really cooperated on anything except the conquest of Poland, and in a couple of years they were at war with each other.

Rating: 8

A tidy and flawless prediction, but not detailed enough to rank high among the Seer's best efforts.

Quatrain II-39: The Dawn of Napoleonic Rule

> One year before the Italian conflict, Germans, Gauls, Spaniards for the fort: The Republican school house will fall. There, except for a few, they will be stifled to death.

Un an devant le conflit Italique,
Germains, Gaulois, Espagnols pour le fort:
Gherra l'école maison de republique,
Ou, hormis peu, seront suffoqués morts.

While the quatrain's second line seems slightly vague, the sense of it has to be that Germans, French, and Spaniards were needed to man the fort, i.e., for military service. The year 1795 was the last year of the French Republic's war against the First Coalition: the armies of Prussia, Austria, and Spain. The next year Napoleon launched his lightning campaign through northern Italy making himself the French national hero. Bonaparte soon put an end to the fledgling French Republic by seizing power for himself and suppressing the assemblies—indeed, all but those of his own inner circle.

Rating: 8.5

This is a good quatrain but not an easy one, which is why it was not solved sooner. The following coupled quatrain (II-40) fits exactly:

Soon after, without a very long interval, by sea and land a great uproar will be raised: Naval battle will be much greater, Fires, excitement, those who will cause greater insult.

This is a clear description of the Napoleonic wars.

Quatrain II-42: Death Finds Robespierre

Cock, dogs, and cats will be satiated with blood; and from the wound of the tyrant judged dead, at the bed of another, legs and arms worn out, he who was not afraid to die a cruel death.

Coq, chiens et chats de sang seront repub,
Et de la plaie due tyran trouvé mort,
Au lit d'un autre jambes et bras rompus,
Qui n'avait peur mourir de crelle mort.

Cheetham sees this one depicting the last days of the revolutionary leader Robespierre. He was in a hotel room ("another's bed") when he was arrested and was shot in the jaw by troops of the Convention. After a painful night, he was guillotined ("cruel death") July 28, 1794. The "cock" here is France, while the "dogs and cats" are taken to represent the Parisian mob. The worn-out legs and arms might simply mean that after being wounded Robespierre lost any will to fight on, but, if so, the phraseology is too abstract.

Rating: 7.5

While the verse is not without weaknesses, it has enough strong points to qualify as a hit.

Quatrain II-47: Air Marshall Göring

> The great old enemy, mourning, dies of poison. The sovereigns subjugated by infinite numbers: stones raining, hidden beneath the fleece. Through death the articles are cited in vain.

> *Le ennemi grand vieil deuil meurt de poison,*
> *Les souverains par infinis subjugues:*
> *Pierres pleuvoir, caches sous la toison,*
> *Par mort articles en vain sont allegues.*

Previously unsolved, this quatrain applies admirably to Herman Göring (or Goering), head of Hitler's Luftwaffe. Following World War II, Göring was captured but swallowed cyanide to avoid being hanged at Nuremberg. Most likely, the old master of aerial warfare was "mourning" the demise of the Third Reich. Because of his suicide, the war crime allegations against him were "in vain." Many sovereigns, of course, were subjugated by the vast armies of World War II. The rain of stones "beneath the fleece" is merely a metaphor for (Luftwaffe) bombs dropping from the clouds.

Rating: 9.5
This is a very incisive quatrain with just the right balance of poetic and specific elements.

Quatrain II-51: London's Great Fire

The blood of the just will cause want in London,
burnt through lightning of twenty threes and six: The
ancient lady will fall from her high place; several of
the same sect will be killed.

Le sang de juste à Londres fera faute,
Brulés par foudres de vingt trois les six:
La dame antique cherra de place haute,
De meme secte plusieurs seront occis.

This famous prediction foretells, and even dates, the Great Fire of London in 1666. The "ancient lady" is most probably the Catholic Church, which did fall from its "high place" in England after Elizabeth's break with Rome in 1570 and the overthrow of Charles I (1649), who was sympathetic to the Catholics. Nostradamus, a Catholic and a Royalist, seemed to see the London fire as divine punishment for the suppression of Catholicism and the execution of Charles. As the last line indicates, a number of Catholic clergymen were executed in England during Elizabeth's reign.

Rating: 9.5
A popular interpretation holds that the "ancient lady" refers to a statue of the Virgin Mary atop St. Paul's Cathedral, which toppled during the fire.

Quatrain II-53: The Great Plague of London

The great plague of the maritime city will not cease
until there be avenged the death of the just blood,
condemned for a price without crime, of the great
lady not outraged by the pretense.

La grande peste de cité maritime
Ne cessera que mort ne soit vengée
Du juste sang, par prix damné sans crime
De la grande dame par feinte n'outragée.

Here Nostradamus forecasts the great plague of London in 1665
and blames it on the execution of Charles I, who was sold by the Scots
to Parliament in 1647 and beheaded in 1649. Charles' principal crime
was that he was politically inept. The only problem with this famous
quatrain has been the identity of the "great lady" in the last line. The
context, though, indicates she was of the same blood line as Charles
("of the just blood . . . of the great lady"). Accordingly, the allusion
must be to Mary Stuart, Charles' grandmother, who was executed on
trumped-up charges in 1587 by Elizabeth I. Mary did face her death
with marvelous equanimity ("not outraged").

Rating: 10

With the solution of the last line, the entire complex prediction is
right on target.

Quatrain II-57: John F. Kennedy

Before the conflict the great wall will fall. The great
one to death too sudden and lamented. Born imper-
fect, he will swim the greater part. Near the river, the
land stained with blood.

Avant conflit le grand mur tombera,
Le grand à mort, mort trop subite et plainte,
Ne imparfait: la plupart nagera:
Aupres du fleuve de sang la terre teinte.

The Berlin Wall, built by the Russians during John F. Kennedy's presidency, came down before the supposedly inevitable war between the United States and the Soviet Union ever occurred. Kennedy's shocking and much lamented assassination happened near the banks of a major river, the Trinity, which flows through the heart of Dallas, Texas. The thorny part of this previously unsolved quatrain is the third line. But Kennedy's health was never very good; he suffered from genetically linked Addison's disease and chronic back problems. The swimming of the "greater part" may merely mean that JFK, an avid swimmer, would complete most, but not all, of his presidential term.

Rating: 8.5
This is a bit abstruse in ways but, on balance, quite a good prophecy.

Quatrain II-59: The Allies Land in South France

> Gallic force through support of the great guard of the great Neptune and his trident soldiers, Provence reddened (bloody) to sustain a great band: more Narbonne war, by javelins and darts.

> *Classe Gauloise par appui de grande garde*
> *Du grand Neptune, et ses tridents soldats*
> *Rougée Prouence pour soutenir grande bande:*
> *Plus Mars Narbone, par javelots et dards.*

Not many quatrains are as immediately obvious as this one. It portrays the Allied invasion of the German-occupied French Mediterranean coast in 1944. Naval and ground forces of the Free French ("Gallic force") and the United States were teamed in the action. The "great Neptune" patently signifies America, the world's preeminent sea power. "Provence" is southern France and "Narbonne" is one of its principal cities. "More Narbonne war" (*Plus Mars Narbone*) is a play on the city's old Roman name, Narbo-Martius. There was, of course, plenty of bloodshed in the landing and the drive north to link with other Allied armies. The "javelins and darts" are merely rockets and bombs.

Rating: 9.5

This is a relatively direct, descriptive, and accurate verse, only slightly fogged by the Seer's wordplay.

Quatrain II-63: The Duke of Parma in France

> The Italian will subjugate the French but little. Pau,
> Marne, and Seine, Parma will carry out (deliverance?).
> He who will build the great wall against them, the
> great one, will lose his life from the least at a wall.
>
> *Gaulois, Ausone bien peu sujuguera,*
> *Pau, Marne et Seine fera Perme l'vrie:*
> *Qui le grand mur contre eux dressera,*
> *Du moindre au mur le grand perdra la vie.*

Despite one unclear word, this prediction is something of a gem because it names its protagonist: Alexander Farnese, duke of the Italian duchy of Parma. After his Flander's campaign in the 1580s, Parma warred along the banks of the Marne and the Seine. He delivered Paris and Rouen from enemy sieges but, overall, "subjugated the French but little." Pau was the capital of his main foe, Henry of Navarre, the ultimate victor. Famed for erecting a wall of ships across the Scheldt to cut off Antwerp (see Quatrain I-33, page 57), Parma was seriously wounded at the walls of Caudebec by an anonymous enemy shot and died a few months later.

Rating: 9

This is a striking verse except that the meaning of *l'vrie* in line two is now uncertain. Most likely it is some colloquial form of the Old French *livree*, meaning "delivery"—the only translation that makes any kind of sense.

Quatrain II-66: The Hundred Days

> Through great dangers the captive escaped: In a short
> time his fortune greatly changed. In the palace the
> people are ensnared; through good omen the city
> besieged.

> *Par grands dangers le captif echappé:*
> *Peu de temps grand la fortune changée.*
> *Dans le palais le peuple est attrapé,*
> *Par bon augure la cité assiegée.*

The first two lines seem to be a very apt depiction of Bonaparte's successful escape from Elba and return to France—which did, in fact, involve considerable dangers. The rest is less obvious but equally adept. Back at the Tuileries ("palace"), Napoleon pledged peace and representative government, and protection for the peasants from the power of the nobility and the Church. In short, he promised whatever was politic to regain power—and the French bought the package ("ensnared"). This last flickering Napoleonic delusion evaporated at Waterloo. Line four, portraying the Allied seizure of Paris, indicates the Seer felt France was well rid of the Corsican.

Rating: 9

The final defeat of Napoleon, of course, meant the reestablishment of the monarchy—the governmental system favored by Nostradamus.

Quatrain II-68: Russia and England circa 1700

> The efforts of Aquilon will be great: The gate on the
> ocean will be opened. The kingdom on the Isle will be
> restored: London will tremble when discovered (sur-
> prised) by sail.

> *De l'Aquilon les efforts seront grands:*
> *Sur l'Ocean sera la porte ouverte,*
> *Le regne en l'Ile sera reintegrand:*
> *Tremblera Londres par voile decouverte.*

The first half of the prediction deals with Peter the Great's successful efforts to open "a window on the sea" for Russia (Aquilon is "the northland"). This he accomplished with his Northern War (1700–1721), which won him the Leningrad area. The "kingdom on the Isle" is England, where the Restoration of the monarchy after Cromwell took place in 1660. In June of 1667, the Dutch fleet alarmed London with a raid up the lower Thames River.

Rating: 9

The prediction is right on. It falls short of full points only because it is a split quatrain.

Quatrain II-70: Modern War and Tyrants

> The dart from the sky will make its extension: deaths
> in speaking, great execution. The stone in the tree; the
> proud nation restored; noise, human monster, purge
> expiation.

> *Le dard du ciel fera son etendue,*
> *Morts en parlant: grande execution.*
> *La pierre en l'arbe, la fiere gent rendue,*
> *Bruit, humain monstre, purge expiation.*

This is an unusual quatrain because it has been accurately fulfilled not just once, but twice. The first two lines are strongly evocative of guided missiles, either the German V-2s or those used in the Persian Gulf. The "stone in the tree" is but a metaphor for explosive force. The "proud nation restored" would be France if the quatrain is applied to World War II, or Kuwait in the case of the Gulf War. "Human monster" is not too strong a description for either Hitler or Saddam Hussein, and both were finally made to pay for their murderous purges.

Rating: 9

The fact that the prediction works for two different wars might seem to indicate it is too general. Still, the images of missile warfare cannot fail to impress.

Quatrain II-72: The Wars for Italian Unification

The Celtic (French) army vexed in Italy; on all sides
conflict and great loss: Romans fled—O, France
repelled! Near the Ticino-Rubicon uncertain battle.

Armée Celtique en Italie vexée
De toutes parts conflit et grande perte:
Romains fuis, Ô Gaule repoussée!
Près du Thesin, Rubicon pugne incerte.

Somehow previous commentators have missed the obvious application of this quatrain to the wars of the Italian Risorgimento. The
French army was involved in these many-sided conflicts and suffered
heavy losses before withdrawing. The Roman and French troops of
the Papal States were routed by the Piedmontese in 1859. The Ticino
River was the boundary ("Rubicon") between the warring Austrians
and Italians, and the scene of several battles in two of the wars. King
Charles Albert and the pope were uncertain, even reluctant, about
launching the first of these (1848), which ultimately ended in a draw.

Rating: 9.5
This is a bulls-eye for the Seer, and a quatrain notable for its remarkable geographic precision.

Quatrain II-76: Tallyrand

Lightning in Burgundy will cause a portentous situation, one which could not have been made by ingenuity. From their Senate the churchman made lame will
make the affair known to opponents.

Foudre en Bourgongne fera cas portenteux,
Que par engin onc ne pourait faire,
De leur senat sacriste fait boiteux
Fera savoir aux ennemis l'affair.

Many commentators believe this prediction must pertain to French diplomatic wizard Tallyrand-Perigord, lamed in a childhood accident. Trained for the church, Tallyrand was Bishop of Autun in Burgundy when an unlikely sequence of situations propelled him into the French Foreign Service, which he came to dominate through the Napoleonic era ("lightning" meaning "destiny striking"). When Bonaparte fell, Tallyrand outflanked his opponents, as usual, by quickly convening a rump session of the Senate to put in motion his plan to restore the Bourbon monarchy. It worked.

Rating: 8.5

With the interpretative aspects developed here, the quatrain qualifies as a successful one.

Quatrain II-83: The Sack of Lyons

The vast trade of great Lyons changed. The greater
part turns to pristine ruin, prey to the soldiers swept
away by pillage. Drizzle through the Jura mountains
and Suevia (Switzerland).

Le gros trafic d'un grand Lyon changé,
La plupart tourne en pristine ruine,
Proie aux soldats par pille vendangé:
Par Iura mont et Sueve bruine.

Nostradamus nailed this one in the year 1793 when the Republican Convention in Paris sent the French army to put down a Royalist revolt in Lyons. After a seven-week siege the city yielded, whereupon there was a savage massacre of Royalists, and the Republicans set about to tear down the town's buildings. Even the name Lyon was abolished. The last line merely says the event would not happen in the summer (when it would be sunny) or in winter (when it would be snowing, not raining, in the areas mentioned). The siege was in September and early October.

Rating: 9.5

The prediction names the place and fits the events remarkably well—a near-perfect quatrain.

Quatrain II-87: A Royal Plum for Hanover House

> Afterward there will come from the outermost countries a German Prince upon the golden throne: The servitude and waters (tears, perspiration) met, the lady serves, no longer fond of her time.

> *Après viendra des extremes contreés*
> *Prince Germain, dessus le trone doré:*
> *La servitude et eaux rencontrées,*
> *La dame serve, son temps plus n'adore.*

The first half of this verse is easily seen to depict the accession of George I of Hanover ("German Prince") to the British throne in 1714. The throne is "golden" because Britain was then the greatest power on the planet. Though analysts have found the rest of the verse obscure, it appears to be a portrait of George's predecessor, Queen Anne, the last of the Stuarts. Anne, conscientious but none too bright, found the monarchy of the British Empire to be ever more laborious and burdensome ("perspiration"); her personal life was unhappy, even tragic ("tears"). In typical English fashion, she stuck it out, but it was said that death was to her "as welcome as rest to a weary traveler."

Rating: 9

The first word of the quatrain is key to its comprehension; "afterward" clearly specifies that the arrival of the German prince occurs on the heels of the lady's service.

Quatrain II-89: Accord between America and Russia

One day the two great masters will be friends. Their
great power will be seen increased: The new land will
be at its high peak; of the bloodthirsty one the number recounted.

Un jour seront demis les deux grands maîtres,
Leur grand pouvoir se verra augmenté:
Le terre neuve sera en ses hauts etres,
Au sanguinaire le nombre raconté.

Since the "new land" (America) is "at its high peak," this quatrain
must refer to the United States over the past half-century. The other
"master" would perforce be Russia, the only other superpower of the
era. Thus, Nostradamus seems to have foreseen the Reagan-Gor-
bachev rapprochement of the 1980s. The identity of the "bloodthirsty
one" is less obvious, but the most likely subject would be Joseph Stalin. Only during the period of *glasnost* did the Russian people finally
learn the full extent of Stalin's mass murders.

Rating: 8.5

The last line is less vague than it might appear since no one but Stalin
really fits the context. It is hard not to give the verse high marks.

Quatrain II-90: The Hungarian Revolt of 1956

Through life and death the realm of Hungary
changed: The law will be more harsh than (of) service. Their great city cries out with howls and laments;
Castor and Pollux enemies in the arena.

Par vie et mort changé regne d'Ongrie:
La loi sera plus apre que service:
Leur grande cité d'hurlements plaintes et crie,
Castor et Pollux ennemis dans la lice.

The significance of this prediction was quickly recognized when Russian tanks rolled into Budapest in 1956 to help put down an anti-Communist revolt. Here Nostradamus identifies the scene exactly, with Budapest being the only great city in Hungary. He also gives the cause: the harsh laws of a police state. "Castor and Pollux" being twins, the implication is that Hungarians fight Hungarians—exactly the case; some supported the reformer Imre Nagy, others the conformist Communist, János Kadár.

Rating: 10

This prophecy is perfectly clear and accurate as well as being quite specific.

Quatrain II-91: The Siege of Leningrad

> At sunrise one will see a great fire, noise, and light
> extending toward Aquilon (the northland): Within
> the circle, death and one will hear cries. Through
> steel, fire, famine, death attending them.

> *Soleil levant un grand feu l'on verra,*
> *Bruit et clarté vers Aquilon tendants:*
> *Dedans le rond mort et cris l'on ouira,*
> *Par glaive, feu, faim, mort les attendants.*

Since "Aquilon" is consistently northern Russia in the *Centuries*, there can be little question that this prophecy describes the heroic "Nine Hundred Day Siege" of Leningrad in World War II. The city was encircled ("within the circle") by the Nazis and their Finnish allies from late 1941 to early 1944, and hundreds of thousands died of famine, disease, exposure, and the blasts of bombs and artillery—perhaps the most horrific siege of a city in history.

Rating: 8.5

An expressive quatrain, but oddly enough it was previously unsolved. The actual death toll in the Leningrad siege is not certain but is estimated at over 700,000.

Quatrain II-92: The Franco-Prussian War

Fire the color of gold from the sky seen on earth.
Struck by the high born one, marvelous deed done.
Great human murder: the nephew of the great one
taken; Deaths spectacular (but) the proud one escapes.

Feu couleur d'or du ceil en terre vu:
Frappé du haut ne fait cas merveilleux:
Grand meutre humain: pris du grand le neveu,
Morts de spectacles echappe l'orgueilleux.

The key to this prophecy lies in "the nephew of the great one," most likely Napoleon III, the nephew of Napoleon I and ruler of France during the Franco-Prussian War. He was captured at the disastrous battle of Sedan in 1870 but escaped death (line four). It was Leon Gambetta who performed the "marvelous deed," escaping from a besieged Paris by balloon and organizing the heroic "Defense Nationale" in the countryside after the regular French army had been routed. The German forces were indeed commanded by a "high born one," Count Von Moltke, whose family was one of ancient nobility. The golden fire from the sky in the first line presumably alludes to artillery.

Rating: 9.5

With the interpretation of the second line provided here, the quatrain becomes highly successful.

Quatrain II-94: Napoleon's Campaigns

Great Po, great evil will be received via the Gauls
(French); vain terror to the maritime Lion. People will
pass by the sea in immeasurable numbers, a quarter
million not escaping (this).

GRAND Pau, grand mal pour Gaulois recevra,
Vaine terreur au maritime Lion:
Peuple infini par le mer passera,
Sans echapper un quart d'un million.

The French army, under Bonaparte, rampaged through Italy's Po valley, but he never managed to carry off his feared invasion of England ("the maritime Lion"), because the British navy maintained control of the sea. The second half of the quatrain appears to deal with the number of troops requisitioned to serve abroad ("by the sea") in the Napoleonic wars. Most were British sent to Spain and Portugal or the Netherlands. Many others were Frenchmen transported to Egypt for the Corsican's campaign there. The figure of a "quarter million" is probably close to the actual grand total.

Rating: 8
The accuracy of the numerical estimate, in particular, is notable.

Quatrain II-95: Vietnam and the Kennedys

> The populous places will be uninhabitable: great discord to obtain fields. Realms delivered to prudent incapable ones; then for the brothers dissension and death.

> *Les lieux peuples seront inhabitables:*
> *Pour champs avoir grande division:*
> *Regnes livres à prudents incapables:*
> *Lors les grands freres mort et dissension.*

Many "populous places" became uninhabitable in Vietnam as the combatants warred back and forth over the rice fields. The governmental leaders of South Vietnam shifted repeatedly, but most, if not all, could fairly be described as "prudent incapable ones." In the United States there was great dissension about the war and, of course, the deaths of John and Robert Kennedy.

Rating: 9
There is little to criticize in this quatrain though the first half is somewhat general. "Prudent incapable ones" might also apply to most of the Johnson administration.

Quatrain II-97: The Death of the Prisoner Pope, Pius VI

> Roman Pontiff beware of approaching the city that
> two rivers water. You will come to spit blood there:
> you and yours when the rose will flourish.

> *Romain Pontife garde de t'approcher*
> *De la cite que deux fleuves arrose,*
> *Ton sang viendra auprès de là cracher,*
> *Toi et les tiens quand fleurira le rose.*

When French republican forces captured Rome in 1798, they took Pius VI prisoner, who was later carried off to Valance, France, at the confluence of the Rhône and Isere Rivers. In the summer of 1799, when the roses were in bloom ("rose will flourish"), the unfortunate pope became violently ill, vomiting and spitting up. Whether he actually spat blood is not clear, but most likely he did before he died on August 29. Regarding the last line ("you and yours"), there were a number of priests who were held prisoner with Pius.

Rating: 9.5

This is an unusually clear and detailed quatrain and highly accurate.

Quatrain II-99: Napoleonic Wars

> Roman land, as the omen interpreted, will be vexed
> too much by the Gallic people: But the Celtic
> (French) nation will fear the hour the fleet has been
> pushed too far by the north wind.

> *Terroir Romain qu'interpretait augure,*
> *Par gent Gauloise par trop sera vexée:*
> *Mais nation Celtique craindra l'heure,*
> *Boreas, classe trop loin l'avoir poussée.*

The French republican armies certainly did vex Rome and most of Italy during Bonaparte's era. The French ("Gallic") conquerors in the peninsula showed poor discipline and were deeply resented by most

Italians. The second half of the quatrain sees the French ("Celtic") navy venturing too far south—as if driven by a north wind. The two most catastrophic defeats suffered by the French fleet both happened far south of France at Trafalgar near Gibraltar and at Aboukir in Egypt.

Rating: 7.5

A shortcoming of this otherwise well-done quatrain is that the last line is somewhat ambiguous in the original French.

Quatrain II-100: Imperial Japan

> Within the isles such horrible uproar, one will hear only a party of war. So great will be the insult of the plunderers that they will come to be joined in a great league.

> *Dedans les îles si horrible tumulte,*
> *Rien on n'ouira qu'une bellique brigue,*
> *Tant grand sera des predateurs l'insulte*
> *Qu'on se viendra ranger à la grande ligue.*

Since there have been only two island nations with any real military power—Britain and Japan—this previously unsolved quatrain is less obscure than it first seems. In the 1930s, Japan fell into a militarist frenzy as warlords took complete control, drowning out any dissenting voices. Ultimately, Japan joined fellow "plunderers," Germany, Italy, and some lesser powers, in the infamous Axis alliance that spawned World War II.

Rating: 8

This quatrain is not long on specifics, but it is correct as far as it goes.

Quatrain III-I: Britannia Rules the Waves

After combat and naval battle, the great Neptune in
his highest belfry: Red adversary pale with fear, putting the great ocean in dread.

Après combat et bataille navale,
Le grand Neptune à son plus haut beffroi:
Rouge adversaire de peur viendra pale,
Mettant le grand ocean en effroi.

The "great Neptune" has to be Great Britain, which ruled the seas
for three centuries. British sea power reached a peak ("highest belfry")
with Nelson's brilliant victory at Trafalgar where he virtually
destroyed the French and Spanish navies. Both navies could be called
"red" adversaries, red being Spain's color and the French being revolutionaries. After Trafalgar, Napoleon held the "ocean in dread," never
again challenging the British at sea.

Rating: 8

This is a simple enough verse, though a little too broad, which has
been misapplied by some commentators.

Quatrain III-5: End of World War II

Near and far, default of the two great luminaries
which will occur during April and March. O, what a
cost! But two great good-natured ones by land and sea
will relieve all parts.

Près, loin dafaut de deux grands luminaires
Qui surviendra entre l'Avril et Mars:
O quel cherté! mais deux grands debonnaires
Par terre et mer secourront toutes parts.

Though not recognized until now, this prediction applies well to
the demise of the two principal Fascist "luminaries," Hitler and Mussolini, both of whom met death in April of 1945 after their bloody

careers had inflicted horrible costs on their foes and their own peoples. The Axis was already in collapse ("default") in March. The two debonair ones would be Roosevelt and Churchill, who combined to free western Europe with both land and sea forces and begin its reconstruction.

Rating: 9

This is a descriptive and accurate quatrain. The phrase "near and far" seems a little vague, but it might refer to the fact that Mussolini died near France while Hitler met his end far away in Berlin.

Quatrain III-7: Refugees in World War II

> The fugitives, fire from the sky on the pikes: conflict
> near the ravens frolicking. From land they cry for aid
> and heavenly relief, when the combatants will be near
> the walls.

> *Les fugitifs, feu du ciel sus les piques:*
> *Conflit prochain des corbeaux s'ebattants,*
> *De terre on crie aide, secours celiques,*
> *Quand près des murs seront les combattants.*

There is some striking imagery here of streams of refugees fleeing the advance of modern armies as in World War II. In particular, the "fire from the sky on the pikes" is strongly suggestive of air-to-ground rockets. The "ravens frolicking" could well represent warplanes overhead, silhouetted black against the sky, planes which sometimes bombed and strafed hapless civilian refugees. What walls might have been in the Seer's vision is unclear, but there are still some cities in Europe that have preserved sections of their old walls.

Rating: 8

While the prophecy might be seen as leaning too heavily toward the poetic, it presents a prescient picture of twentieth-century warfare.

Quatrain III-11: The Fall of Fascist Italy

> The arms to fight in the sky a long time; the tree in
> the middle of the city fallen: Sacred bough clipped,
> steel in the face of the firebrand; then the monarch of
> Adria fallen.

> *Les armes battre au ciel longue saison,*
> *L'arbre au milieu de la cité tombé:*
> *Verbine rogne, glaive, en face tison,*
> *Lors le monarque d'Hadrie succombé.*

Again, the Seer portrays aerial warfare so this is a prediction for our own time. Since "Adria" is Venice or the Adriatic, the scene is Italy. The tree in the city (Rome) has to represent King Victor Emmanuel III, who abdicated when Italy collapsed in World War II. He named his son ("sacred bough") as successor, but the Italian people rejected the monarchy, ending the royal line. "Steel in the face of the firebrand" is a striking metaphor for the Allied military powers that brought down the flamboyant Mussolini. The last line likely applies to Il Duce, though it could mean Emmanuel himself.

Rating: 9.5
Previously unsolved, this is a marvelously accurate prediction, geographically specific and involving a variety of elements.

Quatrain III-13: Vichy France

> Through lightning in the arch gold and silver melted,
> of two captives one will eat the other: The greatest
> one of the city stretched out, when the submerged
> fleet will swim.

> *Par fondre en l'arche or et argent fondu,*
> *De deux captifs l'un l'autre mangera:*
> *De la cité le plus grand etendu,*
> *Quand submergée la classe nagera.*

The last line plainly foresees submarines so this is a quatrain for the modern era. The "lightning in the arch" is a reference to the Nazi blitzkrieg (lightning war) reaching the Arch of Triumph in Paris. The metaphor of the "two captives" is a clever depiction of Vichy France and Occupied France; midway through World War II, Vichy France was absorbed (eaten) into Occupied France by the Nazis. The "greatest one of the city" is Vichy's Admiral Darlan, who was made High Commissioner of French North Africa by the Allies, but was shot dead ("stretched out") in Algiers by an assassin. French money, of course, became almost worthless ("melted") when France fell.

Rating: 9
Once properly interpreted, this is a highly accurate prophecy though perhaps a shade too abstract.

Quatrain III-15: Louis' Luck Runs Out

> The realm will change in heart, vigor, and glory, on all
> points having its adversary opposed: Then through
> death an infancy will rule France; a grand regent will
> then be more adverse.

> *Coeur, vigeur gloire le regne changera,*
> *De tous points contre ayant son adversaire:*
> *Lors France enfance par mort subjuguera,*
> *Un grand Regent sera lors plus contraire.*

People tend to forget that the last years of Louis XIV's long and grandiose reign (post 1700) were decidedly downbeat. France became entangled in the ruinous war of the Spanish Succession and was not faring well against the English ("the adversary"). Debt was piling up and popular support for the king was rapidly eroding. After the Grand Monarch died, things went from bad to worse under Louis XV, who became king at the age of five (line three). His "regent," the Duke of Orleans, was not very capable, and Louis himself was no better. The days of the monarchy were numbered.

Rating: 8.5

Overall, the quatrain holds up well though the last line might be considered slightly vague. The sense seems to be that conditions continued to deteriorate under the regent.

Quatrain III-20: The Morisco Revolt in Spain

> Through the regions of the great river Guadalquiver,
> deep in Iberia to the Kingdom of Grenada, crosses
> beaten back by the Mahometan peoples. One of Cordova will betray his country.

> *Par les contrées du grand fleuve Bethique*
> *Loin d'Ibere au Royaume de Grenade*
> *Croix repoussées par gens Mahometiques*
> *Un de Cordube trahira la contrade.*

Largely unresolved by prior commentators, this is a remarkably accurate quatrain dealing with the Spanish Moriscos ("little Moors") who had nominally accepted baptism but retained most of their Moorish ways. In 1568, the fervently Christian Philip II issued a repressive decree that prompted them to an armed revolt in southern Spain ("Grenada"). After some early successes, the uprising was stifled but only with great difficulty and after prolonged fighting. The leader of the insurrection was one Ferdinand de Cordova.

Rating: 10

The geography in this prediction is extremely precise and the identification of the revolt's leader is a real stunner.

Quatrain III-23: A Warning to France

> If, France, you pass beyond the Ligurian Sea, you will
> see yourself shut up in islands and seas: Mahomet
> contrary, more so the Adriatic Sea, you will gnaw the
> bones of horses and asses.

> *Si France passes outre mer lygustique,*
> *Tu te verras en îles et mers enclos:*
> *Mahommet contraire, plus mer Hadriatique:*
> *Chevaux et d'anes tu rongeras les os.*

This is a cautionary quatrain that the French ignored—to their
own misfortune. The "Ligurian Sea" is the French route to the eastern
Mediterranean, so the Seer is saying that all French efforts to push
into the east Mediterranean are foredoomed—historically correct. In
the 1660s, a French effort to save Crete from the Turks failed.
Napoleon's expedition to Egypt foundered after Nelson smashed the
French navy at Aboukir. Circa 1809, the French attempt to set up a
puppet state in Dalmatia ("the Adriatic") failed and their fleet suffered
another severe defeat. In the twentieth century, the French venture
into Lebanon proved another expensive and profitless exercise.

Rating: 9

One is hard-put to find fault with this one. A coupled quatrain (III-
24) follows:

> Great confusion in the enterprise, loss of people,
> countless treasure: You ought not to extend there.
> France, let what I say be remembered.

Quatrain III-25: King Henry of Navarre

> He who will attain to the kingdom of Navarre when
> Sicily and Naples will be joined: He will hold Bigorre
> and Landes through Foix and Oloron from one who
> will be too closely allied with Spain.

Que au royaume Nauarrois parviendra
Quand le Sicile et Naples seront joints:
Bigorre et Landes par Foix Loron tiendra
D'un qui d'Espagne sera par trop conjoint.

Sicily and Naples were separate states when the quatrains were written but were reunited in 1556. A few years later in 1562, the future Henry IV of France took the throne of Navarre. Bigorre, Landes, Foix, and Oloron were merely parts of Navarre held in fief from the French throne. Under the influence of Catherine de Médici, France was, in fact, working in close cooperation with Spain during this period.

Rating: 8

The quatrain is entirely correct, but its prophetic content is somewhat limited. Essentially, it predicts the reunification of Naples and Sicily and an era of Franco-Spanish coordination.

Quatrain III-28: Elizabeth's Road to the Throne

Of land weak and parentage poor, through extremity
and peace she will attain to the empire. For a long
time a young female to reign; never has a worse one
come upon the kingdom.

De terre faible et pauvre parentelle,
Par bout et paix parviendra dans l'empire.
Longtemps regner une jeune femelle,
Qu'onc en regne n'en survint un si pire.

Nostradamus, a devout Catholic, lets his personal persuasions erupt in the last line of this quatrain. He views Elizabeth I negatively, because she was to bring the triumph of Protestantism to England. Elizabeth attained the throne peacefully (late 1558) despite the fact that her legitimacy was questioned, and she had once been far down in the line of succession. She was the daughter of the scorned (and executed) Anne Boleyn. At one time the future queen, who would reign for forty-five years, had actually been a prisoner in the tower of

London, an "extremity" which, however, may well have been known to Nostradamus.

Rating: 9

The prediction is both specific and accurate, even if judgmental.

Quatrain III-30: The Arrest of Count Montgomery

> He who during the struggle with steel in the deed of
> war will have carried off the prize from one greater
> than he: by night six will carry the grudge to his bed.
> Without armor he will be suddenly surprised.

> *Celui qu'en lutte et fer au fait bellique*
> *Aura porté plus grand que lui le prix:*
> *De nuit au lit six lui feront la pique,*
> *Nu sans harnois subit sera surpris.*

Le Pelletier correctly applied this prophecy to the arrest of Count Montgomery who, years before, had accidentally killed King Henry II of France in a joust. Afterwards, the count retired to his estates but resurfaced later as a Huguenot leader. His luck ran out in 1574 when his small troop was surrounded by Royalist forces at Domfront. Under the terms of his surrender, his life was to be spared, but Catherine de Médici, widow of Henry II, ordered Montgomery to be commandeered from his castle and brought under guard to Paris for trial and execution. It is said the guard numbered six men. Without a doubt, Montgomery was a victim of Catherine's "grudge."

Rating: 9

The exact circumstances of Montgomery's seizure under Catherine's order seem sketchy, but he was in his castle, maybe the bedroom, without armor, and he must have been most unpleasantly surprised.

Quatrain III-32: A Death Blow for France (1940)

> The great sepulcher of the people of Aquitaine (south-
> ern France) will afterwards approach from Tuscany
> (Italy), when Mars will be in the corner of Germany
> and in the land of the Mantuan (Italian) people.

> *Le grand sepulcre du peuple Aquitanique*
> *S'approchera aupres de la Toscane,*
> *Quand Mars sera près du coin Germanique*
> *Et au terroir de la gent Mantuane.*

When France was already reeling from the Nazi's World War II
blitzkrieg in the north, Italy administered the coup de grâce by invading southern France, rendering the French position completely hopeless. "Mars," the god of war, was certainly in Germany's corner at the
time and in Italy's, too. Casualties in the southern campaign were not
heavy though, so the "sepulcher" likely symbolizes the death of the
French republic.

Rating: 8.5

This is just one of a number of predictions dealing with an Italian
invasion of southern France. There can be no question that the Seer
foresaw such an event.

Quatrain III-35: The Specter of Napoleon

> From the very depths of the West of Europe a young
> child will be born of poor people, he who by his
> tongue will seduce a great troop. His fame will
> increase toward the realm of the East.

> *Du plus profond de l'Occident d'Europe,*
> *De pauvres gens un jeune enfant naitra,*
> *Qui par sa langue seduira grande troupe:*
> *Son bruit au regne d'Orient plus croitra.*

There is little doubt that this prediction has to do with Napoleon I, who was born in modest circumstances on the out-of-the-way island of Corsica. Napoleon's troops were captivated by his speeches, and he greatly enhanced his fame through his spectacular expedition to Egypt, and his successful return through seas controlled by the British navy. The quatrain does not apply well to Hitler who was born in central Europe and met frustration and defeat when he pushed eastward into Russia.

Rating: 9
The Seer's foreknowledge of Napoleon, demonstrated in many quatrains, is thoroughly astonishing.

Quatrain III-37: Bonaparte Crosses the Alps

> The speech delivered before the attack, Milan is taken
> by the Eagle through deceptive ambushes: ancient
> wall driven in by cannons, through fire and blood few
> given quarter.

> *Avant l'assaut l'oraison prononcee,*
> *Milan pris a'Aigle par embuches decus:*
> *Muraille antique par canons enfoncee,*
> *Par feu et sang à merci peu recus.*

The speech here is famous in history, delivered by a young Napoleon ("the Eagle") to his ragged, half-starved troops before they crossed the Alps into Italy in 1796. The campaign was a dazzling success, and Bonaparte was soon chasing the Austrians across northern Italy. The Corsican's armies were famous for their rapid and deceptive movements, often appearing suddenly many miles from where they were thought to be. Though Milan was quickly taken, the city's walled citadel held out for several weeks and had to be reduced by siege guns.

Rating: 9.5

The eagle is the Seer's favorite symbol for Napoleon, and all the facts fit, so there is no doubt about the subject of this quatrain.

Quatrain III-38: Mountains of Misery

> The Gallic people and a foreign nation beyond the mountains, dead, captured, and destroyed: In the contrary month and near vintage time, through the Lords brought up in accord.

> *La gent Gauloise et nation étrange*
> *Outre les monts, morts, pris et profliges:*
> *Au mois contraire et proche de vendange,*
> *Par les Seigneurs en accord rediges.*

An astonishing quatrain that has been misapplied, this one describes and gives the exact duration of the major Allied campaign in the War of the Second Coalition ("the Lords brought up in accord"). In 1799, the Russians sent an army under Field Marshall Suvarov to help the Austrians oust the French from north Italy (beyond the Alps from France). The crusty, old warrior did exactly that, thrashing the French at every turn. But later, forcing their way over the mountain passes in Switzerland, the Russians themselves suffered crippling losses—then further decimation in a costly retreat to the Voder Rhine. The six-month campaign ended in early October—"vintage time."

Rating: 9.5

The contrary month here obviously means the opposite month of the year from October, i.e., April, which marked the campaign's start. Chronologically and otherwise, the verse is a near paragon of prophecy.

Quatrain III-41: Huguenot Leader Louis of Condé Murdered

> A hunchback will be elected by the council, a more
> hideous monster not seen on earth. The willing blow
> will put out his eye: the traitor to the king received as
> faithful.

> *Bossu sera elu par le conseil,*
> *Plus hideux monstre en terre n'apercu,*
> *Le coup voulant crevera l'oeil:*
> *Le traitre au Roi pour fidele reçu.*

The Catholic Nostradamus again lets his personal bias show in this famously successful prophecy. The hunchbacked Louis of Condé was elected leader of the Huguenot (Protestant) assembly in 1560. Condé was lacking in neither courage nor competence, but in the ebb and flow of the French religious wars, he did twice turn against King Charles IX after swearing loyalty. Upon giving himself up at the battle of Jarnac (1569), Condé was deliberately shot in the head by Montesquiou, thereby fulfilling all aspects of the Seer's prediction.

Rating: 10

There are enough unlikely elements in the quatrain to just about eliminate coincidence as a possible explanation of its accuracy.

Quatrain III-45: The Fall of Napoleonic France

> The five strangers (or foreigners) entered in the temple,
> their blood will come to pollute the land: To the
> Toulousans it will be a good hard example of one who
> will come to exterminate their laws.

> *Les cinq étranges entrés dans le temple,*
> *Leur sang viendra la terre profaner:*
> *Aux Tholosains sera bien dur exemple*
> *D'un qui viendra ses lois exterminer.*

Cheetham views this quatrain as a parable of the Coalition's conquest of revolutionary France in 1814. If *étranges* is translated as "foreigners," and the "temple" is seen as France itself—not unreasonable—the interpretation fits quite well. There were five foreign armies involved in the invasion: England, Austria, Prussia, Spain, and Russia. Toulouse was the last city to fall to Wellington's forces. The battle was a bloody and ironic affair with several thousand casualties (fought after Napoleon had already abdicated).

Rating: 8

While it could be argued that the imagery in the first line is overly arcane, it nonetheless does work nicely.

Quatrain III-50: Geneva's Night of the Escalade

> The republic of the great city will not want to consent
> to the great severity: The king leaves a city by trumpet
> (sound). The ladder at the wall; the city will repent.

> *La republique de la grande cité*
> *A grand rigeur ne voudra consentir:*
> *Roi sortir hors par trompette cité,*
> *L'echelle au mur, la cité repentir.*

The republic of the great city of Geneva suffered "great severity" in 1601 when it was forced to cede its key granary district per a treaty between Navarre and Savoy. The ruler of Savoy, Charles Emmanuel, then made a treacherous but unsuccessful attack on Geneva itself, scaling the walls with ladders in the dead of night. The king who "leaves by trumpet" then is Charles, setting out from Savoy on his intended conquest. (The king's city referred to in line three is not the city in line one since that city is a republic.) The end of the quatrain is delphic: Which city is to repent? It seems the Seer went blank on who would win the night of the escalade.

Rating: 8
This is an intriguing if somewhat difficult quatrain. The rating is crimped by the Seer's retreat to ambiguity in the final phrase.

Quatrain III-51: The Contract on the Guise Brothers

> Paris conspires to commit a great murder; Blois will
> cause it to be fully carried out: Those of Orleans will
> want to replace their chief. Angers, Troyes, Langres
> will do them a disservice.

> *Paris conjure un grand meurtre commettre*
> *Blois le fera sortir en plein effet:*
> *Ceux d'Orleans voudront leur chef remettre,*
> *Angers, Troye, Langres leur feront un mefait.*

The infamous murders of the Guise brothers were plotted in Paris by Henry III of France, and carried out at Blois (December 1588) during the French religious wars. The deed caused a monumental national uproar and the people of Orleans rose up against Henry's governor, whereupon the third Guise brother, the Duke of Mayenne, took over the city. The last line of the quatrain is more difficult. Nostradamus may only be saying that these cities, though at least two were Guise allies, will not directly assist the people of Orleans in their rebellion.

Rating: 8.5
The rating is hurt by the rather murky last line; otherwise, it is an admirable quatrain.

Quatrain III-53: The Rise of Hitler

> When the greatest one will carry off the prize of
> Nuremberg, of Augsberg, and those of Basle through
> Cologne, the chief French fort retaken; they will cross
> through Flanders right into Gaul.

> *Quand le plus grand emportera le prix*
> *De Nuremberg, d'Ausbourg, et ceux de Basle*
> *Par Agrippine chef Frankfort repris*
> *Traverseront par Flamant jusqu'en Gale.*

When properly interpreted—which it has not been—this quatrain is one of the most arresting. It exactly describes Hitler's career up until the invasion of France. The Bavarian cities of Nuremberg and Augsburg are where the Nazis rose to political power. "Those of Basle through Cologne" defines the Rhineland, the scene of Hitler's first big geopolitical success when he wrested it from French occupation. There is a clever play on "Frankfort" here. It does not mean the German city but the chief Frankish fort, probably Metz, which the Germans had taken in the war of 1870–71 and then was retaken by Hitler in 1941, as his main strike drove through Flanders and into France.

Rating: 10
Though more difficult than most, this is a detailed and virtually perfect prophecy, well beyond the bounds of coincidence.

Quatrain III-54: Franco Seizes Spain

> One of the greatest ones will fly to Spain which will
> thereafter come to bleed of a long wound: armies
> passing over the high mountains, devastating all, and
> then to reign in peace.

> *L'un des plus grands fuira aux Espagnes*
> *Qu'en longue plaie après viendra saigner:*
> *Passant copies par les hautes montagnes,*
> *Devastant tout, et puis en paix regner.*

This is a plain and obvious prediction dealing with Francisco Franco and the Spanish civil war. In 1936, as the Nationalist revolt erupted, General Franco, one of the plotters, was in virtual exile at a remote outpost in the Canary Islands. He immediately flew to Spanish Morocco and later to Spain proper to help direct the struggle. Soon

Franco was the army's supreme commander. The civil war, which lasted three years, was very much a "long wound" for Spain; about a million people perished as the brutal conflict raged across the mountainous country. Afterwards though, during Franco's long reign, Spain remained at peace, avoiding involvement in World War II.

Rating: 10
The prophecy is crystal clear and right on target in all respects.

Quatrain III-55: The Religious Wars in France

> In the year that one eye will reign in France, the court
> will be in very unpleasant trouble. The great one of
> Blois will kill his friend: the realm placed in harm and
> double doubt.

> *En l'an qu'un oeil en France regnera,*
> *La cour sera à un bien facheux trouble:*
> *Le grand de Blois son ami tuera:*
> *Le regne mis en mal et doute double.*

The one-eyed ruler, the only one in French history, was Henry II, whose eye was put out in a joust with Count Montgomery (1559). Henry died shortly thereafter, putting the government of France in jeopardy since all three of his succedent sons were ineffectual and religious strife was rapidly worsening. One of the sons, Henry III, had fellow Catholic leader, the Duke of Guise, murdered while both were at court in Blois in 1588. The event roused such a storm that the already wobbly French monarchy hung by a thread ("double doubt") until Henry III was assassinated and the dauntless Henry of Navarre took the throne.

Rating: 9
This is a well-done quatrain with only trivial shortcomings.

Quatrain III-57: Great Britain in History

> Seven times will you see the British nation change,
> steeped in blood in 290 years: Free not at all its sup-
> port Germanic. Aries doubts his Bastarnian pole.

> *Sept fois changer verrez gent Britannique,*
> *Teints en sang en deux cent nonante ans:*
> *Franche non point appui Germanique.*
> *Aries doute son pole Bastarnan.*

This intriguing quatrain predicts seven changes in British rule. The first ruler of Great Britain as such was James I, so 1603 is the logical start of the 290 years. The seven stages would be the Stuarts, the Council of State, the Cromwell Protectorate, the Restoration, the Glorious Revolution, the Hanovers, and, in 1901, the Windsors. (This spans 298 years, but close enough.) It was Britain's empire-building era with plenty of bloodshed. The Germanic support must refer to Prussia, which aided Britain against Napoleon. But their victory made Prussia a major power soon to become Britain's nemesis. Costly support! The last line is occultish.

Rating: 8

My only suggestion on line four is that Basternia is the borderlands region of old Austria and Russia, both British allies in the Napoleonic era. Britain (the other Aries pole) likely did have doubts about their support at times.

Quatrain III-58: Der Führer

> Near the Rhine from the Noric mountains will be
> born a great one of a people come too late, one who
> will defend Sarmatia and the Hungarians. One will
> not know what will have become of him.

> *Aupres du Rhin des montagnes Noriques*
> *Naitra un grand de gens trop tard venu,*
> *Que defendra Saurome et Pannoniques,*
> *Qu'on ne saura qu'il sera devenu.*

The Noric mountains border the ancient Roman province of Noricum located just south of the upper Danube and east of the upper Rhine. This small region is the exact birthplace of Adolph Hitler. He defended the Hungarians because they were his allies. Sarmatia is old Greater Lithuania, an area Hitler conquered but then had to defend against Russia's counteroffensive. There was great doubt at the time, and there is some still, about whether Hitler really died in his Berlin bunker ("one will not know"). The "people come too late" is cryptic but may allude to the fact that the Germans were among the last in Europe to form a modern nation state—too late for expansionist dreams.

Rating: 8.5

Admirably precise geographically, the quatrain is hurt by the fuzziness of phraseology in the second line.

Quatrain III-61: The Allies in the Gulf War

> The great band and sect of crusaders will be arrayed
> in Mesopotamia (Iraq): light company by the nearby
> river, that the same law will hold for an enemy.

> *Le grande bande et secte crucigere*
> *Se dressera en Mesopotamie:*
> *Du proche fleuve compagnie legere,*
> *Que telle loi tiendra pour ennemie.*

The use of the term "crusaders" clearly indicates the presence of Christian forces, i.e., the American, British, and French contingents in the Gulf War against Iraq, though the crusade in this case was not against Islam but for international law ("that the same law will hold"). A "light company," in military terms, is one designed for high mobility. The Allied units moved with such rapidity in their Persian Gulf offensive that Iraqi forces were thrown into complete confusion and disarray. The "river," of course, is the Euphrates, which the Allies reached in hours.

Rating: 9

This is excellent work by the Seer, though a clue as to the nature of the "law" would have helped to solve this quatrain sooner.

Quatrain III-62: Marshall Soult Meets His Match

> Near the Douro by the closed Tyrian sea, he will come to pierce the great Pyrenees mountains. Short-handed and his opening glossed (defined), he will lead his tracks to Carcassone.

> *Proche del Duero par mere Tyrrene close,*
> *Viendra percer les grands monts Pyrénnés.*
> *La main plus courte et sa perce glose,*
> *À Carcassonne conduira ses menées.*

Though previously unrecognized, this is a phenomenally precise prophecy about the Peninsular War in Spain in Napoleonic times. The protagonist here is France's Marshall Nicolas Soult, who battled the Duke of Wellington in the Douro basin and the Pyrenees. Soult himself crossed the Pyrenees a number of times, and in 1813 launched a major counterattack across the mountains but was repulsed. Back in France, the marshall made a last stand at Toulouse with his depleted army ("short-handed"), but after heavy fighting slipped away in the night to Carcassonne where he found the war was over. The "Tyrian Sea" is merely the Bay of Biscay, reputedly first explored by Tyre.

Rating: 9.5

The Seer is again straining for a rhyme with *glose*, but the sense is fairly clear.

Quatrain III-63: The Rome-Berlin Axis

The Roman power will be thoroughly abased, following in the footsteps of its great neighbor: Hidden civil
hatreds and debates will delay their follies for the buf-
foons.

Romain pouvoir sera du tout a bas,
Son grand voisin imiter les vestiges:
Occultes haines civiles, et debats
Retarderont aux bouffons leurs folies.

Starting in 1936, Mussolini aligned Fascist Italy steadily closer to
Hitler, creating the Rome-Berlin Axis. Ultimately, Italy followed the
fatal footsteps of its more powerful neighbor, Nazi Germany, to
destruction and unconditional surrender ("thoroughly abased"). The
"follies" are the grandiose territorial ambitions and demented doc-
trines of the Fascists. Complete implementation of the Axis accord
was retarded by turmoil in the Tyrol where the majority of German
residents chafed under Italian rule ("civil hatreds and debates"), creating a serious friction between Germany and Italy in the 1930s. The
dispute was settled by a 1939 deal between der Führer and Il Duce.

Rating: 8.5
There was a certain black humor aspect to the wild histrionics of
Hitler and Mussolini, justifying the use of the word *bouffons*.

Quatrain III-66: Trial of the Bailiff of Orleans

The great Bailiff of Orleans will be put (condemned)
to death by one of blood revengeful: Of death
deserved he will not die, nor by chance, being made
captive poorly by his feet and hands.

Le grand Bailli d'Orleans mis à mort
Sera par un de sang vindicatif:
De mor merite ne mourra, ni par sort:
Des pieds et mains mal le faisait captif.

A relatively minor but interesting incident in the 1560s is the basis of this quatrain. One Jerome Groslot, bailiff of Orleans, tried to deliver the city to the Calvinists and was later condemned to death by a tribunal of the Inquisition. He managed to escape, however, eluding his fate. The office of bailiff was hereditary in Orleans so Nostradamus knew his prediction pertained to the Groslot family.

Rating: 8

This quatrain, solved by Le Pelletier, serves to remind us that Nostradamus was not always dealing with world-shaking events.

Quatrain III-68: Fascist Spain and Italy

> Leaderless people of Spain and of Italy dead or over-
> come within the Peninsula: Their (the Italians') dic-
> tator betrayed by irresponsible folly, swimming in
> blood everywhere in the latitude.

> *Peuple sans chef d'Espagne, d'Italie*
> *Morts, profliges dedans le Chersonese:*
> *Leur dict trahi par legere folie,*
> *Le sang nager partout à la traverse.*

Weak leadership in Spain and Italy paved the way for Fascist takeovers in both countries. In Spain, many of the opposition perished ("dead") in a bloody civil war; in Italy, they were merely "overcome" by Mussolini's strong-arm tactics. Later, though, Italy was led into World War II so that there was great bloodshed "everywhere in the latitude." The "dictator betrayed by irresponsible folly" is Mussolini, who was killed by his own people. Franco had sense enough to stay out of the war.

Rating: 8.5

Though it seems a bit slapdash after the first reading, the prophecy is actually fairly well constructed and well fulfilled on all counts.

Quatrain III-70: Britain vs. Italy

> The great Britain including England will come to be inundated by very high waters. The new League of Ausonia will make war, so that they (the British) will come to strive against them.

> *La grande Bretagne comprise d'Angleterre*
> *Viendra par eaux si haut à inonder*
> *La Ligue neuve d'Ausonne fera guerre*
> *Que contre eux ils se viendront bander.*

Grande Bretagne is surprising because there was no Great Britain, as such, in Nostradamus' time; the term was not used until the early 1600s. Since the prophecy clearly centers on an Anglo-Italian war, the inundation may not be strictly literal though there was disastrous flooding along the North Sea coast in 1953. A double meaning here could include the rising tide of fascism that threatened to engulf Britain in World War II. The "new League of Ausonia" is modern Italy, comprised of minor states consolidated in the Risorgimento about 1870, an enemy the British had to "strive against" in the Second World War.

Rating: 8
The quatrain correctly foresees the conflict between Britain and Italy, but the Seer's second line is ambiguous even for him.

Quatrain III-73: Hitler vs. FDR

> When the cripple will attain to the realm, for his competitor he will have a near bastard: He (the latter) and his realm will become so mangy that before it recovers, it will be too late.

> *Quand dans le regne parviendra le boiteux,*
> *Competiteur aura proche batard:*
> *Lui et le regne viendront si fort rogneux,*
> *Qu'ains qu'il guerisse son fait sera bien tard.*

Franklin D. Roosevelt, a victim of polio, and Adolph Hitler are the opponents described in this prediction. Hitler was only one step removed from bastardy; his father, whose original name was Schickelgruber, was illegitimate. The adjective "mangy" may seem an odd choice at first, but it is quite descriptive of down-and-out Germany in the 1930s, and not a bad epithet for Hitler's diseased mentality. Germany, obviously, did not recover its economic and psychological health in time to steer away from its impending cataclysmic fate.

Rating: 8.5
Previous commentators have applied the quatrain to the rather obscure Duke of Bordeaux, but that interpretation is weak on more than a couple of counts.

Quatrain III-75: Napoleon Brings Down the Empire

Pau, Verona, Vicenza, Saragossa—lands wet with blood from distant swords. Very great plague will come to the great shell; relief near, and remedies very far.

Pau, Verone, Vicence, Sarragousse,
De glaives loin terroirs de sang humides:
Peste si grande viendra à la grande gousse,
Proche secours, et bien loin les remedes.

The chronological key to this unsolved verse is Saragossa, scene of the most famous battle of the Peninsular wars of the Napoleonic period. Pau was the site of the termination of that great struggle between the French and Brito-Spanish forces under Wellington. The "great shell" is a perfect description of the Holy Roman Empire at the time; a hollow "empire" brought down by Napoleon's wars ("great plague"). There was much fighting around Verona and Vicenza during Napoleon's Italian campaigns.

Rating: 9
The last line seems obscure but reflects the fact that while the French revolutionary era did not last long, the resolution of its root causes took a very long time.

Quatrain III-77: The Turks and the Persians in 1727

> The third climate included under Aries, the year 1727
> in October, the King of Persia taken by those of Egypt.
> Conflict, death, loss: to the cross great shame.

> *Le tiers climat sous Aries compris*
> *L'an mil sept cent vingt et sept en Octobre,*
> *Le Roi de Perse par ceux d'Egypte pris:*
> *Conflit, mort, perte: à la croix grand opprobre.*

The Seer goes out on a limb on this one and doesn't miss by much. The Turks, whose realm included Egypt as a prominent part, attacked Persia in 1725, but the Persians fought them to a standstill. Ashraf, usurper of the Persian throne, was not captured, but he was surely "taken" in the ensuing peace negotiations in October of 1727. In return for recognition of his dynasty, the new Shah gave the Turks virtually all the territory they wanted. Shortly before the war with Persia, the Turks had, in 1716, captured Morea from the Venetians who got little help from the Christian Moreans (shame to the cross).

Rating: 9
The prophecy is not flawless, but the dating is so extraordinary that it merits high marks.

Quatrain III-80: Britain's King Charles Deposed

> The worthy one chased out of the English realm; the
> adviser through anger put to the fire: His adherents
> will go so low to efface themselves that the bastard
> will be half-received.

> *Du regne Anglois le digne dechassé,*
> *Le conseiller par ire mis à feu:*
> *Ses adherents iront si bas tracer*
> *Que le batard sera demi recu.*

Le Pelletier long ago applied this prediction to Charles I who was driven out of England and later beheaded (1649). Two of Charles' key advisors, Thomas Strafford and Archbishop Laud, aroused such hostility that they were executed but neither was literally "put to the fire." The adherents who "go so low" are the Scots who, for a price, delivered Charles to Parliament for trial and execution. The Seer was no fan of Protestant leaders so "bastard" is seen as an epithet for Oliver Cromwell who was half-received because he never had the full support of the British people.

Rating: 7.5

While the quatrain works well in many ways, it is not without arguable aspects. Yet, the interpretation is reinforced by the following quatrain that deals with Charles' nemesis, Cromwell.

Quatrain III-81: The Rise of Cromwell

> The great shameless, audacious bawler will be elected
> governor of the army: The boldness of his contention,
> the bridge broken, the city faint from fear.

> *Le grand criard sans honte audacieux,*
> *Sera elu gouverneur de l'armee:*
> *Le hardiesse de son contintieux,*
> *Le pon rompu, cité de peur pamee.*

The opening description of Oliver Cromwell may seem harsh, but it is not far from the facts. Cromwell was not a polished speaker but had volume and conviction. He had no military training either, but showed such boldness and tactical insight that in only three years he became the recognized chief of Parliament's army in the war against Charles I. In the last line, "broken bridge" is seen as a play on the city of Pontefract (meaning "broken bridge" in Latin), the scene of multiple sieges during the British civil wars.

Rating: 9

The Pontefract ploy and the fact that this quatrain directly follows one on Charles I leave little room for doubt about the subject of the prophecy.

Quatrain III-83: The French Monarchy Restored

> The long hairs of Celtic Gaul (France), accompanied by foreign nations, will make captive the people of Aquitaine, that these will succumb to their designs.

> *Les longs cheveux de la Gaule Celtique*
> *Accompagnes d'etranges nations,*
> *Mettront captif la gent Aquitanique,*
> *Pour succomber à leur intentions.*

In the wake of Napoleon's defeat, the monarchy returned to France in the form of Louis XVIII, who came in with the baggage of the Allied armies ("foreign nations"). The "long hairs" are merely the French aristocrats whose hairstyles contrasted with the close crops of the republicans. Louis himself was known as *le chevelu*, the long-haired. Normally, "Aquitaine" refers to the southern half of France, but here it stands for France in general. Under Louis, the people of Aquitaine and all of France again had to "succumb" to royalty.

Rating: 8.5

The choice of *Aquitanique* to make the rhyme somewhat blurs a fundamentally solid prophecy.

Quatrain III-84: The Sack of Magdeburg

> The great city will be thoroughly desolated. Of the inhabitants not one will remain there: Wall, sex, temple, and virgin violated; through sword, fire, plague, cannon, people will die.

> *La grande cité sera bien désolée,*
> *Des habitants un seul n'y demeurera:*
> *Mur, sexe, temple et vierge violée,*
> *Par fer, feu, peste, canon peuple mourra.*

The only great walled city since Nostradamus to suffer a disaster of such magnitude was the German Protestant city of Magdeburg, stormed by General Tilly's army in 1631 during the savage Thirty Years' War. The sack stands among the blackest pages in history. Tilly's troops went on a rampage of murder, rape, and burning almost beyond belief. The city was leveled except for a few structures, and most of the inhabitants butchered. The rest fled the apocalyptic scene in terror. While the quatrain has been viewed as geographically vague, the one out-of-place word, *sexe*, provides a cryptic clue; Magdeburg is in the old German province of Saxe.

Rating: 8.5

This quatrain hasn't been solved until now. Though the geographic indicators may be overly subtle, the fact remains that no other city but Magdeburg could qualify as the subject.

Quatrain III-87: A French Naval Disaster

> Gallic fleet, do not approach Corsica, less Sardinia;
> you will rue it. All of you will die frustrated of the
> help of the cape: You will swim in blood; captive, you
> will not believe me.

> *Classe Gauloise n'approches de Corseigne,*
> *Moins de Sardaigne, tu t'en repentiras:*
> *Trestous mourrez frustrés de l'aide grogne:*
> *Sang nagera: captif ne me croiras.*

A storm sank a squadron of French ships near Corsica and Sardinia in 1655. Many of the sailors died, unable to reach safety at nearby Cap de Porceau. The most interesting aspect of the prediction, though, is that the squadron's master pilot, Jean de Rian, at one time a galley slave, was known as "The Captive."

Rating: 9

The interpretation, which is Le Pelletier's, holds up well, though the Seer overstates the death toll. All the ships were lost, but not all of the sailors died in the disaster.

Quatrain III-88: The Spanish Blockade of Marseilles

> From Barcelona such a great army by sea that all Marseilles will tremble with terror: Isles seized, help shut off by sea; your traitor will swim on land.

> *De Barselonne par mer si grande armée,*
> *Toute Marseille de frayeur tremblera:*
> *Îles saisies de mer aide fermée,*
> *Ton traditeur en terre nagera.*

   In 1596, during the French religious wars, Spain's Philip II sent a fleet of twelve ships to seize the isles of Château d'If and Ratonneau in an effort to isolate Marseilles by sea. A consul, Charles de Casau, who wanted to deliver the city to the Spanish, was run through by Pierre Libertat and the traitor's body was dragged through the streets by the citizens.

Rating: 9.5

The interpretation of this incisive prediction goes back a long way, at least to Guynaud in the early 1700s.

Quatrain III-89: The Struggle for Cyprus

> At that time Cyprus will be frustrated of its relief by those of the Aegean Sea (Greeks): Old ones done away with, but by speeches and supplications their king persuaded, the Queen more outraged.

> *En ce temps là sera frustree Cypres*
> *De son secours de ceux de mer Egee:*
> *Vieux trucides: mais par mesles et lyphres*
> *Seduit leur Roi, Reine plus outragee.*

In 1974 a struggle erupted between the ruling Greek military junta and Turkey for control of the island of Cyprus. The Turks invaded the island to protect the Turkish minority, and though the Greek army mobilized, it did not challenge the more powerful Turkish military. The Turks took over nearly half the isle, leaving the Cypriot Greeks "frustrated." About this same time, a referendum was held in which the Greeks voted to abolish the monarchy. King Constantine II agreed to accept the election result and renounced the crown ("king persuaded"). Evidently, the queen was "more outraged" at the loss of the throne than was King Constantine.

Rating: 9

The "old ones done away with" may be the victims of the Greek junta, which imprisoned or killed many opponents, including some veteran political activists.

Quatrain III-92: The Late Great French Empire

> The world near the last period, Saturn will come back
> again late: Empire transferred to the Dusky nation;
> the eye plucked out by the Goshawk at Narbonne.

> *Le monde proche du dernier periode,*
> *Saturne encore tard sera de retour:*
> *Translat empire devers nation Brodde,*
> *L'oeil arraché à Narbon par Autour.*

The arresting part of this prediction is the opening indicator that when French power is shifted toward Africa (the dusky nation?), the planet (or perhaps, civilization) will be close to its final cycle. Such a shift did occur in World War II when the Germans occupied France and the French Empire in Africa was first under Vichy, then stood for a time as the only significant remnant of Free France. The "Goshawk" is apparently Hitler who was content with occupying northern France for a while, but eventually swept all the way to Narbonne on the southern coast, depriving the Allies of an espionage "eye" on the continent. "Saturn" is usually seen as a negative influence by astrologers.

Rating: 8

Obviously, it is not possible to say if the Seer was correct about the world's "final period," though there are indications he might be. The rest of the quatrain looks good.

Quatrain III-95: The Fall of Communism

The law of More will be seen to decline: afterwards
another much more seductive. Dnieper first will come
to give way: through benefits and tongue (discussion)
another more attractive.

La loi Moricque on verra défaillir:
Après une autre beaucoup plus seductive:
Boristhenes premier viendra faillir:
Par dons et langue une plus attractive.

A prophecy for our own time, this quatrain clearly foretells the demise of Communism, i.e., "the law of More" (referring to Thomas More's philosophy of utopian communism with which the Seer was no doubt familiar). "Dnieper" is one of the great rivers of Russia, having its source near Moscow and flowing through western Russia and the Ukraine. This is exactly the area where the anti-Communist revolt erupted in 1991, the people finding the benefits of democracy and freedom "more attractive."

Rating: 9

This is one of two quatrains that specifically predicts the fall of Communism, the other being IV-32 (page 150)—quite impressive.

Quatrain III-96: The Duke de Berry Assassinated

The chief from Fossano will have his throat cut by the
leader of the bloodhound and the greyhound: The
deed executed by those of the Tarpean Rock, Saturn in
Leo, February 13.

Chef de Fossan aura gorge coupee
Par le ducteur du limier et levrier:
Le fait patre par ceux du mont Tarpee,
Saturne en Leo 13. de Fevrier.

A curious quatrain that seems slightly askew in ways but hits the exact date of the Duke de Berry's murder in Paris—February 13, 1820. The duke was not a chief from Fossano but his maternal grandfather was. The knife-wielding assassin, Louis Louvel, was a saddler at the royal stables and may have worked with hunting dogs at times. He was a republican, which justifies the allusion to the "Tarpean Rock" of old republican Rome. The duke's throat was not literally cut; he was simply stabbed.

Rating: 7.5

The prophecy suggests that the Seer's impressions were not always simply right or wrong, but sometimes just slightly indistinct.

Quatrain III-97: Zionist Resettlement of the Holy Land

A new law to occupy the new land towards Syria,
Judea, and Palestine: The great barbarian empire to
decay, before the Moon completes its cycle.

Nouvelle loi terre neuve occuper
Vers la Syrie, Iudée et Palestine:
Le grande empire barbare corruer,
Avant que Phebés son sicle determine.

Among the more obvious of the Nostradamian predictions, this one foretells the resettlement of the Jews in Palestine and even the Golan Heights of Syria. The "great barbarian empire" is that of the Turks whose realm disintegrated in the wake of World War I. (The Christian Seer habitually referred to Muslims as barbarians.) The first Zionist agency for resettling Jews in the Holy Land was established in Palestine in 1908. Well within a cycle of the moon thereafter, 18.6 years, the once great Turkish Empire had collapsed.

Rating: 9
The prophecy combines unusual clarity with great accuracy, leaving the critic virtually empty-handed.

Quatrain III-100: Charles de Gaulle

> The last one honored among the Gauls will be victorious over the enemy man. Force and land in a moment explored, when the envious one will die from the hit of a dart.

> *Entre Gaulois le dernier honoré,*
> *D'homme ennemi sera victorieux:*
> *Force et terroir en moment exploré,*
> *D'un coup de trait quand mourra l'envieux.*

The notion of exploration "in a moment" strongly suggests military aerial reconnaissance, so the time period must be our own. If so, the "last one honored" can only be Charles de Gaulle, who fought a long, lonely, and frustrating battle for Free France during World War II. Eventually, he triumphed over his opponents, in particular, Marshall Pétain, who collaborated with the Nazis. The "envious one" is Admiral Darlan, a rival of de Gaulle's in North Africa who was shot dead by an assassin in December of 1942.

Rating: 8.5
If one accepts the "dart" as a bullet, which is not much of a stretch, the prediction works nicely.

Quatrain IV-1: The Fall of Venice

> That the remainder of the blood not be shed, Venice asks that relief be given. After having waited a very long time, the city delivered up at the first sound of the horn.

Cela du reste de sang non epandu:
Venise quiert secours etre donné:
Après avoir bien longtemps attendu,
Cité livrée au premier cor sonné.

This is a simple quatrain that has been unnecessarily complicated by commentators. It basically describes the final fall of Venice in 1797. As Bonaparte's army chased the Austrians across northern Italy, Venice insisted on its neutrality, asking both sides to respect its non-belligerent status. The Corsican, though, was intent on destroying the Venetian oligarchy since it might threaten his rear as he advanced into Austria. When Napoleon's plan became obvious, the *Doge* (duke) abdicated, surrendering the 1,000-year-old city without a fight.

Rating: 8.5

The phraseology might have been better in spots, but the prediction is basically correct.

Quatrain IV-2: The War of the Spanish Succession

Because of death France will take to making a journey, fleet by sea, marching over the Pyrenees Mountains. Spain in trouble, military people marching: Some of the greatest Ladies taken off to France.

Par mort la France prendra voyage à faire,
Classe par mer, marcher monts Pyrenees,
Espaigne en trouble, marcher gent militaire:
Des plus grandes Dames en France emmenées.

The death of Spain's Charles II in 1700 fractured the European balance of power as the grandson of Louis XIV of France claimed the Spanish throne. A coalition of major powers (including England, Austria, Holland, and Prussia) decided to support the pretensions of the Archduke Charles of Austria and a costly, futile twelve years of war ensued in western Europe. Units of the French army supported by the French navy crossed the Pyrenees to fight in Spain. The whole mad episode could be traced to the fact that two Spanish princesses had married into the French royal line as wives of Louis XII and Louis XIV.

Rating: 9
There is little to critique here except that the last line could be improved.

Quatrain IV-5: Louis XIV and the Spanish Succession

> Cross, peace, under one the divine word accom-
> plished. Spain and Gaul will be united together: great
> disaster near and combat very bitter. No heart will be
> so hardy as not to tremble.

> *Croix, paix, sous un accompli divin verbe*
> *L'Espaigne et Gaule seront uriis ensemble:*
> *Grande clade proche, et combat trés-acerbe:*
> *Coeur si hardi ne sera qui ne tremble.*

The only time France and Spain were "united" in any substantive sense was when the grandson of Louis XIV inherited the Spanish throne, putting Spain under the Bourbons and under strong French influence. The two nations fought as allies in the lengthy ensuing War of the Spanish Succession ("combat very bitter"). The first line is difficult unless Nostradamus' ardent Catholicism is borne in mind. Almost certainly the Seer is referring to the revocation (1685) of the Edict of Nantes by Louis XIV, which ended religious strife in France through the harsh tactic of repressing the Huguenots, driving many out the country and making France solidly Catholic.

Rating: 9.5
The resolution of the previously unsolved first line makes this a particularly strong quatrain.

Quatrain IV-8: The Siege of St. Quentin

The great city by prompt and sudden assault surprised by night, guards interrupted: The guards and watches of St. Quentin slaughtered, guards and the portals broken.

La grande cité d'assaut prompt repentin
Surpris de nuit, gardes interrompus:
Les excubies et veilles saint Quintin
Trucidés, gardes et les portails rompus.

In 1557, only two years after this quatrain was published, a Spanish army suddenly invaded France from the Netherlands, capturing St. Quentin after a short siege. The Spanish move was a surprise, but it is not known whether the St. Quentin garrison, which was in a deplorable state of readiness, learned of the impending assault at night. Alternately, it might be that something akin to line two happened during the siege but, if so, it is lost to history. The hastily improvised defenses only allowed the French to hold out for seventeen days before the guards were slaughtered and "the portals broken" by cannon fire.

Rating: 7.5
Though the second line is dubious, the Seer has to get credit for an essentially correct call.

Quatrain IV-10: Bill Clinton

The young Prince, falsely accused, will plunge the army into trouble and quarrels: The chief bruised for his support, Scepter to pacify: then to cure scrofula.

Le jeune Prince accusé faussement
Mettra en trouble le camp et en querelles:
Meurtri le chef pour ie soutenement,
Sceptre apaiser: puis guerir ecrouelles.

The "army into trouble" indicates President Bill Clinton who threw the armed forces into a furor when he tried to make them accept homosexuals. Line three also fits perfectly since Secretary of Defense Les Aspin was confronted by horrendous pressures due to the policy change and was soon hospitalized for heart surgery ("bruised"). The "scepter to pacify" sums up the compromise in which Clinton backed off to quiet the storm. The first line suggests that some of the many accusations against Clinton in the election campaign of 1992 were untrue. "Scrofula" is technically a form of tuberculosis but once had broader applications; dramatic progress against the AIDS virus was made during the Clinton tenure.

Rating: 9

"Young Prince", i.e., a head-of-state to be, is an apt description of Clinton during the 1992 campaign.

Quatrain IV-12: The Defeat of Napoleon

> The greater army put to flight in disorder, scarcely
> further will it be pursued: Army reassembled and the
> legion reduced, then it will be chased out completely
> from the Gauls.

> *Le camp plus grand de route mis en fuite,*
> *Guere plus outre ne sera pourchassé:*
> *Ost recampé et legion reduite,*
> *Puis hors des Gaules due tout sera chassé.*

This is an apt description of the aftermath of the Battle of the Nations at Leipzig where Napoleon's army was routed and fled back across the Rhine. The Allies, though, did not pursue the retreating foe and only months later, after Bonaparte had foolishly refused an honorable peace, did they venture into northern France. By then, Napoleon had reassembled a semblance of his former legions ("legion reduced"). But the Allies, after some indecisive engagements, finally caught the Corsican out of position and boldly marched directly on Paris, beating him to the capital and forcing his abdication and exile to Elba.

Rating: 9

This quatrain is esoteric enough that it has not previously been fathomed. It works very well though. Interestingly, the last two lines were fulfilled twice; they might also apply to Napoleon's comeback attempt that ended at Waterloo.

Quatrain IV-13: The Greek Defeat at Symrna

> News of the very great loss reported; the report will
> astonish the army: United troops revolt in opposition.
> The double phalanx will abandon the great one.

> *De plus grande perte nouvelles rapportées,*
> *Le rapport fait le camp s'etonnera:*
> *Bandes unies encontre revoltées:*
> *Double phalange grand abandonnera.*

The use of the word "phalanx" in the quatrains usually has to do with a Greek army. War between Greece and Turkey broke out in the wake of World War I over various territories, including Symrna on the coast of Asia Minor. In 1922, the Turkish army struck at Symrna with an attack that utterly crushed the Greek forces there, a defeat so shocking that the government in Athens resigned. Many of the fleeing Greek soldiers landed on the island of Khíos where a military revolt erupted, which forced King Constantine ("the great one") to flee the country. Eleven of the principal Greek ministers were court-martialed in the wake of the disaster and six of them were shot.

Rating: 9.5

Not correctly solved until now, the prediction precisely describes complex events—a prophetic triumph.

Quatrain IV-14: Theodore Roosevelt

> The sudden death of the first personage will have
> caused a change and put another in the sovereignty:
> Soon, late, come so high and of low age, such that by
> land and sea it will be necessary to fear him.

> *La mort subite du premier personnage*
> *Aura changé et mis un autre au regne:*
> *Tot, tard venu à si haut et bas age,*
> *Que terre et mer faudra qu'on le craigne.*

At first this prediction seems quite general; a young man comes to power on the death of another and proves to be a formidable ruler. But the quatrain is tightly qualified by the fact that he is to be feared by sea as well as land. There have only been two fearsome sea powers since the defeat of the Spanish Armada in 1588: Britain and the United States. So, the only person the quatrain really fits is Theodore Roosevelt who succeeded to the "sovereignty" as the youngest ever American president after the assassination of President McKinley. Roosevelt used the big stick of military and naval might to cow Latin America and achieve his dream of a Panama Canal.

Rating: 9

The prevalent application of the prophecy to Charles XII of Sweden is not convincing because Sweden was never a strong sea power.

Quatrain IV-15: The Nazi Submarine Blockade

> From where they will think to make famine come,
> from there will come the surfeit: canine avarice
> through the eye of the sea. For the one the other will
> give oil and wheat.

> *D'où pensera faire venir famine,*
> *De là viendra le rassasiement:*
> *L'oeil de la mer par avare canine*
> *Pour de l'un l'autre donra huile, froment.*

During World War II the German submarine fleet tried to cut Britain's oceanic supply lines to starve the island into submission. The "eye of the sea" is an obvious metaphor for a submarine's periscope. The relentless antisubmarine warfare of the Allies transformed the sea from an obstacle to a broad highway for all that was needed and then some ("surfeit"). Brits used to joke that their island would sink under the weight of all the material the Americans were sending, much of it wheat and oil. The use of "canine" is interesting since the Nazi subs used to travel in "wolf packs."

Rating: 9.5

This is a clever and accurate prophecy, poetic enough but not overly abstruse. "Avarice" here is an allusion to the Nazi greed for conquest.

Quatrain IV-16: Washington, D.C.

The free city of liberty made servile: made the asylum of profligates and dreamers. The king change to them not so violent: from one hundred grow more than a thousand.

La cite franche de liberte fait serve:
Des profliges et reveurs tait asile.
Le Roi change a eux non si proterve:
De cent seront devenus plus de mille.

One could hardly ask for a better description of the United States' capital. The term "free city" not only signifies freedom but also implies a city not in the jurisdiction of another state—just the case with the District of Columbia. Originated by brilliant patriots, it was in time overrun by profligates "servile" to special interests and disconnected from the world of the citizens. The thousand growing out of one hundred represents the multiplication of bureaucrats. "Hundred" may be a geographic clue as well since the District of Columbia originally was exactly 100 square miles. The nonviolent change in line three merely alludes to America's practice of changing its chief executive peacefully by elections.

Rating: 9

Nostradamus is nothing if not opinionated, but in this case his view is hard to refute. (A previously unsolved quatrain.)

Quatrain IV-18: Persecution of Galileo and Bruno

> Some of those most lettered in the celestial facts will
> be condemned by illiterate princes: Punished by
> Edict, hunted, like criminals, and put to death wher-
> ever they will be found.

> *Des plus lettres dessus les faits celestes*
> *Seront par princes ignorants reprouves:*
> *Punis d'Edit, chasses, comme scelestes,*
> *Et mis a mort la ou seront trouves.*

Copernican theory, which revolutionized the whole concept of our universe, caused the princes of the Church great discomfort. The Inquisition soon zeroed in on the two leading exponents of the radical notion that the Earth moved around the sun: Giordano Bruno and Galileo. Bruno was arrested, brought to Rome, and burned at the stake in 1600. Galileo had the good sense to recant and was merely placed under a kind of permanent house arrest during which he continued his research. There were, of course, many other efforts at suppression before Copernicus' ideas finally triumphed.

Rating: 9

Not correctly applied before, the quatrain suggests that Nostradamus may have favored Copernican theory, but he was not about to push his luck. The Inquisition kept a wary eye on the Seer's activities.

Quatrain IV-21: The Breakup of the USSR

> The change will be very difficult: City and province
> will gain by the change: Heart high, the prudent
> established, cunning one chased out. Sea, land, people
> will change their state.

Le changement sera fort difficile:
Cite, province au change gain fera:
Coeur haut, prudent mis, chasses lui habile,
Mer, terre, peuple son etat changera.

This is an amazingly accurate description of the disintegration of the old Soviet Union, certainly a "difficult" change. The extreme centralization of the old regime was dumped and many former provinces gained complete or virtual independence (line two). More prudent people replaced the blind ideologues of the past. The "cunning one" is Gorbachev who tried to placate all elements simultaneously but could not quite carry it off. Many people, such as the Lithuanians, actually did "change their state" as they opted out of the Commonwealth of Independent States altogether.

Rating: 9
The stunning accuracy of the prophecy more than makes up for its lack of a geographic clues.

Quatrain IV-22: Civil War Rends Lebanon

The great army which will be chased out, in one
moment it will be needed by the king: The faith
promised from afar will be broken; he will be seen
naked in pitiful disorder.

La grande copie qui sera dechassee,
Dans un moment fera besoin au Roi:
La foi promise de loin sera faussee,
Nu se verra en piteux desarrol.

The phrase "pitiful disorder" fits few nations better than Lebanon. The refugee massacre of 1982 brought a multinational peacekeeping force to that Middle Eastern country. But heavy casualties inflicted by terrorist bombings "chased out" the peacekeepers, leaving Lebanon's President Gemayel and his country trapped in tragic, protracted chaos (faith broken).

Rating: 8.5

The term "naked" in this prediction means vulnerable or defenseless. (A previously unsolved verse.)

Quatrain IV-25: The Seer as Television Critic

> Lofty bodies endlessly visible to the eye, through these they will come to cloud reasons: Body, brows included, (but) sense and head (judgement) invisible, diminishing the sacred prayers.

> *Corps sublimes sans fin a l'oeil visibles,*
> *Obnubiler viendront par ces raisons:*
> *Corps, front compris, sens, chef et invisibles,*
> *Diminuant les sacrees oraisons.*

This is one of the more interesting quatrains if not one of the more obvious. The only "lofty bodies endlessly visible to the eye" would be stationary earth satellites, such as those used to relay television signals. Nostradamus renders a dim judgment of television fare, predicting these satellites will be used to obscure people's reason and will diminish their interest in religion. Line three is difficult but seems to say that the television screens will show complete human images, but they will lack sense and intellect. (Anyone care to argue?)

Rating: 8

While the verse is quite remarkable in ways, the rating is hurt by the overly murky phraseology of the third line.

Quatrain IV-26: Napoleon Takes Over

> The great swarm of bees will arise, such that one will not know whence they have come. By night the ambush, the sentinel under the vines, city delivered by five babblers not without cover.

> *Lou grand eysseame se leuera d'abelhos,*
> *Que non sauran don te siegen venguddos;*
> *De nuech l'embousque, lou gach dessous las treilhos*
> *Cieutad trahido per cinq lengos non nudos.*

The old Le Pelletier interpretation of this somewhat abstract quatrain is still the best. He applies it to Napoleon's coup of 18 Brumaire, 1799, in Paris. Bees were in fact the emblem of Napoleon's dynasty, and "five babblers" is certainly an excellent description of the French Directors who yielded power to Bonaparte as First Counsel. The coup was planned the previous night, and the conspirators may have had a sentinel posted under some vines, though this is not known. The Directors are described as "not uncovered," because it is said that some were secretly bought off.

Rating: 7.5

This is quite an interesting quatrain, but the third line is not as strong as the rest.

Quatrain IV-31: The Burning of Bruno

> The Moon in the full of night over the high moun-
> tain; the new sage with a lone brain has seen it: By his
> disciples invited to be immortal, eyes to the south.
> Hands on bosom, body in the fire.

> *La Lune au plein de nuit sur le haut mont,*
> *Le nouveau sophe d'un seul cerveau l'a vu:*
> *Par ses disciples etre iminortel semond,*
> *Yeux au midi. En seins mains, corps au feu.*

The Seer is in rare poetic form with this verse about the ill-fated Italian intellectual, Giordano Bruno. This independent thinker ("lone brain") began his professional career in Naples in the shadow of Vesuvius ("high mountain"). There Bruno began to formulate his volcanic ideas: pantheistic concepts of creation and support for the Copernican view of the cosmos (figured here by "the Moon"). After settling in

Zurich, he received an invitation from disciples in Venice ("to the south"). In that city, though, Bruno came into the grasp of the Inquisition and, after several years in prison, was burned at the stake in Rome (1600).

Rating: 9
From a literary aspect, this previously unresolved quatrain is one of Nostradamus' very best. It is almost as good prophetically.

Quatrain IV-32: Communism Collapses in East Europe

> In the places and times of flesh giving way to fish, the
> communal law will be made with opposition: It will
> hold the old ones strongly. Then removed from the
> scene, Communism put far behind.

> *Es lieux et temps chair au poisson donnera lieu,*
> *La loi commune sera faite au contraire:*
> *Vieux tiendra for puis otee du milieu,*
> *La Panta Choina Philon[5] mis fort arrieve.*

Communism was forced on eastern Europe during the era when Catholics held to the now-disregarded rule of eating fish instead of meat on Fridays. The prediction evidently refers to the Catholic eastern European countries: Poland, Czechoslovakia, Hungary, and perhaps Yugoslavia, which has a large fraction of Catholics. Marxist indoctrination converted a whole generation of eastern Europeans, some of whom ("old ones") held to it even after its failure was obvious. But when the USSR began to crumble, younger and more audacious heads saw the opportunity to free their countries from the Soviet tyranny and did so.

---

5. Literally, "love of everything in common."

Rating: 9

This is one of two verses in the *Centuries* clearly forecasting the demise of Communism, which was only an abstract academic theory in Nostradamus' time. (See Quatrain III-95, page 136.)

Quatrain IV-36: The Late 1800s in Europe

> The new games set up again in Gaul, after victory in
> the Insubrian (northern Italy) campaign. In the
> mountains of Hesperia, the great ones tied, trussed
> up. Romaigne and Spain to tremble with fear.

> *Les jeux nouveaux en Gaule redresses,*
> *Après victoire de l'Insubre champaigne:*
> *Monts d'Esperie, les grands lies, trousses:*
> *De peur trembler la Romaigne et l'Espaigne.*

The second modern Olympics ("new games") were held in Paris in 1900, about forty years after Napoleon III's successful campaign to oust the Austrians from northern Italy. In between these two events, Spain experienced almost continuous turmoil with sporadic civil warfare, and the Spanish monarchy was forced to accept a constitution ("great ones tied"). In the same time frame, the Papal States ("Romaigne") were being gobbled up by the new Italy—much to the "fear" and dismay of the pope.

Rating: 9

Despite the clear Olympic Games clue, this excellent verse has not previously been decoded, but it is accurate on all counts.

Quatrain IV-37: Bonaparte Crosses the Alps

> The Gaul will come to penetrate the mountains by
> leaps: He will occupy the great place of Insubria: His
> army to enter at the greatest depth. Genoa and Monaco
> will incite the red forces.

> *Gaulois par sauts, monts viendra pénétrer:*
> *Occupera le grand lieu de l'Insubre:*
> *Au plus profond son ost fera entrer,*
> *Gennes, Monech pousseront classe rubre.*

In May of 1800, Napoleon leaped the Alps with 40,000 troops, in a remarkable passage over the St. Bernard Pass, to occupy Milan ("the great place of Insubria") and reestablish control over northern Italy. In June the amazing French victory at Marengo sent the advancing Austrians reeling backward and suing for peace. Earlier that same year, the Austrians had besieged Genoa, and a British fleet had attacked Monaco. Both the British and the Austrians favored red uniforms.

Rating: 9.5

This highly accurate verse is all the more effective because the geography is unusually specific.

Quatrain IV-39: The Liberation of Rhodes

> The Rhodians will demand relief, through the neglect
> of its heirs abandoned. The Arab empire will lower its
> course; the cause set right by Hesperia (the West).

> *Les Rhodiens demanderont secours,*
> *Par le neglect de ses hoirs delaissee.*
> *L'empire Arabe revelera son cours,*
> *Par Hesperies la cause redressee.*

In 1522, after a bloody siege, the Knights of St. John abandoned the Aegean island of Rhodes to the Turks. The Christian Rhodians suffered much under Turkish domination but got no relief until World War I when the western alliance—Britain, France, Italy, and the United

States—defeated the Turks/Central Powers, whereupon the island was put under Italian rule. When Il Duce was crushed by Anglo-American forces in World War II, Rhodes and its largely Greek population properly became part of Greece ("cause set right").

Rating: 8.5

This is a good prophecy except for the questionable use of "Arab" to denote the Turkish Empire. More than once Nostradamus seems fuzzy on the point that the Turks are not Arabic, though their culture and much of their empire was. (The Seer would likely view all this as nitpicking.)

Quatrain IV-43: The Arab-Israeli Conflict

> Arms will be heard clashing in the sky. That same year
> the divines (are) enemies: They will want unjustly to
> dispute the holy laws: through lightning and war
> many a believer put to death.

> *Seront ouis au ciel les armes battre:*
> *Celui an meme les divins ennemies:*
> *Voudront loix saintes injustement debattre:*
> *Par foudre et guerre croyant a mort mis.*

This is a somewhat difficult quatrain but not insoluble. The "clashing in the sky" takes us to the twentieth century and the quarreling "divines" connote religious warfare; all of which applies to the Israeli-Islamic struggles of the past half-century. "Lightning" and "war" in the last line immediately conjure up the Israeli "blitzkrieg" of the 1967 Six-Day War. The debated "holy laws" likely pertain to the Jews' position that scripture gives them all of Palestine forever—a belief disputed by the Muslims. The Seer seems to say that this argument should not be settled by unjust means, i.e., force and violence.

Rating: 8

This is not a bad overall picture of the Arab-Israeli confrontation, though it leans toward overabstraction.

Quatrain IV-45: Germany in the Wake of World War I

Through conflict a King will abandon his realm. The greatest chief will fail in time of need: Dead, ruined, few will escape it (ruin). All cut up, one will be a witness to it.

Par conflit Roi, regne abandonnera:
Le plus grand chef faillira au besoin:
Morts, profliges peu en rechappera,
Tous destranches un en sera temoin.

This is a remarkably precise depiction of Germany's post-World War I plight. Following its defeat, Kaiser Wilhelm abdicated and Germany ceded large territories whereby eastern Prussia was isolated from the rest of the country ("all cut up"). The French later seized the Rhineland when the Germans could not meet their war debt. President Hindenberg ("the greatest chief") proved unable to cope with the problem, and the economy virtually disintegrated. The last line is chilling; one of the witnesses to all of this was an army corporal named Adolph Hitler who swore vengeance on those he held responsible—the Jews, the Communists, the French, and the British.

Rating: 9.5
This is a masterful prediction throughout, but especially in the foreboding final line, the significance of which has been overlooked.

Quatrain IV-47: The Fall of Mussolini

The savage black (hearted) ruler when he will have tried his bloody hand at fire, sword, and drawn bows: All of his people will be much frightened seeing the greatest ones hung by the neck and feet.

Le noir farouche quand aura essaye
Sa main sanguine par feu, fer, arcs tendus:
Trestous le peuple sera tant effraye,
Voir les plus grands par col et pieds pendus.

This prophecy has been applied to the French King Charles IX who reigned during the infamous St. Bartholomew's Day Massacre. This is really a bad rap since Charles' mother, Catherine de Médici, engineered the massacre. Actually, the quatrain fits Mussolini better, who tried his hand at war with so little success that in the end he and his mistress were shot and hung by their feet by Italian partisans. No doubt this event filled Il Duce's fascist followers with fear—with good reason; some of them were soon to hang by the neck.

Rating: 8

Unfortunately, the verse lacks a geographic clue although the following (coupled?) quatrain is about Italy and probably portrays the rise of the Fascists. Quatrain IV-48 (not listed), though, is overly subtle so it is difficult to be sure of its meaning.

Quatrain IV-49: Television and the Vietnam War

> Before the people blood will be shed; from the high
> heavens only it will come far. But of one for a long
> time nothing will be heard; the spirit of the lone one
> will come to bear witness against it (the bloodshed).

> *Devant le peuple sang sera repandu,*
> *Que du haut ciel ne viendra eloigner:*
> *Mais d'un longtemps ne sera entendu,*
> *L'esprit d'un seul le viendra temoigner.*

Vietnam was the first television war and the first two lines of the quatrain depict how the realities of modern combat were brought home via video, i.e., scenes of bloodshed carried to viewers through the airwaves. The second half of the quatrain applies to Senator Eugene McCarthy who held back for some time but then started what was at first a lonely campaign against a sitting president based on opposition to the continued bloodshed in Vietnam.

Rating: 8.5

Though this previously unresolved verse is not highly specific, the description of television broadcasting is remarkable.

Quatrain IV-50: The Rise of the United States

> Libra will see the Hesperias (the far west) govern, hold-
> ing the monarchy of heaven and earth. No one will see
> the power of Asia perish; only seven will hold the hier-
> archy in order.

> *Libra verra regner las Hesperies,*
> *De ciel et terre tenir la monarchie:*
> *D'Asie forces nul ne verra peries,*
> *Que sept ne tiennent par rang la hierarchie.*

This prophecy has come true with the rise of the United States ("the far west") to world supremacy while Japan ("the power of Asia") ranks as the world's second strongest nation despite its defeat in World War II. The last line of the prediction neatly confines it to our own time; the seven who "hold the hierarchy in order" are the so-called G-7 nations, the great industrial powers of today. The "monarchy of heaven" is illu- minating because it implies an overwhelming air power, further clarify- ing the subject. No nation has ever dominated the skies like the United States.

Rating: 9

This is a brilliant prophecy, not fully appreciated previously. The use of "Libra" seems rather pointless, but it may refer to Britain with the impli- cation that the United Kingdom would see America succeed it as the premier world power. (The Seer seemed to view Britain as under Libra.)

Quatrain IV-54: The Emperor Napoleon

> Of the name which no Gallic King ever had, never was
> there so fearful a thunderbolt. Italy, Spain, and the Eng-
> lish trembling, very attentive to foreign women.

> *Du nom qui onc ne fut au Roi Gaulois*
> *Jamais ne fut un foudre se craintif,*
> *Tremblant l'Italie, l'Espagne et les Anglois,*
> *De femmes étranges grandement attentif.*

Emperor Napoleon had a name completely unlike that of any French king. He was a "thunderbolt" who demolished the old Europe and brought prolonged and bloody warfare to Italy, Spain, and the English. One of his wives was a Creole from Martinique, another an Austrian, and he had at least one foreign mistress, Marie Walewska of Poland.

Rating: 10

The subject of the prediction is instantly apparent and the geographic precision is laudable. This single quatrain is almost enough to establish the Seer's precognition of Napoleon.

Quatrain IV-56: Munich and the Holocaust

> After the victory of the raving tongue, the spirit
> tempted into tranquility and repose: During the con-
> flict the bloody victor makes harangues, roasting the
> tongue and the flesh and the bones.

> *Après victoire de rabieuse langue,*
> *L'esprit tempte en tranquil et repos:*
> *Victeur sanguin par conflit fait harangue,*
> *Rotir la langue et la chair et les os.*

The infamous Munich sell-out is aptly designated here as the "victory of the raving tongue"—the tongue, or course, being Hitler's. The agreement to dismember Czechoslovakia (1938) lulled the world into a false sense of "repose," most thinking that der Führer had been placated: Chamberlain's "peace in our time." The last half of the quatrain depicts Hitler's notorious harangues during his conquests of France and eastern Europe and his extermination and cremation of Jews and other targeted groups.

Rating: 9

This is a clear enough quatrain that seems to have escaped decoding. It would have been improved by some hint of Hitler's final defeat, but the depiction of Hitler as a raving, bloody haranguer is perfect.

Quatrain IV-61: The Tragedy of Pétain

> The old one mocked and deprived of his place by the
> foreigner who will suborn him: Hands of his sons
> eaten before his face, he will betray his brother at
> Chartres, Orleans, and Rouen.

> *Le vieux moqué et privé de sa place,*
> *Par l'etranger qui le subornera:*
> *Mains de son fils mangées devant sa face,*
> *Le frere à Chartres, Orl Rouan trahira.*

The obvious candidate here is Marshall Pétain, aged chief of Vichy France, who was co-opted by the Nazis and then dumped to a nominal role when they forced him to accept the notorious collaborationist, Pierre Laval, as premier. Since Pétain was one of the great World War I generals, "his sons" is a metaphor for the French army that was chewed to pieces by the German war machine in 1940. The last line portrays Pétain as a betrayer of his fellow Frenchmen.

Rating: 8.5

On first reading the verse seems overly abstruse, but it actually represents a pretty fair balance of the poetic and the prophetic.

Quatrain IV-62: Oliver Cromwell

> A colonel with ambition plots: He will seize the great-
> est army. Against his prince false invention; and he
> will be discovered under his arbor.

> *Un colonel machine ambition,*
> *Se saisira de la plus grande armée,*
> *Contre son Prince fainte invention,*
> *Et decouvert sera sous sa ramée.*

Many commentators have favored Oliver Cromwell as the subject of this prophecy but have been unable decode the last line. Most likely, it refers to the fact that when he first came to public notice Cromwell was a gentleman farmer, a man of limited means and education but with a strange genius for things military. He soon obtained control over most of the English army and repeatedly defeated the forces of the king. He was a leader among those who concocted the case against Charles I, which led to the king's eventual execution.

Rating: 9

The resolution of the last line would seem to settle the question of whether it applies to Cromwell, or to Coligny as some have supposed.

Quatrain IV-65: The Fall of Napoleon III

> To the deserter of the great fortress, after he will have abandoned his place, his adversary will exhibit very great prowess. The emperor, soon dead, will be condemned.

> *Au deserteur de la grande forteresse,*
> *Après qu'aura son lieu abandonné,*
> *Son adversaire fera si grande prouesse,*
> *L'empereur tot mort sera condamné.*

The last line of the verse instantly conjures up French Emperor Napoleon III's debacle in the Franco-Prussian War of 1870; it caused him to be officially condemned by the French Assembly. He died a couple of years later. Efforts to identify the emperor as the "deserter" of the first line do not work well. The deserter has to be France's Field Marshall Bazaine who made a scandalous, premature surrender of the great fortress of Metz for which he was court-martialed. For the balance of the war, the highly competent Prussians continued to provide the French (and Bazaine, as onlooker) with lessons in the art of warfare.

Rating: 9

The Prussians captured Napoleon III when they surrounded Sedan; hence, it is very hard to hang the tag of "deserter" on the emperor.

Quatrain IV-68: The Struggle for Malta

> In the place very near, not far, from Venus, the two
> greatest ones of Asia and of Africa, from the Rhine and
> the lower Danube they will be said to have come.
> Cries, tears at Malta and the Ligurian coast.

> *En lieu bien proche non eloigné de Venus,*
> *Les deux plus grands de l'Asie et d'Affrique,*
> *Du Ryn et Hister qu'on dira sont venus,*
> *Cris, pleurs à Malte et coté Ligustique.*

This is an intricate quatrain that portends the legendary siege of Malta in 1565. The "greatest ones of Asia and of Africa" are the Turkish Sultan and Dragut, the great leader of the Barbary pirates of North Africa. Together they attacked the Knights of St. John in Malta with overwhelming numbers but were eventually repulsed. "Venus" here would be the south Italian city of Venosa, site of one of the Knights' great cathedrals. The Turks, at the time, ruled the lower Danube valley. "From the Rhine" evidently alludes to the roots of the Barbary pirates, descendents of the Germanic Vandals, also pirates, who crossed the Rhine in the fifth century and occupied the Barbary (Barbarian) Coast.

Rating: 8

Dragut's pirates raided Italian (Ligurian) shores, so all facets of the verse check out, even though the Rhine reference might be considered overly cryptic.

Quatrain IV-70: Wellington Wins in Spain

> Quite contiguous to the great Pyrenees mountains,
> one to direct a great army against the Eagle: Veins
> opened, forces exterminated. As far as Pau he will
> come to chase the chief.

> *Bien contigue des grands monts Pyrenees,*
> *Un contre l'Aigle grande copie adresser:*
> *Ouvertes veines, forces exterminees,*
> *Que jusqu'à Pau le chef viendra chasser.*

The quatrain neatly describes the Duke of Wellington's victory in the Peninsular campaign where he drove the French out of Spain and pursued them over the Pyrenees into the south of France. The "Eagle," as usual, is Napoleon. Pau was one of the last cities captured by Wellington before the French General Soult ("the chief") surrendered. Casualties were very heavy on both sides as line three indicates.

Rating: 9.5

There are a number of quatrains that describe the Peninsular War so accurately that it is almost impossible to argue that Nostradamus did not foresee it.

Quatrain IV-73: Napoleon III and Italy

> The great nephew by force will test the treaty made by
> the faint heart: The Duke will try Ferrara and Asti,
> when the pantomime will take place in the evening.

> *Le neveu grand par force prouvera*
> *Le pache fait du coeur pusillanime:*
> *Ferrare et Ast le Duc eprouvera,*
> *Par lorsqu'au soir sera le pantomime.*

The verse centers on the involvement in the Italian Risorgimento of France's Napoleon III, nephew of Napoleon I. The "treaty" of line two is the one negotiated with Premier D'Azeglio of Piedmont after the Austrian victory in the War of 1848. D'Azeglio soon resigned in despair ("faint heart") and was succeeded by Cavour who convinced Napoleon III to intervene in Italy. The Austrians were defeated and lost all their gains of 1848 and more. The "Duke" here is Archduke Albert, the great Austrian army leader whose field of action ranged through the Po valley from Ferrara to near Asti. The last line alludes to a famed diplomatic charade between Napoleon and the Austrian ambassador at a social affair.

Rating: 10

This is a remarkable quatrain. It is so complex that it has not been fully comprehended, though Le Pelletier was on the right track.

Quatrain IV-75: Stalingrad

Ready to fight one will desert; the chief adversary will
obtain the victory: The rear guard will make a
defense, the faltering ones dead in white territory.

Pret à combattre fera defection,
Chef adversaire obtiendra la victoire:
L'arriere-garde fera defension,
Les defaillants morts au blanc territoire.

The "white territory" quickly brings to mind the snowy Russian
steppes where the decisive battle of World War II was fought around
Stalingrad in the winter of 1942–43. The phrase "one will desert" refers
to German Sixth Army General Paulus whose forces were cut off by a
Russian pincer movement. Paulus had orders from Hitler to fight to
the last man, but seeing his situation as hopeless, the general surrendered his entire army of 93,000 men. The Russians were Hitler's "chief
adversary" at the time since the United States was just becoming a
major force. After Stalingrad, the Germans were in almost constant
retreat, leaving hundreds of thousands dead on the frozen steppes.

Rating: 9.5

This is a neat fit. Attempts to apply the quatrain to Waterloo are far
from convincing.

Quatrain IV-80: France's Maginot Line

Near the great river, great ditch, earth drawn out; in
fifteen parts the water will be divided: The city taken,
fire, blood, cries, sad conflict, and the greatest part
concerned by the collision.

Près du grand fleuve, grande fosse, terre egeste,
En quinze parts sera l'eau divisee:
La cité prise, feu, sang cris conflit mettre,
Et la plupart concerne au collisee.

The extensive earthworks of France's infamous Maginot line near the Rhine River are depicted here. The second line must refer to the area's many canals that also figured into France's illusory defense plan. The Nazi armies simply went around the whole thing by way of the Low Countries, taking Paris in a matter of days—the saddest defeat in French history. The last line indicates that nearly all the countries of Europe would be involved or affected by the conflict.

Rating: 8

The quatrain has a couple of slightly vague aspects but works well overall.

Quatrain IV-82: The Russians Take Berlin

> A throng approaches from Slavonia; the old Destroyer
> will ruin the city: He will see his "Rome" quite deso-
> lated. Then he will not know how to put out the great
> flame.

> *Amas s'approche venant d'Esclavonie,*
> *L'Olestant vieux cité ruinera:*
> *Fort desolee verra sa Romanie.*
> *Puis la grande flamme eteindre ne saura.*

As the Slavic masses of the Red Army approached Berlin in 1945, it was obvious that Hitler was finished. Der Führer, (the destroyer) though, refused to surrender, a manic decision that doomed the German capital to be "desolated" by Russian artillery and bombs. Hitler's twisted mind actually wanted Berlin destroyed in a *Götterdamerung*. The "great flame" is mostly metaphorical; a poetic portrayal of the forces reducing to ashes Hitler's dream of a 1,000-year Reich (his "Rome").

Rating: 8.5

The verse applies less well to Napoleon because he was only forty-three, not at all "old," at the time of his retreat from Russia. Also, France was never "desolated" to the extent that Germany was.

Quatrain IV-89: Britain's Glorious Revolution

> Thirty of London will conspire secretly against their
> King, the enterprise over the sea. He and his satellites
> will have a distaste for death; a fair King elected,
> native of Frisia.

> *Trente de Londres secret conjureront,*
> *Contre leur Roi, sur le Pont l'entreprise:*
> *Lul, satellites la mort degouteront,*
> *On Roi elu blond, natif de Frize.*

As one of Nostradamus' famous successes, this verse forecasts the overthrow of Britain's King James II in 1688–89 due to his pro-Catholic policies. The exact number of lordly conspirators is not known, but thirty is not far off the mark. Their negotiations with the Protestant William of Orange were carried on through a number of voyages to and fro across the North Sea. When William landed in England, James and his cohorts saw discretion as the better part of valor and fled the country ("distaste for death"). William was from Frisia and was most likely fair-complected if not fair-haired.

Rating: 10

The events forecasted were so unlikely that the prospect of guesswork or chance fulfillment is next to nil. (*Pont* could mean either "sea" or "bridge," but if it means a bridge, it would be a ship's bridge, so the quatrain works either way.)

Quatrain IV-93: The Strange Case of the Duke of Bordeaux

> A serpent seen near the royal bed; it will be by the
> lady at night—the dogs will not bark. Then to be born
> in France a Prince so royal, all the princes will see him
> (as) come from heaven.

Un serpent vu proche du lit royal,
Sera par dame nuit chiens n'aboyeront:
Lors naitre en France un Prince tant royal,
Du ciel venu tous les Princes verront.

The Duke of Bordeaux, an heir to the French throne, was born in September of 1820, seven months after the assassination of his father. He was hailed by royalists as a "gift of God." The "serpent" here is a figure for Louis Philippe, Duke of Orleans, who himself had an eye on the throne and contested the legitimacy of the birth. Louis, having free access among royalty, would not cause the guard dogs to bark. In the end, Bordeaux's claim to the crown came to nothing. He was too reactionary to accept the concept of a limited monarchy and was passed over in favor of Louis.

Rating: 8

The Seer's characterization of Louis as a serpent seems overly harsh, but then Nostradamus was a strict monarchist and would doubtless have favored Bordeaux.

Quatrain IV-95: The American Civil War

The realm allotted to two they will hold it very briefly. Three years and seven months passed by they will make war. The two vestals will rebel in opposition (to each other). The victor the younger in the land of Armenique (Amerique).

Le regne à deux laissé bien peu tiendront,
Trois ans sept mois passés feront la guerre:
Les deux Vestales contre rebelleront,
Victor puine en Armenique terre.

Though unrecognized as such, the verse is an apt outline of the American Civil War; the "two" (in line one) being Abraham Lincoln and Confederate President Jefferson Davis. Lincoln held office barely more than four years, Davis for even less. Being custodians of a nation's hearth and home, the rival vestals stand here for "the house divided against itself"—the North and the South. Lincoln, the "victor," was in fact a year younger than Davis. "Armenique" is a barely disguised anagram for America. The Seer is only a shade off on the length of the struggle. Real warfare did not actually commence until the Battle of Bull Run in late July of 1861, effectively ending with the Battle of Five Forks three years and eight months later.

Rating: 8.5

The slight chronological miscalculation necessarily costs points, but the interpretation is bolstered by the fact that the following (coupled) quatrain also concerns the United States.

Quatrain IV-96: The Rise of America

> The elder sister of the British Isle will be born fifteen
> years before her brother. Because of her promise
> being verified she will succeed to the kingdom of the
> balance.

> *La soeur ainée de l'Ile Britannique*
> *Quinze ans devant le frère aura naissance,*
> *Par son promis moyennant verifique,*
> *Succedera au regne de balance.*

Analysts have long suspected that this verse pertains in some way to America but have been unable to decipher it. The answer comes clear with the realization that Canada is the younger brother of the United States, both nations pictured here as siblings of Britain. America declared its independence in 1776. Parliament created English Canada exactly fifteen years later with the Constitution Act of 1791. The United States did indeed fulfill its early promise, finally becoming preeminent in the world and "succeeding to the kingdom of the balance"; that is, replacing Britain as the great Anglo power. (The Seer sees Britain as a Libra nation.)

Rating: 9.5

The precision of the timeline is so striking, it is difficult to withhold a top rating. (The Seer has been criticized for seeming to pay little attention to the United States, but there are more than thirty unfathomed quatrains like this one that apply to America and/or Americans.)

Quatrain IV-99: Prussia's Iron Prince

> The valiant son of the King's daughter will hurl back
> the Celts very far, such that he will cast thunderbolts,
> so many in such an array, few and distant, then deep
> into the Hesperias (western land).

> *L'ainé vaillant de la fille du Roi,*
> *Respoussera si profond les Celtiques,*
> *Qu'il mettra foudres, combien en tel arroi*
> *Peu et loin, puis profond és Hesperique.*

One of the Prussian leaders in the 1870 war against France was the "Iron Prince," Frederick Charles, eldest son of the daughter of a German state ruler. The prince was an impetuous but resourceful field marshall and played a key role in the destruction of the French regular army in eastern France. He was then dispatched deep into western France to deal with the newly formed Army of the Republic. The prince practically ended French resistance with his victory at Le Mans early in 1871.

Rating: 9.5

The interpretation of this previously unsolved verse is supported by the fact that the following quatrain also deals with the Franco-Prussian War. The use of "Hesperias" here is a little unusual, but not really out of line since Le Mans is quite near the Atlantic.

Quatrain IV-100: The Franco-Prussian War

> With celestial fire on the Royal edifice, when the light
> of Mars will fail, seven months great war; people dead
> through evil. Rouen, Evreux will not fail the King.

> *Du feu celeste au Royal edifice,*
> *Quand la lumiere de Mars defaillira,*
> *Sept mois grande guerre, mort gent de malefice*
> *Rouan, Eureax au Roy ne faillira.*

Prussian artillery rained fire on the Tuileries when Paris was under siege in the Franco-Prussian War, 1870–71. The "light of Mars" certainly failed the French whose army was so poorly trained and directed that the French were beaten in just under seven months. The last line is less obvious though Cheetham says Normandy ("Rouen, Evreux") remained a strongpoint of royalist support during and after the martial fiasco. At any rate, Normandy was one of the few areas not overrun by the Prussians. The war marked the end of the line for the French monarchy; Napoleon III lost the throne and France has been a republic since.

Rating: 9

Nostradamus winds up his impressive fourth Century with two strong, coupled quatrains on the Franco-Prussian conflict.

Quatrain V-I: The Hitler-Stalin Pact

> Before the coming of Celtic (French) ruin, in the temple two will parley. Pike and dagger to the heart of one mounted on a steed; they will bury the great one without making any report.

> *Avant venue de ruine Celtique,*
> *Dedans le temple deux parlementeront*
> *Poignard coeur, d'un monté au coursier et pique,*
> *Sans faire bruit le grand enterreront.*

The year before the fall of France, Ribbentrop and Molotov, foreign ministers of Germany and Russia, hatched the 1939 Hitler-Stalin Pact in a parley at the Kremlin ("the temple"). The "nonaggression treaty" actually included a deal to partition Poland. The figure for Poland— "one mounted on a steed"—is apropos because the Polish army was so outmoded; the Polish cavalry actually charged Nazi mechanized columns. As line three indicates, Poland was attacked simultaneously by its two enemies ("pike and dagger to the heart"). The last line refers to the secret nature of the partition agreement.

Rating: 9

This is a colorful and astute prophecy though possibly a shade too allegorical.

Quatrain V-4: The Early Phases of World War II

A large mastiff expelled from the city will be vexed by
the strange alliance. After having chased the stag from
the fields the wolf and the Bear will defy each other.

Le gros matin de cité dechassé,
Sera faché de l'étrange alliance,
Après aux champs avoir le cerf chassé
Le loup et l'Ours se donront defiance.

A highly allegorical verse that nevertheless well describes the first year of World War II. The "mastiff," known as *le dogue Anglais* in France, is Britain. The "bear" is obviously Russia while the "wolf" is a figure for Nazi Germany. The Brits, who were certainly vexed by the bizarre Hitler-Stalin treaty, were expelled from the city of Dunkirk in 1940 by encircling Nazi armies. The "stag," prey to both the bear and the wolf, stands for Poland, which was chased from the field by the combined forces of Russia and Germany—who went to war with each other shortly afterward.

Rating: 7.5

While too figurative for a top rating, this quatrain is still one of the more intriguing.

Quatrain V-3: A Frenchman Rules Florence

> The successor to the Duchy will come very far beyond
> the Tuscan Sea: A Gallic branch will hold Florence,
> the nautical frog in its lap by agreement.

> *Le successeur de la Duché viendra,*
> *Beaucoup plus outre que la mer de Toscane:*
> *Gauloise branche la Florence tiendra,*
> *Dans son giron d'accord nautique Rane.*

This simple but successful prophecy merely says that the Médici dynasty of Florence is to be replaced by another of French affiliation. This actually happened in 1737 when the Médicis died out and Francis of Lorraine became the Grand Duke. The Tuscan realm continued in his family until 1859, except for a brief episode during the Napoleonic era when it was given to Spanish Bourbons, actually another Gallic branch. The "nautical frog" may refer to some now forgotten legend or coat of arms.

Rating: 7.5

While it is correct, the quatrain does not really hold a great deal of prophetic content.

Quatrain V-5: Napoleon Falls and Falls

> Under the shadowy pretense of removing seritude, he
> will himself usurp the people and the city. He will do
> worse because of the deceit of a young whore. Deliv-
> ered in the field reading a false poem.

> *Sous ombre feinte d'oter de servitude*
> *Peuple et cité l'usurpera lui-meme:*
> *Pire fera par fraude de jeune pute,*
> *Livré au champ lisant le faux poeme.*

The first two lines clearly fit Napoleon; while posing as a loyal son of the Republican Revolution, he plotted to seize total power, and soon did. The third line is fascinating. In 1807, Napoleon fell into an affair with a young married Polish countess—the beginning of the end for his marriage to the popular Josephine. The emperor and his wife were soon divorced, and there was widespread belief that Bonaparte's phenomenal luck then deserted him. In fact, public enthusiasm for Napoleon, on which all depended, did fade. Ultimately, the Corsican was "delivered" to his enemies in the field despite all his speeches promising riches and glory to his followers—in the end a "false poem."

Rating: 9.5

An extraordinary degree of insight is displayed in this previously unsolved verse, one of the most beguiling of them all.

Quatrain V-8: United States' Air Strikes on Japan

> There will be unleashed live fire, hidden death, horrible and frightful within the globes. By night the city reduced to dust by the fleet; the city afire, the enemy amenable.

> *Sera laissé feu vif, mort caché,*
> *Dedans les globes horrible epouvantable,*
> *De nuit à classe cité en poudre laché,*
> *La cite à feu, l'ennemi favorable.*

The words "hidden death" imply a secret weapon—most likely the atomic bomb. They may also allude to radiation that kills through invisible rays. While the first two lines concern Hiroshima and Nagasaki, the rest deals with the massive incendiary raids on Tokyo and other cities by "fleets" of heavy bombers. Often carried out at night, these raids sometimes did as much damage and took as many lives as an A-bomb. The last line has Japan "amenable" to peace talks because of the devastation imposed by the Strategic Air Command.

Rating: 8.5

While there is no clear geographic clue, Japan is really the only feasible candidate for this verse.

Quatrain V-15: The Popes and the Corsican

> The great Pontiff taken captive while navigating, the
> great one thereafter to fail the clergy in tumult. Sec-
> ond one elected, absent his estate declines; His
> favorite bastard to cunning death.

> *En naviguant captif pris grand Pontife,*
> *Grand après faillir les clercs tumultues:*
> *Second elu absent son bien debiffe,*
> *Son favori batard à mort roue.*

Few quatrains are more provocative than this one about Pius VI,
Pius VII, and the death of Napoleon. Both popes were taken captive by
the French while navigating the Fishing Barque (the papacy). There
was extreme tumult among the clergy in the reign of Pius VI, which he
failed to resolve—chaos in revolutionary France and strife with the
Jesuits. In Pius VII's reign, the Papal States were lost to France ("estate
declines"). The arresting last line supports the theory that Napoleon
was slowly poisoned by the British on St. Helena. "Favorite bastard"
summarizes Pius VII's attitude toward Bonaparte, who favored
Catholicism but often clashed with the pope.

Rating: 9
Since the actual cause of Napoleon's death at the age of fifty-one is
uncertain, we cannot give the verse top rating though it may well
deserve it. Bonaparte's "stomach cancer" symptoms were consistent
with arsenic poisoning; all his brothers far outlived him.

Quatrain V-19: Saddam Invades Kuwait

> The great royal one of gold, augmented by brass; the
> agreement broken, war opened by a young man. Peo-
> ple afflicted by a lamented chief, the land covered with
> barbarian blood.

> *Le grand Royal d'or, d'airain augmenté,*
> *Rompu la pache, par jeune ouverte guerre:*
> *Peuple affligé par un chef lamenté,*
> *De sang barbare sera couverte terre.*

"Great royal one of gold" aptly describes the oil-rich Emir of Kuwait while the "brass" perhaps reflects the Seer's impression of the vast array of metallic pipes and fittings involved in his many refineries, oil rigs, and pipelines. The young man who makes war is Saddam Hussein, who invaded Kuwait because it allegedly broke its oil production agreement. Saddam was fifty-three at the time but only forty-three when he launched an earlier war against Iran. He certainly became a "lamented chief" for many Iraqis after the death and devastation of the Gulf conflict. (A fervent Christian, Nostradamus habitually used the term "barbarian" when referring to the Muslims.)

Rating: 8.5

Though the use of "young" in describing Hussein might be questioned, it is, of course, a relative term (Bush was sixty-six in 1990). The rest of this previously unsolved verse holds up well.

Quatrain V-20: Benito and the Count

> A great army will pass beyond the Alps a little before a
> monster scoundrel will be born: Prodigious and sud-
> den he will turn the great Tuscan to his neighboring
> place.

> *Dela les Alpes grande armée passera,*
> *Un peu devant naitra monstre vapin:*
> *Prodigieux et subit tournera*
> *Le grand Tosquan à son lieu plus propin.*

"Monster scoundrel" aptly personifies Benito Mussolini. The army of Napoleon III crossed the Alps in 1859 to help the Italians against Austria. In the context of historical time, Mussolini was born a little later, in 1883. Both Il Duce's personality and his rise to power were "prodigious and sudden." Rash and melodramatic by nature, he rose to supremacy in Italy less than four years after founding his Fascist Party. The "great Tuscan" here is Count Ciano of the Tuscan port of Livorno, Benito's right-hand man and heir apparent until they came to a parting of the ways in 1943. Mussolini then pushed Ciano aside by dismissing the cabinet and making the count ambassador to nearby Vatican City ("neighboring place").

Rating: 9.5

The accuracy of this previously unsolved verse is phenomenal. Count Ciano did not survive the war, but his diary is an invaluable historical resource.

Quatrain V-22: The End of Il Duce

> Before the great one has given up the ghost as to
> Rome, great fright for the foreign army: The ambush
> by squads near Parma; then the two red ones will cele-
> brate together.

> *Avant qu'à Rome grand aie rendu l'ame,*
> *Effrayeur grande à l'armée estrangere:*
> *Par escadrons l'embuche près de Parme,*
> *Puis les deux rouges ensemble feront chere.*

The sudden capitulation (1943) by King Victor Emmanuel of Italy in World War II threw the Nazis into a frightened frenzy. They had to rush troops into Italy to take control, worrying all the while about guerilla activity behind their lines. The "great one" is Mussolini who ran a puppet government in German-occupied Italy until shortly after the fall of Rome in June 1944—which must have ended his last hopes ("ghost given up"). The second part of the verse depicts the capture and execution of Il Duce by pro-Communist partisans not far from Parma in northern Italy—a coup for the Italian "reds," who were no doubt joined in their elation by the "reds" of Russia.

Rating: 9

While the city of Parma is about 100 miles from the scene of Mussolini's death, Parma was formerly a sizable duchy whose northern boundaries extended quite "near" the capture site. (A previously unsolved verse.)

Quatrain V-23: The Rome-Berlin Axis

The two satisfied ones will be united together, when
for the most part they will be conjoined with Mars:
The great one of Africa trembles in terror; Duumverate disjoined by the fleet.

Les deux contents seront unis ensemble,
Quand la plupart à Mars seront conjoint:
Le grand d'Affrique en effrayeur tremble,
DUUMVIRAT par la classe dejoint.

An easy enough quatrain, this one has Hitler and Mussolini pleased with their Axis alliance of 1936 and the settlement of their sticky Tyrolean boundary dispute. Thus the way was cleared for their joint plans of conquest ("conjoined with Mars"). At about the same time, Mussolini overran Ethiopia, so the "great one of Africa" in fear is clearly Haile Selassie, the Ethiopian emperor. The duumvirate of der Führer and Il Duce was "disjoined" by the Allied seaborne invasion of Italy in 1943—hence, the reference to "the fleet."

Rating: 10

A solid, plain, and tidy quatrain with no ragged edges.

Quatrain V-26: The Rise of Russia

> The Slav people through luck in war will become ele-
> vated to a very high degree: They will change their
> Prince, one born a provincial. An army raised in the
> mountains to pass over the sea.

> *La gent esclave par un heur martial,*
> *Viendra en haut degré tant elevee:*
> *Changeront Prince, naitra un provincial,*
> *Passer la mer copie aux monts levee.*

Their tenacious struggle against the Nazis in World War II established the Russians as one of the world's two superpowers. They had in
truth changed their "Prince" to a "provincial"; after the revolution,
Joseph Stalin, from the remote border province of Georgia, became
dictator. The armies crossing the sea must be the Allied armies that
landed in the Soviet Union in 1918–20, to help the White Russians
against the Reds—a futile effort as it turned out.

Rating: 9

The argument can be made that *esclave*, since it is not capitalized,
means "slave" rather than "Slav." Even so, the verse would not be inval-
idated since the Russian peasants were virtual slaves under the old
czarist feudal system.

Quatrain V-29: Mussolini and Hitler

> Liberty will not be recovered; a proud villainous,
> wicked, black ruler will occupy it, when the matter of
> the pontiff will be opened. The republic of Venice will
> be vexed by Hister (Hitler).

> *La liberté ne sera recouvree,*
> *L'occupera noir, fier, vilain, inique,*
> *Quand la matiere du pont sera ouvree,*
> *D'Hister, Venise fachée la republique.*

The bulk of this verse deals with Mussolini's rise to power in Italy, but the most striking aspect is the reference to Hitler in the last line. (The change of a single letter in a name was a common anagrammer's ploy.) The "matter of the pontiff" alludes to Il Duce's concordat with the pope regarding Vatican City in 1929. Since Hitler was not yet in power, the first two lines of the quatrain must, quite aptly, refer to Mussolini. The adjective "black" may be significant since the Fascists were known as "blackshirts." "Venice" here stands for northern Italy, vexed by Hitler when he occupied it in World War II after Italy's surrender.

Rating: 9.5

Curiously, the verse even works (though less well) for conservatives who would translate Hister as *Ister* (meaning "the Danube") since it was from the general area of the Danube that Nazi troops moved into Italy.

Quatrain V-30: Liberty, Equality, Pillage

> All around the great city soldiers will be lodged
> throughout the fields and towns: Paris, Rome incited
> to give the assault; then upon the pontiff great pillage
> carried out.

> *Tout alentour de la grande cité,*
> *Seront soldats loges par champs et villes:*
> *Donner l'assaut Paris, Rome incité,*
> *Sur le pont lors sera faite grande pille.*

During the French Revolution, Paris was hotly incited against the Church. After Napoleon's invasion of northern Italy, French agents whipped up similar sentiments in Rome and, late in 1797, a revolutionary riot broke out resulting in the death of General Duphot of the French embassy. A French army then overran the Papal States ("soldiers lodged throughout"), took Pius VI prisoner, and pillaged the Vatican of many priceless works of art. Some of the best treasures at the Louvre are souvenirs of this episode.

Rating: 10
While a beautifully accurate prophecy, the quatrain is also geographically precise. The solution goes back at least as far as Le Pelletier.

Quatrain V-31: France and the Papacy

> Through the Attic land, fountain of wisdom, at present
> the rose of the world: The pontiff ruined, and his great
> preeminence to be subjected, a wreck amidst the waves.

> *Par terre Attique chef de la sapience,*
> *Qui de present est la rose du monde:*
> *Pont ruiné, et sa grande preeminence*
> *Sera subdite et naufrage des ondes.*

This is an extension of the previous verse, Quatrain V-30. The "Attic land" here is not Greece but France, considered by the Seer to be the cultural heir of ancient Attica. He predicts that France will humiliate the papacy, which it did more than once during the French revolutionary era. Two popes were shanghaied by the French, and the Vatican under French domination was subjected to a variety of indignities, looting included.

Rating: 8.5
This is a satisfactory quatrain but not detailed enough to rate among the Seer's elite calls.

Quatrain V-33: The Infamous Nantes Massacre

> Of the principal ones of the city in rebellion who will
> strive mightily to recover their liberty: The males cut
> up, unhappy fray; cries, groans at Nantes pitfall to see.

> *Des principaux de cité rebellee*
> *Qui tiendront fort pour liberté ravoir:*
> *Detrancher males infelice melee,*
> *Cris, hurlements à Nantes piteux voir.*

In 1793 a counter-revolutionary movement broke out at Nantes, which was put down by the notorious French revolutionary terrorist, Jean-Batiste Carrier. He guillotined about a thousand prisoners ("males cut up") and had many others shot in cold blood without trial. His most sadistic ploy was tying priests and women together naked on barges and sinking them. But what goes around, comes around; Carrier himself soon died under the guillotine.

Rating: 10

This is a virtually perfect quatrain, complete with precise geography.

Quatrain V-35: The British Fail at La Rochelle

> For the free city of the great Crescent Sea, which still
> carries the stone in its stomach, the English fleet will
> come under the drizzle to seize a branch (subdistrict).
> War opened by the great one.

> *Par cité franche de la grande mer Seline,*
> *Qui porte encore à l'estomac la pierre,*
> *Angloise classe viendra sous la bruine*
> *Un rameau prendre, du grand ouverte guerre.*

This is a cleverly styled quatrain partially solved by Leoni. It deals with the city of La Rochelle on the crescent-shaped Bay of Biscay. *Roche* means "rock" in French; the city was named for its stony surroundings. In 1627, during the era of religious mayhem, the Duke of Buckingham set out from England with a sizable force to relieve La Rochelle, a Protestant free city under French siege. He landed on the harbor island of Re but was repulsed. No doubt there was some drizzle at times during the escapade. Politically, *rameau* means a subdistrict, in this case La Rochelle itself. The "great one" is presumably Richelieu, who ordered the French assault on the city.

Rating: 9.5

The "great one" could hardly be Buckingham who was a bumbling scoundrel eventually stabbed to death by someone who served with him at Re.

Quatrain V-38: Louis the Dud(e)

> He who will succeed the grand monarch on his death
> will lead an illicit and wanton life: Through noncha-
> lance he will give way to all, so that in the end the
> Salic law will fail.

> *Ce grand monarque qu'au mort succedera,*
> *Donnera vie illicite lubrique:*
> *Par nonchalance à tous concedera,*
> *Qu'à la parfin faudra la loi Salique.*

The Seer scores big with this one. It is a flawless description of the reign of the inept Louis XV, successor to the Grand Monarch, Louis XIV. A weak-willed lightweight, Louis XV catered to the whims of mistresses like Madame Pompadour and Madame du Barry with disastrous results for France. The public dissatisfaction with his reign set the stage for the French Revolution and the fall of the monarchy. The succession to the throne of France was governed by the Salic law.

Rating: 10

The use of the term "the grand monarch," the precise nickname of Louis XIV, is noteworthy.

Quatrain V-40: Ike Pulls the Reins

> The royal blood will be so very mixed; Gauls will be
> constrained by Hesperia (western land): One will wait
> until his term has expired and the memory of his
> voice has perished.

> *Le sang royal sera si trés melé,*
> *Contraints seront Gaulois de l'Hesperie:*
> *On attendra que terme soit coulé.*
> *Et que memoire de la voix soit perie.*

The first line confines the time frame to the era when the nobility has been much diluted, i.e., the twentieth century. The one instance when the French were really constrained by a western land was during the Eisenhower administration when France, combined with Britain and Israel, invaded Egypt to seize the Suez Canal. Ike blew his stack and pressured the Allies into backtracking. But seven years after Eisenhower's term ended, Israel ("the one who waits"), launched its six-day blitz against neighboring Arab states, regaining the Sinai and much other territory.

Rating: 9.5

The prediction is perhaps not quite complex enough for a perfect rating but it's a close call. (A previously unsolved verse.)

Quatrain V-41: The Reagan Era

> Born in the shadows and during a dark day, he will be
> sovereign in influence and kindness. He will cause his
> blood to rise again in the ancient urn, renewing the
> age of gold for that of brass.

> *Ne sous les ombres et journée nocturne,*
> *Sera en regne et bonté souveraine:*
> *Fera renaitre son sang de l'antique urne,*
> *Renouvelant siecle d'or pour l'airain.*

The opening phrase indicates one born in obscurity and in mid-winter; this is true of Ronald Reagan who was born February 6, 1911, to a small town, middle-American family. Reagan was surely one of the most influential presidents, and even his enemies would concede his generally good-natured disposition. The third line may allude to Reagan's remote relationship to old Irish royalty, whose blood "rose again" in the sense that he became the nearest thing to a royal president in some time. His administration was marked by prosperity and a preoccupation with material wealth, qualifying as an age of gold compared to the lackluster '70s—an age of brass.

Rating: 8.5

Some might consider the Seer's review of the Reagan era as overly generous, but then Nostradamus was, after all, a true conservative.

Quatrain V-42: The Struggle for North Italy

> Mars raised to his highest belfry will redeem the Savoyards of France: The Lombard people will cause very great terror to those of the Eagle included under the Balance (Libra).

> *Mars eleve en son plus haut beffroi,*
> *Fera retraire les Allobrox de France:*
> *La gent Lombarde fera si grand effroi,*
> *A ceux de l'Aigle compris sous la Balance.*

Napoleon III, in order to obtain the return of French-speaking Savoy to France, agreed to help Italian Piedmont oust Austria from northern Italy (Lombardy). The plan worked. French and Piedmontese forces defeated the Austrian army ("causing terror") in 1859 and Savoy was transferred to France. The "Lombard people" here include those of the modern provinces of Lombardy and Piedmont, both part of the old Lombard kingdom. Austria is described as the "Eagle under the Balance" because the eagle was an Austrian emblem, and astrologically Austria is supposed to be ruled by Libra.

Rating: 9.5

This is a complex quatrain and quite correct, though it does require the broad definition of Lombards.

Quatrain V-45: The Nazis Blitz France

> The great Empire will soon be desolated and transferred near the Ardennes forest: The two bastards beheaded by the elder, and Bronzebeard, the hawknose, will reign.

> *Le grand Empire sera tot desolé*
> *Et translaté près d'arduenne silue:*
> *Les deux batards par l'ainé decollé,*
> *Et regnera Aenobarbe, nez de milve.*

The main spearhead of Hitler's lightning western offensive in 1940, which transferred France to Nazi control, was through the Ardennes. France did have an empire at the time. The two who are decapitated would be the two successive Allied high commanders, generals Gamelin and Weygand, both badly beaten and severely criticized ("bastards"). Notably, the Allied left wing was literally "decapitated" from the main body, cut off and hemmed in by aging General Von Rundstedt's thrust from the Ardennes to the sea. Rundstedt was then sixty-five (*l'ainé*). "Bronzebeard" may not be a specific individual but a figure of the Teutonic conquerors.

Rating: 9

Possibly, "Bronzebeard" might be Von Rundstedt himself—an archetypal Prussian—if "reign" is broadly used. Von Rundstedt reigned as "high priest" of the German military after this campaign.

Quatrain V-52: Martin Luther King, Jr.

There will be a King who will give opposition, the exiles raised as to the realm: The poorer caste people to swim in blood, and for a long time he will flourish under such an ensign.

> *Un Roi sera qui donra l'opposite,*
> *Les exiles eleves sur le regne:*
> *De sang nager le gent caste hypolite,*
> *Et fleurira longtemps sous telle enseigne.*

This is a novel quatrain that appears to contain a translinguistic pun as a clue; Nostradamus certainly knew that the French *roi* means "king" in English. For a decade and a half, Martin Luther King, Jr. led the opposition to segregation in the United States, a crusade that was eventually successful as the "exiles" (the segregated) were raised to legal equality. The bloodshed cited here most likely includes the lynchings in the old South as well as those who died in the Civil Rights movement in the 1950s and '60s. King himself, of course, was assassinated as he was formulating a new Poor People's Campaign. His ensign was the same as Gandhi's: nonviolent resistance.

Rating: 9

At times Nostradamus is almost too clever at word games. This one has gone right over the heads of commentators for decades.

Quatrain V-56: The Surprising John XXIII

> Through the death of the very old Pontiff a Roman of good age will be elected. Of him it will be said that he weakens his see, but long will he hold on and in biting activity.

> *Par le trepas du trés-vielliard Pontife*
> *Sera elu Romain de bon age,*
> *Qui sera dit que le siege debiffe,*
> *Et long tiendra et de piquant ouvrage.*

When elected in 1958 the elderly Pope John XXIII, who succeeded the elderly Pius XII, was seen as an interim pope, expected to do little but hold down the desk for a brief time. Instead, he jolted the Church with vigorously progressive programs including groundbreaking ecumenical initiatives. His Vatican II Council changed the Church more than anything since the Reformation. John XXIII could fairly be called a Roman since he was an Italian who had spent most of his career at the Vatican. His five-year tenure, about the papal average, would seem less than the quatrain suggests. But he did "hold on" well beyond normal life expectancy, reaching the age of eighty-two.

Rating: 8

In a way, John XXIII held on even beyond his demise since his Vatican Council continued to work for two years afterward. His impact even continues to this day.

Quatrain V-58: The Duke and the Aqueduct

By the aqueduct of Uzes over the Gard, through the
forest and inaccessible mountain, in the middle of the
bridge it will be cut by hand; the chief of Nimes who
will be very terrible.

De l'aqueduc d'Uticense Gardoing,
Par la foret et mont inaccessible,
Emmy du Pont sera tranché au poing
Le chef nemans qui tant sera terrible.

The "aqueduct" here is a famous Roman ruin extending from Uzes
to Nimes. The Duke de Rohan, to relieve fellow Huguenots besieged at
Nimes in 1627, moved his artillery over the aqueduct. At one point,
part of the supports of the bridge over the Gard had to be cut away to
make way for the cannons. Upon his arrival at Nimes, Rohan was put
in command. The adjective "terrible" would be justified in Nostradamus' Catholic eyes since Rohan was a formidable Calvinist warrior for decades, finally dying of a battle wound in 1638.

Rating: 9.5

This is another case of the Seer focusing on a relatively minor event; a
tendency that may account for a good many unsolved quatrains.

Quatrain V-60: A Tale of Two Tyrants?

By the cropped head a very bad choice will come to be
made. Overextended, he will not pass the gate: He will
speak with such great fury and rage that he will con-
sign the entire sex to fire and blood.

Par tête rase viendra bien mal elire,
Plus que sa charge ne porte passera:
Si grande fureur et rage fera dire,
Qu'à feu sang tout sexe tranchera.

This is one of those odd quatrains that seems to have two fulfill-ments. In this case, the subject could be either Hitler or Napoleon, whose careers have obvious parallels. Both made the "very bad choice" of invading Russia. The gate not passed would be Stalingrad for Hitler, Moscow for Napoleon. Both were fiery speakers though Hitler had a clear edge for sheer fury. Both sacrificed huge numbers of their young men in their wars. While their close-cut hairstyles were almost identi-cal, Napoleon was actually known in his youth as "the little crop-head." On the other hand, *fureur* in line three could be a hint at der Führer.

Rating: 8

The verse works so well for both subjects that we have to wonder if it was written for double fulfillment. The ambiguity, though, necessarily hurts the rating.

Quatrain V-62: The Dark Days of World War II

> One will see blood to rain on the rocks; Sun in the
> East, Saturn in the West. Near Orgon war, at Rome
> great evil to be seen; ships sunk to the bottom and the
> Trident taken.

> *Sur les rochers sang on verra pleuvoir,*
> *Sol Orient, Saturne Occidental:*
> *Près d'Orgon guerre, à Rome grand mal voir,*
> *Nefs parfondrées, et pris le Tridental.*

The opening of the verse indicates a rocky harbor, almost surely Pearl Harbor, while "Sun in the East" is a clear reference to Nippon. The attack on Pearl Harbor gave the Japanese temporary superiority over the seas as symbolized by Neptune's "Trident taken." Saturn, a negative influence, implies bad war news for the West. The great evil at Rome is plainly fascism. The reference to the insignificant French town of Orgon is most interesting. It is not far from where Mussolini assaulted France in 1940; also, the coast of Oregon is about the nearest mainland to Pearl Harbor ("war near").

Rating: 9

If the double play on Orgon is intentional, this is an extremely clever quatrain, worthy of a 10. Unfortunately, we cannot be sure. (A previously unsolved verse.)

Quatrain V-63: The Anzio Beachhead

> From the vain enterprise honor and late complaint,
> boats tossed about among the Latins: cold, hunger,
> waves. Not far from the Tiber the land stained with
> blood, and diverse plagues will be upon mankind.

> *De vaine emprinse l'honneur indue plainte,*
> *Galiotes errants par latins, froids, faim, vagues*
> *Non loin du Tymbre de sang la terre teinte,*
> *Et sur humains seront diverses plagues.*

The Anzio beachhead in Italy was one of the most controversial episodes of World War II. The Allies' amphibious landing there in January of 1944 just south of the Tiber was supposed to outflank the Gustav line. But the Nazis soon hemmed in the landing force and turned the beachhead into a killing field ("stained with blood"). In the main, Anzio qualified as a "vain enterprise" and was much criticized ("late complaint"), but the Allied troops held on with honor. The "boats tossed about" are the hundreds of landing and supply crafts that hit the beach under bomb attack over several months. Though Anzio was plague enough in itself, the "plagues" here most likely refer to the overall setting of World War II.

Rating: 10

This is a precise, descriptive, almost obvious quatrain, largely overlooked.

Quatrain V-65: The Holocaust

Come suddenly the terror will be great, hidden by the
principal ones of the affair: And the woman in the live
embers will no more be in sight, so little by little will
the great ones be angered.

Subit venu l'effrayeur sera grande,
Des principaux de l'affaire cachés:
Et dame en braise plus ne sera en vue,
Ce peu à peu seront les grands fachés.

Hitler's "final solution" to the "Jewish problem" was kept secret
from the world and even most Nazi Party members until the discovery
of the extermination camps by liberating Allied armies. Rumors of the
"terror" had begun to leak out "little by little" via diplomatic and intelligence sources during the war, angering Allied leaders ("the great
ones"), but the massive scale of the killings was not grasped. The
"woman in the live embers" is an obvious figure of the victims, many
of them women, who were gassed and then cremated in the ovens of
the death camps.

Rating: 9
The only mysterious thing about the quatrain is the fact that it was not
solved long ago.

Quatrain V-68: The Archduke Charles

In the Danube and of the Rhine the great Camel (or
"slickster") will come to drink, not repenting it: Those
of the Rhone to tremble, and much more so those of the
Loire. Near the Alps the Cock (France) will ruin him.

Dans le Danube et du Rhin viendra boire,
Le grand Chameau, ne s'en repentira:
Trembler du Rosne, et plus fort ceux de Loire,
Et près des Alpes Coq le ruinera.

The "Camel" here has been assumed to mean the Arabs, but the geography makes this unlikely. *Chameau* can also mean a fake-out artist, roughly, "that dirty dog!"—often used in grudging admiration. The verse describes the career of the Austrian Archduke Charles, a wily military tactician and the only commander considered a match for Napoleon. Raised in Italy, Charles fought many battles along the Rhine and Danube, consistently outmaneuvering the French until the climactic 1809 Battle of Wagram near the Austrian Alps. Though barely bested by Bonaparte, the archduke never fought again. His exploits along the Rhine and in Italy surely rattled those of the Loire and Rhône.

Rating: 9.5

While Charles constantly preached caution in warfare, in actual battle he would often turn wildly audacious, much to the consternation of his French enemies. The Seer, being French, might well have seen the archduke as a chameau.

Quatrain V-69: The French Take Algeria

No longer will the great one be in his false sleep;
uneasiness will come to replace tranquility: a phalanx
arrayed in gold, azure, and vermilion to subjugate
Africa and gnaw it to the bone.

Plus ne sera le grand en faux sommeil,
L'inquiétude viendra prendre repos:
Dresser phalange d'or, azure et vermeil
Subjuguer Afrique la ronger jusqu'os.

For some years after the first French intrusions onto the Algerian coast, France's King Louis Philippe displayed a desultory, indecisive policy towards North Africa. But when Abd-el-Kader declared a holy war against the French the response was vigorous. A full-scale effort was launched in 1841 to subdue all Algeria as a matter of national policy. The effort was long and wearisome but ultimately successful. The red and blue ("azure and vermilion") of the French tricolors are mentioned here, but gold is substituted for the white. Since white stands for honor, the Seer may be saying that the conquest of Algeria was less a matter of honor than of greed.

Rating: 8

The phrase "gnaw to the bone" seems to confirm that Nostradamus saw the Algerian conquest as exploitive, but still the verse reads a shade too arcane.

Quatrain V-70: The Forever War: Turkey vs. Austria

> Of the regions subject to the Balance (Libra), they will
> trouble the mountains with great war: Captives, the
> entire sex enthralled and all Byzantium, so that at
> dawn they will cry from land to land.

> *Des regions sujettes à la Balance,*
> *Feront troubler les monts par grande guerre,*
> *Captifs tout sexe du et tout Bisance,*
> *Qu'on criera à l'aube terre à terre.*

Astrologers regarded the region of Austria-Hungary as subject to Libra. The quatrain focuses on the long series of wars that raged intermittently through the sixteenth, seventeenth, and eighteenth centuries between Austria and Turkey (Byzantium) in the mountainous Balkans. Millions of men in the region were impressed into service ("entire sex enthralled") to fight these seemingly endless conflicts. Different areas were involved in the struggles at different times accounting for the cries "from land to land."

Rating: 8.5

The quatrain, until now undecoded, is somewhat general, but there is still considerable merit to it.

Quatrain V-79: Abraham Lincoln

> The sacred pomp will come to lower its wings,
> through the coming of the great legislator: He will
> raise the humble, he will vex the rebels. His like will
> not appear on this earth.

> *La sacree pompe viendra baisser ies ailes,*
> *Par la venue due grand legilateur:*
> *Humble haussera, vexera les rebelies,*
> *Naitra sur terre aucun emulateur.*

President Abraham Lincoln "raised the humble" by freeing the slaves and vexed the "rebels" by defeating the Confederacy. He can legitimately be called a "great legislator" and was so unique and extraordinary a character that the last line is probably quite true. The opening line is more difficult, but it probably presages Lincoln's assassination; the "sacred pomp" with lowered wings may be the Seer's figure for a presidential funeral service.

Rating: 8.5
Curiously, the phraseology can be made to apply to Napoleon fairly well, but that interpretation goes against the overall grain of the quatrain, and the phrase "vex the rebels" would be hard to fit.

Quatrain V-81: The Battle of France (1940)

> The royal bird over the city of the Sun, seven months
> in advance will deliver a nocturnal omen. The Eastern
> wall will fall—lightning, thunder; (in) seven days the
> enemy directly to the gates.

> *L'oiseau royal sur la cité solaire,*
> *Sept mois devant fera nocturne augure:*
> *Mur d'Orient cherra tonnerre eclair,*
> *Sept jours aux portes les ennemis à l'heure.*

The "city of the Sun" is Paris, which Nostradamus saw as the center of the universe. The "royal bird" evokes the Royal Air Force (RAF), some planes of which probably flew patrols in the vicinity of Paris during the so-called "phony war" from October 1939 through April of 1940 (ca. seven months). In April of 1940, the Nazis launched their blitzkrieg (lightning war). After a direct strike westward to trap the British armies against the Channel, German armies paused to regroup. Then on June 5 they struck south and were at the gates of Paris within seven days. The "Eastern wall" would be the Maginot line.

Rating: 8

The "omen" aspect here is slightly fuzzy unless Nostradamus viewed the RAF planes as an augury of the Luftwaffe to come.

Quatrain V-83: United States' Embassy Seized in Iran

> Those who will have undertaken to subvert an unparalleled realm, powerful and invincible: They will act through treachery, three nights to warn, when the greatest one will read his Bible at the table.

> *Ceux qui auront entreprise subvertir,*
> *Nonpareil regne, puissant et invincible:*
> *Feront par fraude, nuits trois avertir*
> *Quand le plus grand à table lira Bible.*

The unparalleled and invincible realm has to be the United States. Since Jimmy Carter was the president most known as a born-again (Bible reading) Christian, he is the evident "greatest one" here. The verse, then, is focused on the 1979 seizure of the American embassy in Teheran by a Muslim fundamentalist mob after the Ayatollah designated America as Islam's number one villain. The Seer is not kind to either side. He calls the takeover an act of treachery. While at the same time, he observes that the Carter administration should have seen it coming at least three days prior because of the rabid demonstrations staged in the preceding days.

Rating: 8.5

Would history have been different if Carter had read this verse before-hand? Would he have caught the drift of it? Most likely he would not have; few quatrains have been correctly revealed in advance.

Quatrain V-85: The Air War/Failure of the League

> Through the Swabians and neighboring places, they
> will be at war over the clouds: a swarm of marine
> locusts and gnats; the faults of Geneva laid quite bare.

> *Par les Sueves et lieux circonvoisins,*
> *Seront en guerre pour cause des nuees:*
> *Camp marins locustes et cousins,*
> *Du Leman fautes seront bien denuees.*

The Swabians were one of the old German tribes living in south-west Germany so Nostradamus is talking about the Franco-German border region, an area of frequent conflict. This one, though, involves aerial warfare (as seen from the ground) with the reference to swarms of gnats and locusts symbolizing combat aircraft. Since the war is laid to the faults of Geneva—the failure of the League of Nations—the scene is patently World War II. The heaviest aerial activity in the germane region was during the Nazi invasion of France and the later Allied invasion of western Germany.

Rating: 9

Some of the old Swabians eventually became the Swiss, but Nostradamus is clearly dealing here with the German branch.

Quatrain V-93: The Ill-Starred Charles I

> Under the land of the round lunar globe when Mercury will be dominating, the Isle of Scotland will produce a luminary, one who will put the English into confusion.

> *Sous le terroir du rond globe lunaire,*
> *Lors gue sera dominateur Mercure:*
> *L'ile Escosse fera un liminaire,*
> *Qui les Anglois mettra à deconfiture.*

This uncomplicated quatrain is customarily applied to Britain's Charles I who was born in Dunfermline, Scotland in 1600, before his father, James I, succeeded to the British throne. On attaining the monarchy himself, Charles displayed a combination of unpopular religious leanings and political ineptitude that threw England into ultimate confusion: civil war. Eventually, he lost his head to the axe. The Seer seems to draw a comparison between Charles and the moon—an inconsistent light. In fact, the luckless king's great failing was his lack of reliability, such that he finally lost the trust of all.

Rating: 7.5

While there is nothing really wrong about the verse, it is a little light on prophetic content. Nostradamus presumably had something in mind with Mercury's dominance (line two), but it is hard to say exactly what.

Quatrain V-94: Hitler and Stalin

> He will transfer into great Germany Brabant and Flanders, Ghent, Bruges, and Boulogne. The truce feigned, the great Duke of Armenia will assail Vienna and Cologne.

> *Translatera en la grande Germanie,*
> *Brabant et Flandres, Gand, Bruges, et Bolongne:*
> *La treve feinte, le grand Duc d'Armenie*
> *Assaillira Vienne et la Cologne.*

Brabant and Flanders, Ghent, and Bruges are Belgian locales while Boulogne is the name of two cities in northern France. All were occupied by Hitler's armies at the time of the German westward blitz in 1940. The "truce feigned" is the phony Hitler-Stalin nonaggression pact that disintegrated with the Nazi invasion of the USSR. Especially interesting is the reference to the "Duke of Armenia" who can only be Stalin. As head of the Soviet Union, he ruled Soviet Armenia, and he was actually born on the old Armenian-Georgian border. Toward the close of World War II, Stalin's armies did assail Austria ("Vienna") and Germany itself ("Cologne").

Rating: 9.5
There are complex elements here that are all pretty much on the mark. Hitler often used the phrase "greater Germany." The rhyme factor was likely involved in the Seer's choice of Cologne as a figure for Germany.

Quatrain V-96: Vienna Under the Nazis

(At) the rose upon the middle of the great world,
public shedding of blood for new deeds: To speak the
truth one will have a closed mouth. Then at the time
of need the awaited will come late.

Sur le milieu du grand monde la rose,
Pour nouveaux faits sang public epandu:
A dire vrai, on aura bouche close,
Lors au besoin viendra tard l'attendu.

Nostradamus was, of course, entirely Eurocentric in his outlook so the middle of his world would be central Europe and the "rose" surely Vienna, easily the region's greatest city in every way. As the Nazis consolidated power after their Austrian takeover in 1938, they issued new edicts outlawing many accepted activities of a free society. Violators could be summarily shot. Freedom of speech disappeared so people feared to speak the truth ("closed mouth"). The Viennese hoped to be liberated by American troops ("the awaited"), but the much-feared Red Army got there first.

Rating: 8.5

This quatrain is perhaps overly subtle in ways but correct in all respects. (A previously unresolved verse.)

Quatrain V-99: France and Austria Contend in Italy

> Milan, Ferrara, Turin, and Aquileia (Venice), Capua,
> Brindisi vexed by the Celtic nation, by the Lion and
> his eagle's phalanx, when Rome will have the old
> British chief.

> *Milan, Ferrare, Turin, et Aquilleye,*
> *Capue, Brundis vexes par gent Celtique:*
> *Par le Lion et phalange aquilee,*
> *Quand Rome aura le chef vieux Britannique.*

In the years around 1800, Italy was trampled by the armies of revolutionary France, particularly in the north (cities listed in line one). The principal French opponents, equally vexing to the Italians, were the Austrians and their allies. The "Lion" here is an excellent figure for the doughty old Field Marshall Suvarov, who with a combined force of Austrians and Russians drove the French from northern Italy in 1799. Both Austria and Russia used the eagle in their national emblems. The last line refers to Cardinal York, the last of the Stuarts, who died in Rome in 1807.

Rating: 9.5

This is an admirably specific quatrain with good imagery. (Some have interpreted the "Lion" as Napoleon, but Nostradamus did not use that figure for Bonaparte.)

Quatrain VI-2: The Fortunes of France

> In the year five hundred and eighty more or less, one
> will await a very strange century. In the year seven
> hundred and three the heavens witness that several
> kingdoms, one to five, will make a change.

En l'an cinq cent octante plus et moins,
On attendre le siecle bien étrange:
En l'an sept cent et trois cieux en temoins,
Que plusieurs regnes un à cinq feront change.

In 1580 France was a political basket case, racked by religious warfare and bitter rivalries among factions of the nobility. No one expected much of a future for it. Yet, strangely, a century later, under the Grand Monarch, Louis XIV, France was the great nation of Europe, the acknowledged vital center of the world. But by 1703, the ruinous War of the Spanish Succession was under way, which caused great changes to several nations: Spain, Austria, Britain, the Netherlands, and, most of all, to France itself. Notably, 1703 was the very year the tide of the war turned against the French.

Rating: 8

Overall, this description of conditions is apropos enough, but the phrase "strange century" is too subjective for top credits.

Quatrain VI-7: The Fascist Twins

Norway and Dacia (Romania) and the British Isle will
be vexed by the united brothers: the Roman chief
sprung from Gallic blood and his forces hurled back
into the forests.

Norneigre et Dace, et l'ile Britannique,
Par les unis freres seront vexés:
Le chef Romain issu de sang Gallique
Et les copies qux forets repoussées.

The three nations cited in the first line were all vexed by the Fascist team of Hitler and Mussolini: Norway invaded, Britain attacked, Romania dominated, forced to give up Transylvania. The statement about Mussolini ("Roman chief") being of Gallic blood is not as odd as it seems. Il Duce was born in the area of northern Italy that was in ancient times overrun and settled by the Celts, so he very likely did have some "Gallic blood." The Greeks in fact hurled Mussolini's armies back into heavily forested Albania when he attempted to invade their country in 1940.

Rating: 8.5

If it were possible to be sure whether Mussolini actually did have some Gallic ancestors the verse could be rated higher.

Quatrain VI-8: Hitler's Crackdown on Dissent

> Those who were in the realm for knowledge will
> become impoverished at the change of government:
> some exiled without support, having no gold. The let-
> tered and the letters will not be at a high premium.

> *Ceux qui etaient en regne pour savoir,*
> *Au Royal change deviendront appauvris:*
> *Uns exiles sans appui, or n'avoir,*
> *Lettres et lettres ne seront à grand prix.*

The quatrain describes Hitler's war on intellectuals, such as writers, professors, artists, etc., who did not fall into line with Nazi ideology. Soon after Hitler took power they found themselves out of work, forced out of the county, or in concentration camps, especially if they happened to be Jewish. Even those who were lucky enough to get out of the Third Reich before the war started often had to leave most of their assets behind. There was no regard for "the lettered or the letters" unless they conformed to Nazi dogma.

Rating: 8.5

The application of this previously unsolved quatrain borders on the obvious, but a geographical clue would have been a plus.

Quatrain VI-9: The Inquisition

> In the sacred temple scandals will be perpetrated:
> They will be reckoned as honors and commenda-
> tions. Of one whom they engrave on medals of silver
> and gold (i.e., a hero) the end will be in very strange
> torments.

> *Aux sacres temples seront faits scandales,*
> *Comptes seront par honneurs et louanges:*
> *D'un que l'on grave d'argent d'or les medailles,*
> *La fin sera en tourments bien etranges.*

The persecutions and burnings of dissidents by the Inquisition are the "scandals perpetrated" that earned plaudits for inquisitorial churchmen. Though the Inquisition was active before Nostradamus wrote, it was then directed mainly against Muslims and Jews (so perhaps tolerable to the ardently Christian Seer). It was after Philip II came to power in Spain (1556) that the Inquisitors became all-pervasive "thought police," victimizing scholars, writers, and scientists—a prospect that apparently alienated Nostradamus. The second part of the verse must refer to the Inquisition's most famous target, Galileo, who spent his last several years under house arrest.

Rating: 8
Though Galileo was never tortured, it must have been a constant torment to him that he had been made to recant what he knew to be true. (A previously unsolved verse.)

Quatrain VI-11: Bad King Henry and the Guise Boys

> The seven branches will be reduced to three: The
> elder ones will be surprised by death. The two will be
> seduced to fratricide; the conspirators will be dead
> while sleeping.

> *Des sept rameaux à trois seront reduits,*
> *Les plus aines seront surpris par morts,*
> *Fratricider les deux seront seduits,*
> *Les conjures en dormant seront morts.*

In France, 1575, only the three youngest of Catherine de Médici's seven children were still alive: Henry III, Francois d'Alencon, and Marguerite of Navarre. Henry and Francois ("the elder ones") did engage in fratricidal warfare in the complex chaos of the French religious wars. The last line refers to the two Guise brothers who were killed on Henry's orders because their Catholic League was a threat to his supremacy. The term "conspirators" is not out of line for the Guises. They were not actually sleeping when they were assassinated, but Le Pelletier takes the meaning to be that they were unwary due to a false sense of security.

Rating: 8.5

One of the Guise brothers was actually told of the King's murderous intentions, but he would not believe the warning; he walked right into Henry's trap.

Quatrain VI-13: The Carter Administration

A doubtful one will not come far with the realm. The greater part will want to uphold him: A Capitol will not want him to reign at all. He will be unable to bear his great burden.

> *Un dubieux ne viendra loin du regne,*
> *La plus grande part le voudra soutenir:*
> *Un Capitole ne voudra point qu'il regne,*
> *Sa grande charge ne pourra maintenir.*

Jimmy Carter probably had the most frustrating time in office of any American president since Hoover. He was seriously challenged from within his own party for renomination, but "the greater part" (a play on party?) voted to uphold him. He was not popular with Congress and the political establishment in Washington, D.C., a factor in his defeat in the 1980 general election ("Capitol will not want him"). Carter seemed always to sound an uncertain trumpet ("doubtful one"), most notably in his unsuccessful grappling with the Iran hostage crisis, the issue that sealed his presidential fate.

Rating: 8.5

The last line is most appropriate. Few presidents showed the strain of office as much as Carter did, who went from young to old in four years.

Quatrain VI-14: Lost in Russia: Sweden's Charles XII

> Far from his land a King will lose the battle, at once
> escaped, pursued, then captured. The unwary one
> caught under the golden mesh, under false cover, and
> the enemy surprised.

> *Loin de sa terre Roi perdra la bataille,*
> *Prompt echappé poursuivi suivant pris,*
> *Ignare pris sous la doree maille,*
> *Sous feint habit, et l'ennemi surpris.*

Several hundred miles from his Swedish homeland in 1709, Charles XII rushed his army headlong into Peter the Great's trap at Poltava and got clobbered. Charles escaped with a remnant of his forces into Turkish territory, briefly pursued by Peter. The Turks then got annoyed with Charles and seized him in a raid, the "golden mesh" being a metaphor for the Sultan's protective custody. For over three years though, Charles and his troop camped on Turkish land ("false cover"). Peter was no doubt "surprised" by Charles' ability to influence the Turks. Three times he persuaded them to declare war on Peter before the Sultan tired of the whole business.

Rating: 9

In 1714, Charles went back to Scandinavia where he was killed during a siege. This previously unsolved quatrain deals with one of history's truly bizarre episodes.

Quatrain VI-16: De Gaulle and the Nazis

That which will be carried off by the young Hawk, by
the Normans of France and Picardy: The black (hearted) ones of the temple of the Black Forest area will
make an inn and fire of Lombardy.

Ce que ravi sera du jeune Milve,
Par les Normans de France et Picardie:
Les noirs du temple due lieu de Negrisilve
Feront auberge et feu de Lombardie.

When Allied forces hit the beaches of Normandy in 1944, Eisenhower proclaimed that his officers would temporarily govern liberated
areas. But de Gaulle slipped into Normandy and, almost before the
Allies realized what was happening, set up his own provisional government, which expanded in the wake of the Allied advance through
Picardy and all of France. Thus, de Gaulle carried off with the victor's
prize. At that time the Nazis ("the black hearted") had occupied northern Italy ("Lombardy") where the warfare caused much damage and
fire. The Black Forest temple is probably Hitler's castle at Berchtesgaden—a ways east of the forest but in very similar terrain.

Rating: 8

Did the Seer get a mental image of Berchtesgaden and its surroundings
and slightly misguess its location? It seems likely. (A previously
unsolved verse.)

Quatrain VI-21: World War and Revolution

When those of the arctic pole are united together,
great terror and fear in the East: Newly elected, the
great trembling supported; Rhodes, Byzantium
stained with Barbarian blood.

> *Quand ceux du pôle arctique unis ensemble,*
> *En Orient grand effrayeur et craine:*
> *Élu nouveau, soutenu le grand tremble,*
> *Rodes, Bisance de sang Barbare teinte.*

The major powers with territory around the Arctic pole are Russia, United States, and Canada, all allies against the Central Powers in World War I. Late in the war, Russia ("the East") was rocked by revolution and terror; in 1917, the new Congress of Soviets elected Lenin as premier, but the whole Soviet state trembled on the brink of collapse for the next three years while Lenin feverishly maneuvered to garner the support to sustain the regime. Turkey ("Byzantium") lost Rhodes to Italy in 1912 and suffered great losses in World War I. ("Barbarian" is the Seer's consistent epithet for Muslims.)

Rating: 9

Commentators have poked around the edges of this specific and accurate verse without quite finding the solution.

Quatrain VI-22: A Mysterious Nephew

> Within the land of the great celestial temple (Stone-
> henge?), a nephew murdered at London through
> feigned peace: The bark will then become schismatic,
> sham liberty will be widely proclaimed.

> *Dedans la terre du grand temple celique,*
> *Neveu à Londres par paix feinte meurtri:*
> *La barque alors deviendra schismatique,*
> *Liberte feinte sera au corn et cry.*

This is a verse that looks easy but has forever frustrated the commentators. The answer lies in the career of the Duke of Monmouth, who was beheaded by James II of Britain (1685). Monmouth was a nephew of James by way of Charles II's dalliance with Lucy Walters. He was favored by some Protestants to succeed Charles as king because

James had declared himself a Catholic. In the end, the nation rallied behind James' clear claim to the throne, and Monmouth's subsequent coup attempt was easily defeated. This apparent settlement soon proved illusory ("feigned peace") due to James' pro-Catholic policies, and he was driven out. A year later, Parliament granted religious toleration to all except Catholics and Unitarians ("sham liberty").

Rating: 9

The use of "schismatic" seems odd at first since the estrangement of England with Catholicism began ca. 1530. But when the quatrains were written, England had a Catholic queen, Mary Tudor. The ouster of James was the final break; Catholic monarchs were then outlawed.

Quatrain VI-23: The Impending Storm in France

> Coins depreciated by the spirit of the realm, and people will be stirred up against their King: New peace made, holy laws deteriorate. Paris was never in such a severe array.

> *D'esprit de regne numismems decries,*
> *Et seront peuples emus contre leur Roi:*
> *Paix fait nouveau, saintes lois empirees,*
> *RAPIS onc fut en si trés dur arroi.*

During the reign of Louis XVI, France was hurtling toward revolution as frustration with the monarchy steadily mounted. Finances were a disaster, inflation rampant. Churchmen were preoccupied mainly with enhancing their political influence and position while the resentment of the peasants neared the flash point. About the only plus in Louis' reign was a reconciliation with England ("new peace") through the 1786 commercial treaty after the hostilities of the American Revolution. The roof fell in on the monarchy in 1789 with the storming of the Bastille.

Rating: 8.5

RAPIS is an obvious anagram for Paris so there is no doubt about location here.

Quatrain VI-25: The 18 of Brumaire

> Through adverse Mars (war) the monarchy of the
> great fisherman will be in ruinous trouble: The young
> black and red ruler will seize the hierarchy. The trai-
> tors will act on a day of drizzle.

> *Par Mars contraire sera la monarchie*
> *Du grand pecheur en trouble ruineux:*
> *Jeune noir rouge prendra la hierarchie:*
> *Les prodíteurs iront jour bruineux.*

The Napoleonic Wars did put the "great fisherman" (the pope) in ruinous trouble; at one point he was deprived of all his lands. For a time, Pius VII was a captive in France and the Church was treated like a mere department of the empire. Napoleon is described as the "black and red ruler" because he was villainous and a revolutionary. The last line is striking; Napoleon and his cohorts seized power in France on 18 of Brumaire (revolutionary calendar)—Brumaire means "the month of drizzle."

Rating: 10

"Hierarchy" here probably implies both that of the Church and of France. This is an insightful and flawless quatrain.

Quatrain VI-33: Sad Straits for Saddam Hussein

His latest hand bloody through Alus, he will be unable
to protect himself by the sea: Between two rivers he
will fear the military hand. The black (hearted) ruler,
the irate one will make him repent.

Sa main derniere par Alus sanguinaire,
Ne se pourra par la mer garantir:
Entre deux fleuves craindre main militaire,
Le noir l'ireux le fera repentir.

The mysterious "Alus," never decoded, is an anagram for l'USA, the nation that bloodied Saddam Hussein's hand when he reached out to grab Kuwait. Perhaps the most-feared weapons of the Gulf War were the deadly guided missiles launched from American navy ships against which Saddam was practically helpless. Iraq is, of course, "The Land of Two Rivers," since most of the people live near or between the Tigris and the Euphrates. The "irate one" is clearly President George Bush who made the "black hearted ruler" repent his aggressions.

Rating: 10

Noir (line four) is the Seer's customary shorthand for "villainous ruler," since it means "black" and contains the letters for *roi* (French for "king"). The quatrain, which is coupled with the following one also about the Gulf War, is so ingeniously factual it has to get top rating.

Quatrain VI-34: The Persian Gulf War

The device of flying fire will come to trouble the great
besieged chief: Within there will be such sedition that
the profligate ones will be in despair.

De feu volant la machination,
Viendra troubler un grand chef assieqe:
Dedans sera telle sedition,
Qu'en desespoir seront les profligez.

Certainly, "device of flying fire" is an apropos description of the guided rockets and smart bombs used by the Allies in the Persian Gulf conflict. The rest of the quatrain also fits. Saddam Hussein, surrounded by hostile forces and without an ally, was indeed "besieged." After the defeat of his army, insurrections by both Kurds and Shiites brought Saddam's regime to the brink of collapse. Though he managed to survive, his clique must have despaired at times. The use of "profligate ones" is appropriate since Saddam wasted billions of dollars in oil revenues on arms build-ups and to support the plush lifestyle of the Baghdad elite.

Rating: 9.5

There are complex elements in this prophecy that are all quite correct, and the "device of flying fire" is strikingly modern in concept.

Quatrain VI-38: The French Directory and Bonaparte

> By the profligates, the enemies of peace, after having
> conquered Italy, the bloodthirsty black and red one
> will be fully seen. Fire, blood shed, water colored by
> blood.

> *Aux profligez de paix les ennemis,*
> *Après avoir l'Italie superee:*
> *Noir sanguinaire, rouge, sera commis,*
> *Feu, sang verser, eau de sang coloree.*

The five-man French Directory ("the profligates"), which ruled France in the midst of the revolution, was a fiscal disaster. It pursued war while debts skyrocketed until the government's money was practically worthless. The only real success of the Directory's tenure was Napoleon's conquest of Italy, which made the Corsican so popular that he became a threat to the Directory itself. The Directors, like everyone else, perceived the Napoleonic apparition, but they were like deer frozen in the headlights of an oncoming truck; Napoleon seized power in 1799. The last line depicts the French revolutionary wars.

Rating: 9

As usual, the colors black and red apply to Bonaparte—mean, villainous, and revolutionary. This is a fine quatrain that has been almost totally ignored by commentators.

Quatrain VI-40: The Archbishops' Dignity

> To quench the great thirst the great one of Mainz will
> be deprived of his great dignity: Those of Cologne
> will come to complain so loudly that the great rump
> will be thrown into the Rhine.

> *Grand de Magonce pour grande soif eteindre,*
> *Sera privé de sa grande dignité:*
> *Ceux de Cologne si fort le viendront plaindre,*
> *Que le grande groppe au Rhin sera jeté.*

The archbishops of Mainz and Cologne exercised temporal power and were Electors of the Holy Roman Empire. Both became victims of the "great thirst" of revolutionary France: a determination to make the Rhine River the country's frontier. France annexed the Mainz territory west of the Rhine in 1797. It took the west bank of the Cologne Archbishopric in 1801, and a couple of years later the remnant ("rump") was divided up among the other German states.

Rating: 8

As he quite often did, Nostradamus deals here with what is essentially only a footnote in history, but he does so with acuity.

Quatrain VI-44: War and Science in the Late
Twentieth Century

> By night the Rainbow will appear for Nantes, by
> marine arts they will stir up rain. At an Arabian Gulf a
> great force will founder; in Saxony a monster will be
> born of a bear and a sow.

De nuit par Nantes l'Iris apparaitra,
Des arts marins susciteront la pluie:
Arabiq gouffre grande classe parfondra,
Un monstre en Saxe naitra d'ours et truie.

Clearly a current-era quatrain since the technology to artificially "stir up rain" (through cloud seeding) has only been known in recent decades. Similarly, it is only with modern, high-intensity urban lighting that one might indeed see a rainbow at night. The "great force" that founders at a Gulf of Arabia is evidently Saddam Hussein's huge but ineffective army, which was soundly defeated in the Gulf War. The "monster" in Saxony is East Germany's long-time leader, Erich Honecker, builder and defender of the infamous Berlin Wall. He is described aptly as born of a "bear" (Russia) and a pig (epithet).

Rating: 8

This seems to be a sort of catchall quatrain for our generation, therefore not very cohesive but featuring some insightful aspects.

Quatrain VI-45: Azana Faces Fascism

The very learned governor of the realm, not wishing to consent to royal fiat: The force at Melilla (in Spanish Morocco) through contrary wind will deliver him to his most disloyal one.

Le gouverneur du regne bien savant,
Ne consentir voulant au fait Royal:
Mellile classe par le contraire vent
Le remettra à son plus deloyal.

The "learned governor" is Manuel Azana, president of Spain at the time of Franco's right-wing takeover. An avid antimonarchist, Azana was a prize-winning writer, essayist, and legal scholar ("very learned"), in addition to being a leader of the political left. Melilla actually was the very city at which Franco (the "disloyal one") started his Fascist revolution. The actions of the civil war went steadily against Azana's popular front ("contrary wind"), and by 1939 Franco was dictator of all of Spain.

Rating: 10

A high-quality quatrain that has been largely ignored.

Quatrain VI-49: The Subjugations of the Swastika

> The great Pontiff of the party of Mars will subjugate
> the confines of the Danube: The cross to pursue,
> through iron hook or crook, captives, gold, jewels,
> more than a hundred thousand rubies.

> *De la partie de Mammer grand Pontife,*
> *Subjuguera les confins du Danube:*
> *Chasser la croix, par fer raffe ni riffe,*
> *Captifs, or, bagues plus de cent mille rubes.*

The "party of Mars" is a perfect designation of the Nazi Party, and its "Pontiff," of course, would be Hitler, who did in fact subjugate the whole length of the Danube valley. "Cross ... iron hook or crook" is, as Cheetham pointed out, highly suggestive of the Nazi swastika. Iron "crooked crosses" were featured on Nazi war medals, pursued by all true followers of der Führer. The Nazis confiscated millions in gold and jewels from conquered territories and from victims sent to concentration camps.

Rating: 8

The context of "Pontiff" here is so unusual that it may be a mischievous ploy by the Seer to mislead analysts. However, the title does carry overtones of "chief dogmatist," which Hitler certainly was for the Nazi Party.

Quatrain VI-51: Hitler Escapes Assassination

People assembled to see a new spectacle; Princes and
Kings among many bystanders. Pillars, walls to fall:
But as by a miracle the King saved and thirty of the
ones present.

Peuple assemblé, voir nouveau expectacle,
Princes et Rois par plusieur assistants,
Piliers faillir, murs: mais comme miracle
Le Roi sauvé et trente des instants.

In late 1939, a powerful bomb was planted in a pillar behind the
rostrum where Hitler was to speak at a Munich hall. Hitler's retinue
included several top party members including the Nazis' "crown
prince," Rudolph Hess. Hearing rumors of a plot, Hitler decided to cut
his usual harangue short and catch an earlier train. The bomb went
off eight minutes after he and his lieutenants left. Several people were
killed, and it is reasonable to suppose that about thirty more could
have died had he still been at the scene.

Rating: 8.5
Hitler was shown this quatrain after the event and was quite convinced that it was a presage of his narrow escape.

Quatrain VI-57: A Bad Choice for Pope

He who was well forward in the realm, having a red
chief (cardinal) close to the hierarchy, harsh and
cruel, he will make himself much feared. He will succeed to the monarchy.

Celui qu'etait bien avant dans le regne,
Ayant chef rouge proche à la hierarchie,
Apre et cruel, et se fera tant craindre,
Succedera à sacrée monarchie.

This verse describes someone who becomes pope because he has a powerful cardinal as his mentor. Such was the case with Paul IV who rose to the papacy through the influence of his cardinal uncle who was also Grand Inquisitor. Paul, of noble family ("well forward in the realm"), was bad-tempered, officious, and a zealous promoter of the Inquisition. His imperious treatment of Queen Elizabeth ended any chance of reconciliation between Rome and England. When he died in 1559, a Roman mob demolished Paul's statue, freed the prisoners of the Inquisition, and scattered its records.

Rating: 7.5

Unfortunately, we cannot be sure the verse was written before Paul's investiture as pope (mid-1555). Regardless, the Seer did predict the character and tendencies of Paul's papacy. "Monarchy" in line four is not inapt since the pope was then temporal ruler of the Papal States.

Quatrain VI-58: A Rivalry of Kings

Between the two distant monarchs, when the Sun is
lost through clear Selin (the moon): great enmity
between two indignant ones but liberty is restored to
the Isles and Sienna.

Entre les deux monarques eloignes,
Lorsque le Sol par Selin clair perdue:
Simulte grande entre deux indignes,
Qu'aux îles et Sienne la liberté rendue.

The "two distant monarchs" are Emperor Charles V, whose emblem was the Sun, and Henry II of France, who chose the crescent moon as his—to honor his mistress, Diana. As the verse indicates, Henry did best Charles in war ("Sun is lost") but then pushed his luck too far. After Charles abdicated, his son, Philip II of Spain, beat the French at St. Quentin, and France lost its Italian territories and the recently conquered isle of Corsica (1559). Liberty was restored to Sienna in the sense that Philip turned it over to the compatriot Italian state of Florence, which allowed the city to have a separate administration.

Rating: 7.5

The quatrain is not especially well composed, but "the two indignant ones" are more likely to be Henry and Philip than Henry and Charles.

Quatrain VI-63: Catherine de Médici

> The lady left alone in the realm by the unique one
> extinguished first on the bed of honor: Seven years
> will she be weeping in grief, then long life at the realm
> through great good luck.

> *La dame seule au regne demeuree,*
> *D'unique eteint premier au lit d'honneur:*
> *Sept ans sera de douleur eploree,*
> *Puis longue vie au regne par grand heur.*

All hands agree this verse concerns Catherine de Médici whose husband, Henri II of France, died in a jousting accident shortly after the *Centuries* were written. She did in fact stay in mourning for seven years, plus a few weeks, though it is possible Catherine read herself as the subject of this quatrain and chose to abide by it. Catherine lived to be seventy, and for most of the thirty years following Henri's death she was de facto ruler of France.

Rating: 8.5

Nostradamus usually disguised his predictions well enough that they would not influence the future, but in this case he may have slipped; after Henri's death, this quatrain was fairly transparent.

Quatrain VI-67: Louis XV

Quite another one will attain to the great Empire,
goodness distant, more so happiness: Ruled by one
sprung not far from the brothel, realms to decay, great
bad luck.

Au grand Empire parviendra tout un autre,
Bonté distant plus de felicité:
Regi par un issu non loin du peautre,
Corruer regnes grande infelicité.

Though unrecognized as such, this is a deftly drawn portrait of the reign of Louis XV of France. Compared to his predecessor (the Grand Monarch), Louis XV was weak in both intellect and character. He inherited a true "empire" but lost much of it. His foreign policies were a disaster, and the nation's finances soon fell into utter chaos. Happiness became a distant memory for the French people. Louis was strongly influenced, even in vital matters of state, by his mistresses, especially Madame Pompadour, who was actually brought up to be a paramour ("not far from the brothel").

Rating: 9

The key to the verse is understanding the second line; the lack of "goodness" applies to Louis, and the lack of "happiness" to the empire.

Quatrain VI-68: The Duke of Alba

When the soldiers in a seditious fury will cause steel
to flash by night against their chief, the enemy Alba
acts with a furious hand; then to vex Rome and
seduce the principal ones.

Lorsque soldats fureur seditieuse,
Contre leur chef feront de nuit fer luire:
Ennemi d'Albe soit par main furieuse,
Lors vexer Rome et principaux seduire.

This is a curious quatrain since all the facets were fulfilled but out of sync. The Duke of Alba was made governor-general of the Netherlands by Spain's Philip II to repress sedition there. The duke met a series of armed revolts with merciless ferocity ("furious hand"). One of his many notorious actions was to lure the malcontent Counts Egmont and Holtz into his power ("seduce the principal ones"), and then have them executed. Alba also vexed Rome in 1559 when he thrashed the army of the pope, but this was before his tenure in the Netherlands. So, the only thing wrong with the whole quatrain is the single word "then" (*lors*) in the last line.

Rating: 8

It could be that "then" means "at that (future) time" rather than "afterwards," but at best there is an ambiguity that impairs the rating.

Quatrain VI-69: The Flight of the French Clergy

> The great pity will occur before long. Those who gave will be obliged to take: Naked, starving, bent with cold and thirst, to pass over the mountains causing a great scandal.

> *La pitié grande sera sans loin tarder,*
> *Ceux qui donnaient seront contraints de prendre:*
> *Nus affames de froid, soif, se bander,*
> *Les monts passer commettant grand esclandre.*

The French Revolution was vehemently anticlerical, and many of the French clergy in 1792 fled over the snowy Alps to refuge in Italy. Formerly distributors of alms, they had to beg for their daily bread and shelter along the way. Though some of these unfortunates probably deserved their fate, Nostradamus, a religious man, would view such a situation as utterly scandalous and pitiful.

Rating: 8.5

It is almost incontestable that the Seer foresaw the French Revolution in nearly all it aspects—this being just one more. The solution of the verse goes back to Le Pelletier.

Quatrain VI-72: The Rascal Rasputin

> Through feigned fury of divine emotion the wife of
> the great one will be violated: The judges wishing to
> condemn such doctrine, she is sacrificed to the igno-
> rant people.

> *Par fureur feinte d'emotion divine,*
> *Sera la femme du grand fort violee:*
> *Juges voulant damner telle doctrine,*
> *Victime au peuple ignorant emmolee.*

The advent of the "Mad Monk" (Rasputin) at the Russian court in 1912 fulfilled this quatrain. Rasputin seemed to have supernatural abilities and soon gained total dominance over the Czar's wife, Alexandra. She was certainly "violated" psychologically, and perhaps physically. The "judges" here are evidently the Bolshevik leaders who, condemning the doctrine of divine right, decided to execute the Russian royal family. Thus, Alexandra was "sacrificed to the ignorant people," the Russian proletariat.

Rating: 8.5

It is noteworthy that the Seer implies that Rasputin was a fake (*feinte*). The vagueness of "such doctrine" (line three) undermines the rating.

Quatrain VI-74: Elizabeth I

> She, chased out, will return to the realm, her enemies
> found to be conspirators: More than ever her time
> will triumph; three and seventy to death most sure.

La dechassee au regne trournera,
Ses ennemies trouvés des conjurés:
Plus que jamais son temps triomphera,
Trois et septante à mort assure.

One of England's great times of "triumph" was the reign of Elizabeth I, who as a child had only the dimmest prospects of attaining the throne. After her mother, Anne Boleyn, was beheaded, Elizabeth became something of a nonperson, losing her right of royal succession. After being reinstated, she was the center of more than one conspiratorial plot and at one point was imprisoned in the tower with some calling for her head. She died at the age of seventy in 1603.

Rating: 9

Certain aspects of the prophecy can be nitpicked, but the overall impact is quite strong.

Quatrain VI-75: Coligny Goes Over

The great Pilot because of the King will be obliged to leave the fleet to fill a higher post: After seven years he will be rebelling; Venice will come to fear the barbarian army.

Le grand Pilote par Roi sera mandé,
Laisser la classe pour plus haut lieu atteindre:
Sept ans après sera contrebandé,
Barbare armée viendra Venise craindre.

Gaspard de Coligny, after being converted to Protestantism, left his position as French admiral in 1559 to become a leader of the Huguenot cause. The move was mandated by the fact that the king supported the Catholic faction. Coligny, who had held the admiralty post for seven years, continued fighting for the Huguenots until his death in the infamous St. Bartholomew's Day Massacre (1572). About this same time, the Turks captured Cyprus from Venice (1570) and Barbary pirates were raiding the Adriatic coast.

Rating: 8.5
The "higher post" here would be more in the sense of a higher calling than a matter of official rank. This is another Le Pelletier solution.

Quatrain VI-79: Bonaparte at Lodi?

> Near the Ticino the inhabitants of the Loire, Garonne, and Saone, the Seine, the Tain, and Gironde: They will erect a promontory beyond the mountains. Conflict given, Po seized, submerged in the wave.

> *Pres de Tesin les habitants de Loire,*
> *Garonne et Saone, Seine, Tain et Gironde:*
> *Outre les monts dresseront promontoire,*
> *Conflit donné, Pau granci, submergée onde.*

All the rivers mentioned, except the Italian Ticino, are French, so the verse simply means the French will invade northern Italy. The Po valley has been seized or "submerged in the wave" of French troops more than once since Nostradamus, so the question is which intrusion is involved. Commentators think they have found the deviously disguised answer in the last line where they see a double meaning; Pau is used in another quatrain (VIII-1) as part of an anagram for Napoleon. Thus, the last line is applied to an incident at the battle of Lodi where Napoleon fell into the Adda River ("submerged") and had to be pulled out ("seized").

Rating: 8
The two-way interpretation of the final line is almost too clever (Stewart Robb, 1942). Even so, the thrust of the verse is historically correct.

Quatrain VI-81: The Terror Exported

> Tears, cries, and laments, howls, terror, heart inhu-man, cruel, black, and chilly: Lake Geneva, the Isles, the notables of Genoa, blood to pour out, wheat famine, mercy to none.

Pleurs, cris et plaintes, hurlements, effrayeur,
Coeur inhumain, cruel noir et transi:
Leman, les Îles, de Gennes les majeurs,
Sang epancher, frofaim à nul merci.

It is not well known but Geneva had its version of revolutionary terror in the 1790s as the unrest in France seeped across the canton's borders. Aristocrats were persecuted—some killed. The terror also spread to the isle of Corsica. There it was opposed by the Corsican leader Paoli, resulting in open warfare and British intervention. Genoa was transformed into a republic by invading French armies bringing an end to the old order there. Slightly later, in 1800, the Genoans underwent terrible privations ("wheat famine") when the Austrians besieged the city.

Rating: 9.5

This is a graphic and completely accurate quatrain with specific geography. (A previously undecoded verse.)

Quatrain VI-83: Philip II and the Low Countries

He who will have so much honor and flattery at his entry into Belgian Gaul: A while after he will act with much harshness. And he will be very warlike against the flower.

Celui qu'aura tant d'honneur et caresses
A son entree en la Gaule Belgique:
Un temps après fera tant de rudesses,
Et sera contre à la fleur tant bellique.

When Philip II of Spain became ruler of Belgium/Holland in 1556, he was at first well received. But in a few years his religious intolerance and repressive policies led to a bloody Protestant revolt. The "flower" of the last line is the fleur-de-lis of France against which the Spanish king waged war in the 1590s. Philip's stubborn foolishness eventually succeeded in reducing Spain to a second-class power.

Rating: 9

This is an unusually straightforward prophecy that is on target and presents no difficulties.

Quatrain VI-84: Tallyrand: Diplomat Extraordinaire

> He, the Lame One, who in Sparta could not reign, he
> will do much through seductive means: So that by the
> short and long, he will be accused of making his per-
> spective against the King.

> *Celui qu'en Sparte Claude ne peut regner,*
> *Il fera tant par voie seductive:*
> *Que du court, long, le fera araigner,*
> *Que contre Roi fera sa perspective.*

Tallyrand, because of a childhood injury, was lame and therefore could not have reigned in Sparta. Yet as foreign minister of France he accomplished much through his subtle diplomacy. The "short and long" are, by hairstyles, the French revolutionaries and the aristocrats. Tallyrand, a pragmatic moderate, was accused at times by both sides. While serving in the national assembly, he turned against King Louis. Later, disapproving of Bonaparte's policies, he resigned as the emperor's foreign minister and subsequently engineered the return of the Bourbon monarchy to France.

Rating: 9

Tallyrand may have been the only sane man in the mad world of the French Revolution. Unfortunately, his advice too often went unheeded.

Quatrain VI-90: The Munich Betrayal

> The stinking abominable disgrace, after the deed he
> will be congratulated: The great one excused for not
> being favorable, when Neptune will not be persuaded
> to peace.

> *L'honnissement puant abominable,*
> *Apres le fait sera felicité:*
> *Grande excusé pour n'etre favorable,*
> *Qu'à paix Neptune ne sera incité.*

This is an unusually astute quatrain that has not been understood. After the disgraceful sell-out of Czechoslovakia at Munich in 1938, Britain's Neville Chamberlain was congratulated by the appeasement crowd on his attainment of "peace in our time." But the great one, Winston Churchill, severely criticized the deal, convinced that Hitler would have to be forcibly stopped sooner or later. Events soon proved Winston right and thereby "excused" his stubborn hard-line stance. Neptune's disinclination for peace here may have a double meaning: as a portent of impending naval warfare, and as a figure of Churchill himself who twice served as Lord of the Admiralty and also saw war ahead.

Rating: 9.5

There are some remarkably insightful aspects to this quatrain, reflecting a deep grasp of the predicted events.

Quatrain VI-92: The Fall of Louis XVI

> Prince of beauty most comely, around his head a plot, made second, betrayed: The city to the sword, in powder the face burnt. Through too great a murder the head of the king hated.

> *Prince de beauté tant venuste,*
> *Au chef menee, le second fait trahi:*
> *La cité au glaive de poudre face aduste,*
> *Par trop grand meurtre le chef du Roi hai.*

The hapless Louis XVI cut a handsome figure as a young man but became the center of plots during France's revolutionary movement. He was made second in the sense that he was subordinated to the National Assembly in 1791. Paris certainly took "to the sword" during the revolution. The phrase "the face burnt in powder" is intriguing;

the hated head of King Louis was thrown into quicklime after he was guillotined.

Rating: 9
This is a widely accepted interpretation, 200 years old, about which there is very little argument.

Quatrain VI-94: Home-Grown Terrorists

> A King will be angry with the seditious breakers (ter-
> rorists) when the arms of war will be prohibited: The
> poison taint in the sugar for the breakers, bruised by
> tears, dead, saying "land, land!"
>
> *Un Roi iré sera aux sedifragues,*
> *Quand interdits seront harnois de guerre:*
> *Le poison teint au sucre par les fragues,*
> *Par eaux meurtris, mort, disant terre terre.*

Sedifragues is one of the Seer's coined words from Latin, but the meaning is fairly plain—basically, "seditious terrorists." The second line, referring to recently enacted restrictions on the possession of military-style assault weapons, shows the verse to be for the present-day United States. The "king" then, is Bill Clinton, angered by the bombing of the federal building in Oklahoma City. The rest deals more broadly with right-wing paramilitary and white separatist groups, noting their attractive (to some) preachments are poisoned with hatred and paranoia. They are to suffer tears and death in their war for their own separate "land."

Rating: 8.5
Only recently fulfilled, the verse has been previously unsolved. The third line is accurate enough but could be seen as overly abstract. More trouble with extremist groups is predicted in Future Quatrain X-81, page 32.

Quatrain VI-96: The Fall of Paris

> Great city abandoned to the soldiers; never was
> mortal tumult so close to it: O, what a hideous
> calamity approaches. Except one offense nothing will
> be spared it.

> *Grande cité à soldats abandonnée,*
> *Onc n'y eut mortel tumulte si proche:*
> *O quelle hideuse calamité s'approche,*
> *Fors une offense n'y sera pardonnee.*

The "great city" is Paris, of course, which was declared an open city and abandoned to the advancing Nazi armies in World War II in order to prevent its destruction. For four years the French capital was downtrodden by the tyranny of German occupation. It was spared one calamity, however, as the Seer says. With the advance of the Allied armies in 1944, Hitler ordered the city burned. The German general in charge could not bring himself to carry out the maniacal command and managed to stall long enough for liberating forces to reach the city.

Rating: 8.5
The quatrain has received other applications but World War II-Paris is easily the most appropriate subject.

Quatrain VI-98: The Trials of Toulouse

> Ruin for the Volcae (Languedoc) so very terrible with
> fear. Their great city (Toulouse) stained, pestilential
> deed: To plunder the Sun and Moon and to violate
> their temples, and to redden the two rivers flowing
> with blood.

> *Ruine aux Volsques de peur si fort terribles,*
> *Leur grande cité teinte, fait pestilent:*
> *Piller Sol, Lune et violer leurs temples:*
> *Et les deux fleuves roughir de sang coulant.*

This is a remarkably accurate verse that has been unsolved because it deals with half-forgotten events in Toulouse during the French Revolution. Toulouse is home to the church of St. Sernin, the largest Romanesque basilica (temple) anywhere, which once housed rich gold and silver shrines. These ("the Sun and Moon") were plundered by revolutionary mobs—the "pestilential deed." At the close of the revolutionary era (1814), the last major battle was fought at Toulouse on the banks of the Garonne, the River Hers, and the Languedoc Canal. It was a bloody affair with over 6,000 casualties—vain losses since Napoleon had abdicated a few days earlier.

Rating: 10

The verse is not overly obscure and is exactly on target in all aspects. This is a most impressive quatrain.

Quatrain VII-7: Lawrence Trounces the Turks

> Upon the combat of the great light horses, they will proclaim the great crescent confounded: To kill by night, mountains, shepherds' garb, red gulfs in the deep ditch.

> *Sur le combat des grands chevaux legers,*
> *On criera le grand croissant confond:*
> *De nuit tuer monts, habits de bergers,*
> *Abimes rouges dans le fossé profond.*

Arabs led by the fabled Lawrence of Arabia, mounted on light horses and dressed in ordinary Bedouin garb (which Lawrence himself wore), carried out a successful revolt against the Turks—symbolized by the "great crescent"—during World War I. Unorthodox guerilla tactics were utilized, striking when and where the Turks least expected ("kill by night"), and then hiding out in the hills. The Turks tried everything to combat this hit-and-run strategy but without success ("confounded").

Rating: 9

So descriptive is this verse that one has to think Nostradamus could virtually "see" Lawrence's troop in action. (A previously unsolved verse.)

Quatrain VII-10: Patton in World War II

> By the great Prince bordering on Le Mans, doughty
> and valiant chief of the great army: By sea and land of
> Bretons and Normans, to pass Gibraltar and
> Barcelona, the isle sacked.

> *Par le grand Prince limitrophe du Mans*
> *Preux et vaillant chef du grand exercite:*
> *Par mer et terre de Gallots et Normans,*
> *Calpre passer Barcelonne pillé l'ile.*

Le Mans was the immediate objective of the great Third Army's famed Normandy breakthrough in World War II, so the subject here is General George Patton. The term "prince" is quite descriptive of the flamboyant, autocratic warrior. The Third Army's advance, after crossing the Channel, was through the lands of the Normans and Bretons. Earlier in the war, Patton had passed by Gibraltar and Spain ("Barcelona") on his way to the conquest ("sack") of the isle of Sicily.

Rating: 9

The second line of the quatrain in particular is beautifully descriptive.

Quatrain VII-11: Louis XIII and Momma Marie

> The royal child will scorn his mother; eye, feet wounded; rude, disobedient: Strange and very bitter news to
> the lady, more than five hundred of her followers will
> be killed.

> *L'enfant Royal contemnera la mere,*
> *Oeil pieds, blessés, rude, inobeissant:*
> *Nouvelle à dame étrange et bien amere,*
> *Seront tués des siens plus de cinq centes.*

This verse clearly deals with a feud between a royal male and his mother. The most notable episode of this kind involved France's Louis XIII and Marie de Médici. Marie tried to retain power after Louis came of age, thereby spawning a long-running contention during which Marie mounted two revolts against the king, the most serious one in 1620. But Marie's forces were handily defeated at Ponts-de-Ce, and Garencieres[6] says over 500 of her followers were killed, a likely enough number. Louis ended up exiling his mother, which must indeed have been strange and bitter news to her.

Rating: 8.5

The phrase "eye, feet wounded" is not without difficulties. The eyes might be Louis' or Marie's since both wept as he sent her into exile. Marie, grossly overweight, fell from a ladder while escaping one of her confinements and may well have injured her feet.

Quatrain VII-13: The Reign of Bonaparte

From the marine and tributary city the shaven head
will take the satrapy: To drive away the sordid one
who will then be against him. For fourteen years he
will hold the tyranny.

De la cité marine et tributaire
La tête rase predra la satrapie:
Chasser sordide qui puis sera contraire,
Par quatorze ans tiendra la tyrannie.

Napoleon actually did shave his head as a young man due to an itch, thus gaining the nickname "the little crophead." The marine city is Toulon, where the Corsican first gained recognition for his role in liberating the British-occupied ("tributary") port. Napoleon held absolute power in France for fourteen years, from late 1799 to early 1814. The thorny aspect of the verse is the identity of the "sordid one."

---

6. Theophilus de Garencieres was a seventeenth-century commentator on Nostradamus. His book *The True Prophecies* (1672) is now a collector's item.

He could well be the crafty, unscrupulous Tallyrand who was driven away from the Foreign Ministry by Napoleon's cavalier dismissals of his recommendations. Sure that Napoleon's course must fail, Tallyrand began plotting for the return of the Bourbon monarchy.

Rating: 9

Le Pelletier interprets "the sordid one" as the Directory, which is not bad except that the Directory was composed of five members. The appellation would apply though to Paul Barras, a particularly venal and corrupt Director who was in fact marginalized by Napoleon.

Quatrain VII-14: Revolutionary Fever

> They will come to set forth the false topography; the urns of the tombs will be opened: Sect and holy philosophy to multiply, black for white, and the unripe for the ancient.

> *Faux exposer viendra topographie,*
> *Seront les crushes des monuments ouvertes:*
> *Pulluler secte, sainte philosophie,*
> *Pour blanches noires, et pour antiques vertes.*

The resourceful Le Pelletier chalks up another winning interpretation with this one. He points out that the French revolutionary National Assembly arbitrarily changed the names and boundaries of the traditional provinces of France in 1789, converting them into "departments." Sepulchres of the French kings at St. Denis were violated during the revolutionary frenzy and anti-Christian sects and sentiments flourished, thus substituting "black for white" and novelties for the ancient traditions.

Rating: 8.5

While Le Pelletier was sometimes guilty of overreaching, he was well within the bounds of reasonableness with this perceptive interpretation.

Quatrain VII-16: Calamity at Calais

> The deep entry made by the great Queen will render
> up the powerful and inaccessible place: The army of
> the three Lions will be defeated, causing within a
> hideous and terrible event.

> *Entrée profonde par la grande Reine faite*
> *Rendra le lieu puissant inaccessible:*
> *L'armee des trois Lions sera defaite,*
> *Faisant dedans cas hideux et terrible.*

After holding Calais for many decades, the British lost it to the French in 1558 during the reign of Mary Tudor. The city was taken after a hard siege by the Duke of Guise, and the British regarded its capture as a major disaster. There are three lions on the coat of arms of England so the defeated army here is very clear. Less so is the "deep entry" mentioned in line one. It probably refers to Mary's ill-advised entry into the continental power struggle via her alliance with Spain, which led to the war with France and the loss of the prized city.

Rating: 8.5

Despite the vagueness of the first line, the quatrain is essentially on target.

Quatrain VII-20: Cavour Comes to France

> Ambassadors of the Tuscan tongue, in April and May
> to pass the Alps and the sea: He of the calf (Taurus)
> will deliver the harangue about not coming to wipe
> out Gallic life.

> *Ambassadeurs de la Toscane langue,*
> *Avril et Mai Alpes et mer passer:*
> *Celui de veau exposera l'harangue,*
> *Vie Gauloise ne venant effacer.*

In 1856, in the very months designated by the Seer, Cavour led the Piedmontese delegation ("Tuscan tongue") to the Congress of Paris. It was there that Cavour first broached the idea to Napoleon III of a joint French-Italian effort to oust the Austrians from north Italy. The two had a follow-up meeting soon after to seal the deal. A notable aspect of this quatrain is that "he of the calf" could be either Napoleon or Cavour: Napoleon was born under Taurus; Cavour was a native of Torino, city of the bull. Napoleon seems to fit better here since he must have stressed the need to hold French casualties to a minimum in the campaign.

Rating: 9.5

It is possible that the second part of the verse is a picture of Cavour reassuring Napoleon that French casualties would not be excessive. So, this extraordinary quatrain works either way.

Quatrain VII-22: Bonaparte Subverts Spain

> The citizens of Mesopotamia angry with their friends
> of Tarraconne (Spain): Games, rites, banquets, a
> whole people lulled to sleep. Vicar at the Rhône, city
> taken and those of Ausonia (Italy).

> *Les citoyens de Mesopotamie*
> *Irez encontre amis de Tarraconne:*
> *Jeux, rites, banquets, toute gent endormie,*
> *Vicaire au Rosne, pris cité, ceux d'Ausone.*

Napoleon's takeover of Spain was a masterpiece of stealth conquest. While the Spanish slept, Bonaparte gradually achieved complete dominance over the Spanish queen and her advisors. He was soon in total control of the country. "Mesopotamia" (between the rivers) cannot be Iraq in this context; it is apparently Portugal, which is straddled north and south by the rivers Duero and Guadiana. The Portuguese warred against neighboring Spain during the Napoleonic era ("angry with their friends"). At the same time, Pius VI was held captive at Valance on the Rhône River and the French seized Rome ("city taken") and much of Italy ("Ausonia").

Rating: 9.5
Once "Mesopotamia" is properly identified, the complex quatrain falls neatly into place. The "games, rites, banquets" most likely allude to activities at the Spanish court while Bonaparte was taking over the country. (A previously unsolved verse.)

Quatrain VII-33: The Sell-Out of Czechoslovakia

> Through guile the realm stripped of its forces; the fleet blocked, passages for the spy: Two feigned friends will come to assemble, hatred long dormant to awaken.

> *Par fraude regne, forces expolier,*
> *La classe obsesse, passages à l'espie:*
> *Deux feints amis se viendront rallier,*
> *Eveiller haine de longtemps assoupie.*

This quatrain has been applied to France in World War II, but it fits Czechoslovakia much better. Through the infamous Munich Treaty, Hitler stripped Czechoslovakia of its fortified frontiers, leaving it wide open to invasion. The British and the French ("two feigned friends") might have been of some help, but since Czechoslovakia was landlocked ("fleet blocked"), there was no way to get reinforcements into the country, so they simply sold it out. Czechoslovakia was heavily infiltrated with German spies. The last line probably refers to the old hatred between the Slavs and the Germans being reawakened by Hitler's aggression.

Rating: 9
The verse is correct in all particulars, but a specific geographic clue would have helped.

Quatrain VII-34: French Defeat in 1870

In great grief will the Gallic people be. Vain and light
of heart, they will trust in rashness: bread, salt, no
wine, water, whisky, or ale. The most great one captive—famine, cold, and need.

En grand regret sera la gent Gauloise,
Coeur vain, leger croira temerité:
Pain, sel, ni vin, eau, venin ni cervoise,
Plus grand captif, faim, froid, necessité.

The tendency to casually ascribe this one to the fall of France in
1940 is most likely wrong. The "most great one" here can only be
Emperor Napoleon III who actually was captured by the Germans in
the Franco-Prussian War. Furthermore, Napoleon's foreign policy was
rash to the point of folly. He had ample opportunity to avoid the war
but plunged ahead anyway under the delusion that the ill-prepared
French army was a match for the Prussians. The last half of the verse
well describes the four-month siege of Paris during which the city suffered from food shortages and a cold winter.

Rating: 9.5

This prediction is a specific and highly accurate account of the Franco-Prussian War. Its misapplication to World War II is difficult to
understand.

Quatrain VII-35: Poland Makes a Poor Catch

The great fisher will come to complain and weep over
the choice it has made, deceived by his age. He will
scarcely want to remain with them at all. He will be
deceived by those of his own tongue.

La grande peche viendra plaindre, pleurer,
D'avoir elu, trompés seront en l'age:
Guere avec eux ne voudra demeurer,
Deçu sera par ceux de son language.

Le Pelletier made a good case for applying this verse to Henry III of France. Young Henry, while still Duke of Anjou, was selected to be Poland's king in hopes that he would found a new dynasty there. Poland was not fortunate in its royal lines and became notorious for fishing around for new monarchs. In this case the Poles were badly deceived indeed for Henry turned out to be homosexual. Upon the death of his brother Charles, Henry gladly hurried back to France to assume the throne there, marking an end to the Valois line. In 1589, Henry was duped into granting an audience to a French monk, Jacques Clement, who proceeded to stab him to death.

Rating: 8.5

While Henry's death was unlamented, he salvaged some historical honor by naming as his successor Henry of Navarre, perhaps the greatest of all French kings.

Quatrain VIII-l: The Emperor and the Pope

> PAU, NAY, OLORON will be more of fire than blood,
> to swim in praise; the great one to fly to the conflu-
> ence: He will refuse entry to the magpies. Villains will
> keep those of the Durance confined.

> *PAU, NAY, LORON plus feu qu'à sang sera,*
> *Laude nager, fuir grand aux surrez:*
> *Les agassas entree refusera,*
> *Pampon, Durance les tiendra enserres.*

Surely one of the most curious quatrains, this one appears to contain an anagram for Napoleon. Pau, Nay, and Oloron are French towns, but the capitalization does suggest an anagram for "Napaulon Roy" (King Napoleon). The context also indicates an individual and certainly Napoleon did "swim in praise." The one flying to the confluence is Pius VI, who was held in protective custody at Valance where the Rhône and Isere rivers meet. "Magpies" is likely just an epithet for the French revolutionaries to whom Pius refused to turn over his temporal powers. In 1791, revolutionaries seized the papal city of Avignon on the Durance River and captured or killed many supporters of the pope.

Rating: 9

The resolution of the undeciphered last line confirms the rest of the interpretation, producing a generally strong quatrain. *Pampon* is from the Greek *pamponeros*, meaning "most villainous."

Quatrain VIII-4: Mazarin and the Rise of France

> The Cock will be received into Monaco. The Cardinal of France will appear: By the Roman Legate he will be deceived. Weakness for the Eagle and strength for the Cock will develop.

> *Dedans Monech le Coq sera recu,*
> *Le Cardinal de France apparaitra:*
> *Par Logarion Romain sera decu,*
> *Faiblesse à l'Aigle, et force au Coq naitra.*

Though widely dismissed as a failure, this verse is remarkably prophetic. In Nostradamus' time, Monaco was under Spanish domination, but it came under French protection in 1641. Very soon thereafter, Cardinal Mazarin became the power behind the throne in France, dominating both foreign and domestic policy. He was undone by another churchman, Jean Retz, who turned the Parisians against the government. During his career, Retz served more than once as French envoy to Rome ("Roman Legate"). Mazarin eventually regained power, and during his tenure France did indeed replace "the Eagle," Austria, as the leading power of Europe.

Rating: 9.5

A conspicuous success, the quatrain is marred only by the fact that the exact meaning of *Logarion* is not known. It is almost surely connected with "legate" or "legation."

Quatrain VIII-10: The Dawn of International Communism

> A great stench will come out of Lausanne (Switzer-
> land), such that one will not know the source of the
> fact. The one will put out all the far off people; fire
> seen in the sky, foreign people defeated.

> *Puanteur grande sortira de Lausanne,*
> *Qu'on ne saura l'origine du fait,*
> *L'on mettra hors toute la gent lointaine,*
> *Feu vu au ciel, peuple etranger defait.*

It was from Switzerland during World War I that Lenin promulgat-
ed his theories of a world-wide Communist revolution; an idea that
would bedevil the world for seventy years. The town of Claren, near
the city of Lausanne, was a major Communist headquarters. "The
one" in line three is Lenin himself, who soon routed all the would-be
revolutionary leaders in Russia to seize total control for himself. The
defeated "foreign people" would be the Allied and Czech military
forces that intervened in revolutionary Russia but were forced to
retire. The second line of the quatrain may refer to the fact that many
of Lenin's dispatches to Russia during his Swiss exile were signed with
pseudonyms.

Rating: 8.5

It has been suggested that the verse could apply to Calvinist Geneva, a
particular peeve of the Seer, but the allusion to fire in the sky clearly
puts the prophecy in the time of aerial warfare, which began in World
War I.

Quatrain VIII-14: Ted Kennedy

> The great credit, the abundance of gold and silver will
> cause honor to be blinded by lust. Known will be the
> offense of the adulterer, which will occur to his great
> dishonor.

Le grand credit, d'or et d'argent l'abondance
Fera aveugler par libide l'honneur,
Sera connu d'adultere l'offense,
Qui parviendra à son grand deshonneur.

This quatrain describes someone of enormous wealth and prestige, whose stature is severely damaged by a scandalous episode. The scenario aptly applies to the career of Ted Kennedy and the Chappaquiddick incident. Obviously, the circumstances outlined in the verse have occurred in other times and places but not with comparable historical impact. It is a near certainty that Ted Kennedy would have become president of the United States if it had not been for the drowning of Mary Jo Kopechne in his automobile. Thus, it is likely that this was the instance the Seer had in mind.

Rating: 7.5

The quatrain works, but it should be more specific. There should be a hidden clue in the wording, but, if so, it is too subtle for this commentator to detect.

Quatrain VIII-15: The Rise of Red Russia

Great exertions about Aquilon (Russia) by masses of men, to vex Europe and almost all the world. It will put the two eclipses into utter rout, and reinforce life and death on the Pannonians (Hungarians).

Vers Aquilon grands efforts par hommasse,
Presque l'Europe et l'Univers vexer,
Les Deux eclipses mettra en telle chasse
Et aux Pannons vie et mort renforcer.

This is a very lucid and accurate verse that has received rather clumsy treatment from other commentators. The quatrain plainly describes the mighty war efforts of the massive Red Army in World War II. While the Russian victory disposed of the Fascist evil, it immediately presented another in the form of a fearsome and aggressive new superpower on Europe's eastern flank. For half a century, the USSR did indeed "vex almost all the world." The two dispelled eclipses are Hitler and Mussolini, who cast the dark shadow of fascism over Europe. The Red Army did enforce "life and death" upon the Hungarians with its bloody suppression of the Hungarian anti-Communist revolt in 1956.

Rating: 9

While the imagery in the third line might be considered a shade too arcane, the verse is uncannily correct.

Quatrain VIII-17: A Crumbling House of Bourbon

Those well-off will be suddenly removed; through
three brothers the world put in trouble. The enemies
will seize the marine city—famine, fire, flood, plague,
and all evils doubled.

Les bien aises subit seront demis,
Par les trois freres le monde mis en trouble,
Cité marine saisiront ennemis,
Faim, feu, sang, peste, et de tous maux le double.

Three brothers in turn ruled France during the turbulent, final era of the Bourbon monarchy, none of whom had much aptitude for the job. The bumbling Louis XVI lost his head in the French Revolution as the "well-off" aristocracy was almost obliterated. After twenty-five years of unparalleled troubles, the European powers managed to put Louis XVIII on the restored throne, but he steadily lost effectiveness. He was succeeded by the inept Charles X, who was soon deposed. The "marine city" is Toulon, which was seized by the British during the revolutionary wars.

Rating: 8.5

The inability of the Bourbon brothers to adapt to the social currents of their time led to the collapse of the old order throughout Europe.

Quatrain VIII-23: The Casket Letters

In the Queen's coffers letters found, no signature,
without any name of the author: The offers will be
concealed by the government, so that they will not
know who the lover is.

Lettres trouvees de la Reine les coffres,
Point de souscrit sans aucun nom d'auteur:
Par la police seront cachés les offres,
Qu'on ne saura qui sera l'amateur.

The most notorious episode of its kind described in this verse was
the case of the Casket Letters involving Mary, Queen of Scots. The letters, apparently in Mary's handwriting, implicated Mary and Earl of
Bothwell in the death of Mary's husband, Darnley. Mary and Bothwell
were married soon after Darnley's demise. The letters, of course, had
been kept secret but were discovered in a silver casket in the possession of Bothwell's retainer. It should be added that the authenticity of
the letters has always been questioned.

Rating: 7.5

Letters were a source of much trouble for Mary. She was eventually
beheaded because of alleged correspondence with Babington, who
was plotting the assassination of Elizabeth I.

Quatrain VIII-31: Victor Emmanuel and Il Duce

First great fruit of the Prince of Peschiera, but then
will come one very cruel and evil: Within Venice he
(the prince) will lose his proud glory and be put to
evil by the more youthful "Celin."

Premier grand fruit le Prince de Pesquiere,
Mais puis viendra bien et cruel malin:
Dedans Venise perdra sa gloire fiere,
Et mis à mal par plus jeune Celin.

In the early years of his reign, Victor Emmanuel III of Italy enjoyed considerable popularity and success, had gained Libya, and even showed a budget surplus. But the town of Peschiera marked a turning point. In World War I, Austro-German forces broke the Italian lines at Caporetto in Venezia ("Venice"). The king held an emergency staff meeting at Peschiera and decided on a general retreat of 100 miles. Though the situation was finally salvaged, Caporetto was a long-term calamity for the prestige of the Italian monarchy ("glory lost"). Shortly, the "cruel and evil" Mussolini ("Celin") arrived on the scene and conned Victor into accepting him as Italy's needed strongman.

Rating: 9

"Selin" usually means a Turkish potentate, but the odd spelling here may imply a different nationality; Il Duce was essentially an Eastern potentate in a Western country. This is a fascinating if somewhat cryptic verse.

Quatrain VIII-33: Il Duce Gets Taken

> The great one will be born of Verona and Vicenza, he
> who will bear a most unworthy surname; he who at
> Venice will want to take vengeance, he himself taken
> by the man of the watch and sign.

> *Le grand naitra de Veronne et Vicence,*
> *Qui portera un surnom bien indigne,*
> *Qui à Venise voudra faire vengeance,*
> *Lui-meme pris homme du guet et signe.*

Since one cannot be born in two places, "Verona and Vicenza" must mean northeast Italy, the area of Il Duce's birth. Mussolini, which literally means "Muslin maker," met Hitler in Venice in 1934. At that time, Mussolini was aggravated with the Nazis because he knew they had designs on Austria, which Italy wished to maintain as a buffer state. So line three is not far off, though "vengeance" is too strong of a word. In time, of course, Mussolini was sucked into the orbit of "the man of the watch and sign," the sign being the swastika. The French *guet* has apropos overtones of ambush—"watching to ensnare."

Rating: 8

The word "vengeance" is bothersome since what Duce wanted in Venice was for Hitler to just back off on the Austrian issue. Is this another case of the Seer reaching for a rhyme?

Quatrain VIII-37: Execution of Charles I

> The fortress near the Thames will fall when the King is
> locked up within: Near the bridge in his shirt will be
> seen one confronting death, then barred inside the fort.

> *La forteresse aupres de la Tamise*
> *Cherra par lors le Roi dedans serré:*
> *Après du pont sera vu en chemise*
> *Un devant mort, puis dans le fort barré.*

A justly famed quatrain that describes the last days of England's Charles I in 1649. After his capture by parliamentary forces, Charles was taken to Windsor Castle on the Thames, a couple of miles from London Bridge, for trial. The hapless "king" was convicted and, on January 30, beheaded. However, the castle could only be said to have fallen in the sense that it was in parliamentary control; it had not been the object of any siege.

Rating: 9

This is a nicely descriptive quatrain and is accurate enough to merit a high rating. It is clearly tied to Quatrain IX-49, page 265, which predicts that London will put its king to death.

Quatrain VIII-41: The Sly Ayatollah

A Fox will be elected without saying a word, playing
the saint in public, living on barley bread. Afterwards
he will very suddenly tyrannize, putting his foot on
the throats of the great ones.

Elu sera Renard ne sonnant mot,
Faisant le saint public vivant pain d'orge,
Tyranniser après tant à un cop,
Mettant à pied des plus grand sur la gorge.

Playing the saintly ascetic to the hilt, the Ayatollah Khomeini was
swept into power in Iran in 1979. No campaign speeches were needed;
Iranian religious fervor and antipathy towards the Shah sufficed. Once
in power, Khomeini cracked down mercilessly on all, great and small,
who differed with his brand of Islamic fundamentalism, using even
executions and torture to achieve absolute power.

Rating: 8.5

This quatrain has generally been applied to Napoleon III, but it is a
stretch to accuse the rather liberal-minded French emperor of tyranny or even to say that he tried to play the saint.

Quatrain VIII-43: The Rise and Fall of Napoleon III

Through the fall of two illegitimate things the nephew
by blood will occupy the realm. In lectoyre there will
be blows by lances; the nephew through fear will fold
his standard.

Par le decide de deux choses batards,
Neveu du sang occupera le regne,
Dedans lectoyre seront les coups de dards,
Neveu par peur pliera l'ensiegne.

Nostradamus seems to have foreseen the career of Napoleon III,
nephew of Bonaparte, with astonishing clarity. Following the govern-

ments of Louis Philippe and of the 1848 National Assembly, both of which might well be described as illegitimate, Napoleon III came to power. His reign ended with his surrender to the advancing Prussians at Sedan, where he ran up the white flag somewhat prematurely. *Lectoyre* is a perfect anagram for Le Torcey, a suburb of Sedan near which the formal French surrender took place.

Rating: 10

This is a multifaceted quatrain in which virtually everything works. This is one of Le Pelletier's most notable interpretations since he solved the verse (except for *lectoyre*) before the battle of Sedan.

Quatrain VIII-50: Don Juan of Austria

> The pestilence around Capellades, another famine
> approaches Sagunto: The knight bastard of the good
> old man will cause the great one of Tunis to lose his
> head.

> *La pestilence l'entour de Capadille,*
> *Une autre faim près de Sagont s'apprete:*
> *Le chevalier batard de bon senile,*
> *Au grand de Thunes fera trancher la tête.*

Leoni makes a rather convincing application of this quatrain to the eminent soldier Don Juan (or Don John) of Austria, bastard son of the great emperor Charles V, who probably merited the appellation "good old man." In 1573, acting for Philip of Spain, Don Juan recaptured Tunis from the Algerian corsairs who had taken the city in 1570. It is not certain whether the Algerian chief lost his life in the fray or possibly was executed in its wake, but there is a good probability. Capellades and Sagunto are both in Spain where pestilence was recorded in 1570 and 1574.

Rating: 8

There is no information of famine in Spain around this period, but there may have been a localized case now forgotten.

Quatrain VIII-53: Napoleon Miscalculates

> Within Boulogne he will want to wash away his
> errors; at the temple of the sun he cannot: He will fly
> away doing things very mighty. In the hierarchy there
> was never one to equal him.

> *Dedans Bolongne voudra laver ses fautes,*
> *Il ne pourra au temple du soleil:*
> *Il volera faisant choses si hautes,*
> *En hierarchie n'en fut onc un pareil.*

In 1803, Napoleon began marshalling a huge army toward Boulogne for the invasion of England. He planned to fake the British fleet out of position long enough to get his troops across the British Channel, a foolish error since the English easily saw through his scheme. Forced to abandon the whole project, Napoleon went off to do mighty things, i.e., his conquest of continental Europe. Earlier, the Corsican had also been frustrated by the British navy in his invasion of Egypt ("temple of the sun"). The last line is obviously true even if it is applied to the religious hierarchy; Napoleon dominated even the pope himself.

Rating: 8.5

About the only thing to criticize here is the reference to the "temple of the sun," which might be considered a trifle obscure.

Quatrain VIII-55: Saddam in a Jam

> He will find himself shut up between two rivers, casks
> and barrels joined to pass beyond: Eight bridges bro-
> ken, the chief raked (as by gunfire) many times. Per-
> fect children have their throats cut on the knife.

> *Entre deux fleuves se verra enserré,*
> *Tonneaux et caques unis à passer outre:*
> *Huits ponts rompus chef à tant enferré,*
> *Enfants parfaits sont jugules en coultre.*

The classic land between two rivers is Mesopotamia—modern Iraq—where Saddam Hussein found himself sealed off without an ally during the Persian Gulf War. The "casks and barrels joined" are the Seer's description of the pontoon bridges used by advancing American armies to cross rivers. There were at least eight key Iraqi bridges over the Tigris and Euphrates that were blown away by American air strikes, which also raked Saddam's capital of Baghdad. The "children" here are probably those of the Kurds, massacred by Saddam in the wake of the war.

Rating: 9

The number of verses on the Persian Gulf War is a little surprising, suggesting that history may view it as more important than we now perceive. (A previously unsolved quatrain.)

Quatrain VIII-56: Cromwell Wins at Dunbar

> The weak band will occupy the land; those of the high
> place will utter horrible cries. The large herd (or
> "troop") of the outer corner will be troubled. Near
> "Dinebro" it (the herd) falls; the scripts discovered.

> *La bande faible la terre occupera,*
> *Ceux du haut lieu feront horribles cris:*
> *Le gros troupeau d'estre coin troublera,*
> *Tombe près Dinebro decouverts les escris.*

This is a marvelous depiction of the battle of Dunbar, near Edinburgh, where Cromwell defeated Charles II's Scots in 1650. "Dinebro" is an anagram for the phonetic "Edinb'ro." Cromwell's forces are well described as the "weak band." Many were ill, and they were outnumbered two to one. Further, the Scots, under Leslie, held the high ground of the battlefield, including Doon Hill ("high place"). Still, Cromwell managed to roll up the enemy line, herding the Scots back upon their own left wing into a pocket ("the outer corner") between the hill and a ravine. The result was an utter rout that cost Cromwell barely twenty men. The "scripts" would be the papers of the Scottish War Office captured by Cromwell.

Rating: 9.5

Nostradamus' description of this famous battle is startling. It is almost as though the Seer was standing atop Doon Hill watching the battle unfold. Though basically solved almost 300 years ago, the extraordinary precision of this verse has not been recognized.

Quatrain VIII-57: Napoleon ... or Cromwell?

> From simple soldier he will attain to empire; from
> short robe he will attain to the long: Valiant in arms,
> in the Church the very worst, to vex the priests as the
> water does the sponge.

> *De soldat simple parviendra en empire,*
> *De robe courte parviendra à la longue:*
> *Vaillant aux armes en Eglise ou plus pire,*
> *Vexer les pretres comme l'eau fait l'eponge.*

Commentators are split over whether the subject here is Napoleon or Cromwell, but the evidence seems to favor Bonaparte, who actually did become an emperor, adopting many outward imperial trappings ("long robe"). Such was not the case with Cromwell even though he was a de facto dictator. Both men vexed the priests in the sense of being troublesome to the Catholic Church, but the metaphor of the last line again suggests Napoleon. He attempted to permeate the Church as water does a sponge, treating the Church as an adjunct of the empire. (While Cromwell could be said to have permeated the Church of England, he did not vex it since he was its great savior.)

Rating: 9

The verse fits Napoleon almost perfectly; the fact that it has an alternate possible application is the only aspect that hurts the rating.

Quatrain VIII-58: A Surprised King

> Realm in quarrel divided between brothers, to take
> the arms and the name of Britain: The Anglican title
> will be advised too late, surprised by night—off to the
> Gallic air.

> *Regne en querelle aux freres divisé,*
> *Prendre les armes et le nom Britannique:*
> *Titre Anglican sera tard avisé,*
> *Surpris de nuit mener à l'air Gallique.*

The last line of the verse immediately brings to mind King James II of Great Britain who fled to France after being deposed in 1688. James was advised too late that his support was evaporating. When he returned to London from Salisbury on November 26, he found that he had been abandoned by all in favor of William of Orange. This was indeed the period during which England, with Scotland and Ireland, assumed the name Great Britain (line two). The realm was assuredly "in quarrel" since there was intense religious strife, setting brother against brother. James badly underestimated the opposition to his pro-Catholic policies.

Rating: 9
Commentators have been confused by the first line assuming it to mean two specific brothers. It most likely refers to the British people being badly divided by intense religious differences.

Quatrain VIII-59: East vs. West

> Twice high, twice lowered, the East and also the West
> will weaken: Its (the West's) adversary after several
> struggles, routed by sea will fail in the pinch.

> *Par deux fois haut par deux fois mis à bas,*
> *L'Orient aussi l'Occident faiblira:*
> *Son adversaire après plusieurs combats,*
> *Par mer chassé au besoin faillira.*

Previously unsolved, this verse is an accurate description of the interminable struggle between Western Christendom and Islam. Twice the Muslims appeared on the verge of triumph, but both times were beaten back. The initial Arab expansion was repulsed at Tours in 732. Subsequently, the West weakened under the Turkish intrusion that was finally halted at Vienna in 1683, the Turks then being pushed out of Europe altogether. Much of the Turkish expansionist momentum was lost when their huge navy was virtually destroyed in the great naval battle of Lepanto in 1571.

Rating: 8.5
The verse is quite correct, but the phraseology could be considered somewhat general in nature.

Quatrain VIII-60: Napoleon III Wins and Loses

> First in Gaul, first in Roman territory, by land and sea
> to the English and Paris; marvelous deeds by that
> great troop. Violating, the wild one will lose Lorraine.

> *Premier en Gaule, premier en Romanie,*
> *Par mer et terre aux Anglois et Paris,*
> *Merveilleux faits par cette grand mesnie,*
> *Violant, terax perdra le NORLARIS.*

Since Louis Napoleon was the only French ruler to really "lose Lorraine," commentators have seen him as the subject of this verse though they have had trouble with other aspects. Actually, there is little difficulty. Louis, first in France, was also a leader in Italy's independence movement, and he sent troops to protect the Papal States (*Romanie*) during the Risorgimento. Earlier, he had fled to England after a failed coup attempt, returning to Paris in 1848. Louis' army did perform a marvelous deed in liberating Italy from Austria. He had a definite "wild" streak, often acting rashly or unrealistically, which is how he lost Lorraine.

Rating: 8

Since the Allies overran Lorraine on their way to Paris in 1814, Bonaparte could qualify as the subject here, except that he never visited England.

Quatrain VIII-61: The Great One: Henry IV

> Never by light of day will he attain to the scepter-
> bearing sign until all his sieges are at rest, bearing to
> the cock the gift of the armed legion.

> *Jamais par le descouvrement du jour,*
> *Ne parviendra au signe sceptrifere:*
> *Que tous ses sieges ne soient en sejour,*
> *Portent au coq don du TAG armifere.*

This is a fairly simple quatrain that has somehow eluded commentators. It deals with Henry of Navarre's long struggle for the throne of France. On the death of Henry III during the French religious wars, the king of Navarre was in line for the French crown. However, it would take Henry years of battles and sieges before he could claim the prize. Finally, to collapse the remaining opposition, he converted to Catholicism ("Paris is well worth a mass"). He was recognized as Henry IV of France (1594), and his legions became the army of France ("the cock"). After soon disposing of the remaining residual resistance, the rest of Henry's sixteen-year reign was remarkably peaceful ("sieges are at rest") and highly successful.

Rating: 8.5

The first line may suggest that Henry's conversion to Catholicism was less than sincere. Nonetheless, the affable and able monarch became the most popular in French history.

Quatrain VIII-64: England in World War II

> Within the Isles the children transported, two out of
> seven will be in despair: Those of the soil will be sup-
> ported by it, the name "cropper" taken, the hope of
> the leagues fading.

> *Dedans les Îles les enfants transportes,*
> *Les deux de sept seront en desespoir:*
> *Ceux du terrouer en seront supportes,*
> *Nom pelle pris des liques fui l'espoir.*

The thrust of this quatrain is very suggestive of Britain's World War
II program to move children away from areas being bombed by the
Luftwaffe. The only hitch has been the unresolved word *pelle* in line
four, which usually means "shovel," but it can also mean "cropper"
(one who raises crops). So this part of the verse is about the wartime
"victory gardens" that helped combat food shortages in Britain. Tens
of thousands of urban and suburban citizens became small-scale
"croppers." The "leagues" with faded hopes during these dark days
would be the Allies and the moribund League of Nations.

Rating: 9
Once the *pelle* problem is disposed of, this becomes a very clear and
strong quatrain.

Quatrain VIII-65: The Pétain Regime

> The old one frustrated in his principle hope, will
> attain to the head of his empire: Twenty months he
> will hold the realm with great power. Tyrant, cruel in
> giving way to one worse.

> *Le vieux frustré du principal espoir,*
> *Il parviendra au chef de son empire:*
> *Vingt mois tiendra le regne à grand pouvoir,*
> *Tyran, cruel en delaissant un pire.*

Aged Marshall Pétain briefly attained to the head of the French empire during World War II, becoming chief of the Vichy regime in July of 1940. In April of 1942, he retired to a nominal role after being pressured by Hitler into accepting Pierre Laval, a more enthusiastic Nazi collaborator, as head of state. Pétain had hoped to transform France into a bulwark of ultraconservatism and a major player in Hitler's New Order for Europe, but was soon and grievously disappointed.

Rating: 9.5
Pétain was convicted of treason after the war but was never executed. Laval faced a firing squad.

Quatrain VIII-68: Richelieu Wins Again

The old Cardinal deceived by the young one, will find himself disarmed out of his dignity: (while) Arles does not show the duplicate to be perceived. Both "Liqueduct" and the prince embalmed.

Vieux Cardinal par le jeune decu,
Hors de sa charge se verra desarmé:
Arles ne montres double soit apercu,
Et Liqueduct et le Prince embaumé.

The aging Cardinal Richelieu lost royal favor due to the machinations of young Cinq-Mars, his former protégé. Just when it appeared that Richelieu was finished, he received from Arles a copy of a treasonous agreement negotiated by Cinq-Mars with Spain. When the copy was shown to Louis XIII, he immediately had Cinq-Mars arrested, tried, and executed (1642). Both Richelieu and the king died soon after. "Liqueduct" (conducted by water) is probably Cinq-Mars, or possibly Richelieu himself. The ailing cardinal conveyed Cinq-Mars up the Rhône by barge for trial at Lyon.

Rating: 9
This could have been a top-rated verse had the phraseology been a little crisper.

Quatrain VIII-70: Saddam vs. Democracy

> He will enter ugly, wicked, infamous, tyrannizing over
> Mesopotamia (Iraq). All made friends of the illegiti-
> mate lady; the land horrible black in physiognomy.

> *Il entrera vilain, mechant infame,*
> *Tyrannisant la Mesopotamie:*
> *Tous amis fait d'adulterine dame,*
> *Terre horrible noir de physionomie.*

The first two lines are an almost self-evident description of dictator Saddam Hussein of Iraq, old-time Mesopotamia. The "illegitimate
lady" is more difficult, but it is most likely the personification of Liberty, always portrayed in sculpture and paintings as a woman. Since
the Seer was a confirmed monarchist, he would naturally view
democracy as an illegitimate form of government (especially since it is
usually established by ousting a monarch). In the Gulf War, world
opinion was overwhelmingly with the democratic powers ("all made
friends"), while Saddam was without allies. The verse ends with a
plain picture of the effects on Iraq and Kuwait from the Gulf War
fighting and the great oil fires that followed.

Rating: 9.5

The imagery of the third line may be a shade abstruse (the verse has
been unsolved), but this is a very strong and descriptive quatrain.

Quatrain VIII-71: Astronomers Afflicted

> The number of astronomers will become very
> great—driven out, banished, and their books
> condemned: The year 1607 by the holy assemblies, so
> that none will be safe from the holy ones.

> *Croitra le nombre si grand des astronomes*
> *Chasses, bannis et livres censures:*
> *L'an mil six cent et sept par sacrees glomes,*
> *Que nul aux sacres ne seront assures.*

Though dismissed as a failure, this dated quatrain is actually so close to the mark that it qualifies as a borderline hit. The number of astronomers did increase greatly after Galileo popularized the telescope in the early 1600s. At the same time, a severe clash erupted between the Church and astronomers over the Copernican concept of a heliocentric solar system. The supporters of the new view were censured and their works condemned; Galileo himself was effectively "banished." The Seer misses the actual year the Theologians of the Holy Office declared Copernicus' theory to be heresy; it was 1613, not 1607.

Rating: 7.5

The chronological miscalculation here is not very great, and the rest of the quatrain is quite accurate. (Commentators have been led astray by translating *astronomes* to mean astrologers.)

Quatrain VIII-74: The Misfortunes of Maximilian

> A King entered very far into the new land, while his
> fellows come to welcome him. His perfidy will have
> such an effect as (to be) grounds for festival and
> assembly for the citizens.

> *En terre neuve bien avant Roi entré,*
> *Pendant sujets lui viendront faire accueil:*
> *Sa perfidie aura tel rencontré,*
> *Qu'aux citadins lieu de fete et recueil.*

Royalists, backed by the direct intervention of France, were able to make European nobleman Ferdinand Maximilian the emperor of Mexico ("the new land") in 1864. Though welcomed at first by conservative elements, Maximilian subsequently refused to back their program ("perfidy") and lost their allegiance. As a foreigner he was unable to command the loyalty of the peasants, so with no base of support, Maximilian's regime was soon toppled after French troops were withdrawn. His defeat, dethronement, capture, and execution occasioned festive assemblies. The Cinco de Mayo celebration dates from this era.

Rating: 8.5
Though the French phraseology is a bit hazy in spots, the prophecy nonetheless works neatly.

Quatrain VIII-76: Oliver Cromwell

> More Butcher than king in England, born of obscure
> place he will have the empire through force: Dastard
> without faith, without law, he will bleed the land. His
> time approaches so near that I sigh.

> *Plus Macelin que Roi en Angleterre,*
> *Lieu obscure ne par force aura l'empire:*
> *Lache sans foi sans loi saignera terre,*
> *Son temps s'approache si près que je soupire.*

Universally applied to Cromwell, this quatrain is one of the Catholic Seer's more negative reviews. Cromwell being anathema to the Roman Church, and vice versa, England's Protestant Lord Protector would have been seen by Nostradamus as a heretic leader ("without faith . . . law"). With uncanny military talents, Cromwell rose from obscurity to take the empire by force and bloodshed, and he was born only forty-some years after the *Centuries* were written.

Rating: 9
Although a striking verse in some ways, the fact remains that Cromwell was as fervent about his Church as Nostradamus was about his, so the phrase "without faith" does not come off as quite apropos even given the Seer's point of view.

Quatrain VIII-77: Stalin's Reign of Terror

> The Antichrist very soon annihilates the three. Seven
> and twenty years of blood will his war last: the
> heretics dead, captives exiled, blood, human bodies,
> reddened water, hail on the land.

> *L'antechrist trois bien tôt annihiles,*
> *Vingt et sept ans sang durera sa guerre:*
> *Les heretiques morts, captifs exiles,*
> *Sang corps humain eau rougie greler terre.*

This is a remarkably precise quatrain that, oddly, has not been grasped. Joseph Stalin was probably the most notorious Antichrist since Attila, doing his best to obliterate the Christian Orthodox Church during his reign of exactly twenty-seven years. By 1926, the Communist dictator had seized complete control of his party and nation by ousting his three rivals—Trotsky, Zinoviev, and Kamenev— all subsequently executed. The Soviet "Man of Steel" ruled with unrelieved bloody power until his death in 1953, waging continual war on all enemies of his regime. Dissenters from Stalinist ideology were branded as heretics and killed or exiled to the Gulag (line three).

Rating: 10

The last line of the quatrain may refer, in part at least, to the massive toll of battlefield deaths in Russia during World War II. The mention of hail may be a clue implying a cold country.

Quatrain VIII-80: The Stalinist Era

> The blood of the innocent, of the widow and virgin,
> so many evils committed by way of the greatest Red
> One: Holy images dipped in burning candles. Frightened by terror, none will be seen to move.

> *Des innocents le sang de veuve et vierge,*
> *Tant de maux faits par moyen se grand Rouge:*
> *Saintes simulacres trempes en ardent cierge,*
> *De frayeur crainte ne verra nul qui bouge.*

The "greatest Red One," in this villainous context, can hardly be anyone but Communist dictator Joseph Stalin. The verse depicts the fear that pervaded all Russians under his regime, especially those who tried to cling to the suppressed Orthodox religion (holy images burned). No transgressors or suspects were exempt from reprisal, not even the young or the widows. The last line is a chilling summation of life under Stalinism; no one dared make a move without the approval of the state.

Rating: 8.5

While a shade too general to rate top marks, the verse is both accurate and graphically descriptive.

Quatrain VIII-81: Problems for Philip IV

> The new empire in desolation, it will be changed from
> the northern pole: From Sicily will come the distur-
> bance to trouble the enterprise tributary to Philip.

> *Le neuf empire en desolation,*
> *Sera changé du pole aquilonaire:*
> *De la Sicile viendra l'emotion,*
> *Troubler l'emprise à Philip tributaire.*

This is a stunningly successful prophecy that seems to have been completely missed by previous commentators. In 1647, revolts broke out in Palermo and Naples in the Two Sicilies, which were "tributary" to Spain's King Philip IV. Citizens, agitated by new taxes, murdered many nobles before the uprisings were put down. The revolts were one more stage in the rapid disintegration of the great Spanish Empire built up during the 1500s. The empire was by then on the verge of collapse under the blows of the northern powers: England, France, and Holland. ("From the northern pole" merely indicates, poetically, a northerly direction.)

Rating: 10

The quatrain, written almost a century before the events, names names and places and is 100 percent accurate.

Quatrain VIII-87: The End of Il Duce

Death conspired will come into full execution, charge
given and journey of death: Elected, created, received,
defeated by his followers. Blood of innocence before
him in remorse.

Mort conspiree viendra en plein effet,
Charge donnee et voyage de mort:
Elu, crée, recu par siens defait.
Sang d'innocence devant soi par remords.

There are many more verses pertaining to Mussolini than commentators have realized. Italian partisan leaders had planned the summary execution of Il Duce well before they captured and shot him as he was attempting to flee Italy in a German convoy ("journey of death") in 1945. Mussolini had been elected to the Italian parliament, created and received by the Italian people, and then defeated by the Grand Fascist Council, which voted for his ouster after the Allies invaded Sicily. As he faced the firing squad, the blood of many innocent people was before him and perhaps Il Duce even experienced some remorse.

Rating: 9

Le Pelletier saw this one as applying to Louis XVI, but the last line clearly paints the protagonist as responsible for the death many innocents—much more true of Mussolini. As a king, Louis was never really "elected" to anything and the "journey of death" also fits Benito better.

Quatrain VIII-88: Charles Emmanuel Opts Out

A noble King will come to Sardinia, one who will hold
the kingdom only three years. He will join several
colors to himself. After care, sleepiness and scorn
afflict him.

Dans la Sardaigne un noble Roi viendra,
Qui ne tiendra que trois ans le royaume,
Plusiers couleurs avec soi conjoindra,
Lui-meme après soin sommeil marrit scome.

After losing his mainland possessions to Bonaparte, Charles Emmanuel IV retired to his Sardinian realm. Then, after only three more years, he abdicated (1802) in favor of his brother and entered a religious order. The "several colors" phrase, which has troubled commentators, probably refers to the French tricolor. While on the mainland, Charles had foolishly agreed to join a confederation with France and soon lost all semblance of any real power. The last line alludes to Charles' indifference and scorn of the world after his abdication.

Rating: 8.5

Ironically, after Charles dropped out, his House of Savoy not only recovered his lost lands but went on to unify Italy and rule the entire Italian nation.

Quatrain VIII-92: A Venture Too Far

Far beyond his realm set on a hazardous journey, he
will lead for himself the occupying grand army: His
followers the King will hold captive and hostage.
Upon his return he will ransack the entire country.

Loin hors de regne mis en hasard voyage
Grand ost duira pour soi l'occupera
Le Roi tiendra les siens captif otage,
A son retour tout pays pillera.

The improbable adventures or Sweden's Charles XII are the subject of this quatrain. After subduing Poland, Charles, in 1707, led a grand army of about 50,000 men into Russia. At Poltava, almost 1,000 miles from home, he battled Peter the Great and was badly beaten. Charles retreated with the remnants of his army into the Turkish Sultan's territory where they encamped in a strange limbo of protective custody for four years (line three) before the Turks seized the camp. When Charles finally returned to Sweden, he had to ransack his already impoverished country for more money and men to fend off the Danes and Norwegians.

Rating: 8.5

Charles' costly career was instrumental in pushing the Swedes toward a limited monarchy and a more pacific foreign policy.

Quatrain VIII-94: A Costly Beating for Spain

> Before the lake where the dearest of seven months was put in, and its army routed, there will the Spaniards be destroyed by the Albanese (English)—loss through delay in giving battle.

> *Devant le lac ou plus cher fut getté*
> *De sept mois, et son ost deconfit*
> *Seront Hispans par Albanois gastez,*
> *Par delai perte en donnant le conflit.*

Charles Ward[7] and others have applied this verse to the sack of Cadiz by the English in 1596, which works well enough. The "lake" is actually the Bay of Cadiz where the Spanish had a treasure-laden fleet ("dearest one") that just returned from a seven-month voyage to the New World. English naval forces under Raleigh, Essex, and Howard sank forty galleons and thirteen Spanish warships, and then pillaged the city. Ward concludes, perhaps correctly, that the Spanish waited too long before giving battle.

Rating: 8

The Albanese must certainly be the English, but the use of the word "lake" in this verse is somewhat curious.

---

7. Charles Ward wrote *Oracles of Nostradamus* (London, 1891). See bibliography.

Quatrain VIII-95: The Greatest Modern Pope

The seducer will be put in the dungeon and bound for some time: The scholar joins the chief with his crozier. The sharp right will attract the contented ones.

Le seducteur sera mis en la fosse,
Et attaché jusqu'à quelque temps:
Le clerc uni le chef avec sa crosse,
Piquante droite attraira les contents.

This verse foretells a period when satanic influence will be contained during the lengthy reign of a very highly regarded pope. This pope, symbolized by the "crozier," is to be a first-rate scholar. The conservative right will be dominant and the world relatively placid. This scenario was fulfilled during the tenure of the brilliant and dedicated Pope Leo XIII, a conservative with a social conscience who held the papacy from 1878 to 1903. During these peaceful and contented years, he brought the church to its highest level of prestige in many centuries.

Rating: 9
The four decades between the Franco-Prussian War and World War I constituted one of those rare periods when Western civilization really seemed to be getting its act together, but, alas, it was only the calm before the storms of the twentieth century.

Quatrain IX-11: Charles' Revenge?

Wrongly they will come to put the just one to death, in public and in their midst extinguished: So great a pestilence will come to arise in this place that the judges will be forced to flee.

Le juste à tort à mort l'on viendra mettre,
Publiquement et du milieu eteint:
Si grande peste en ce lieu viendra naitre,
Que les jugeants fuir seront contraints.

This is an obvious verse on the death of England's Charles I who was publicly beheaded in 1649. Nostradamus, disapproving of regicide—especially since Charles had Catholic sympathies—sees the Great Plague of London in 1665 as a divine punishment. Some of the judges, the Cromwellians who condemned the king, doubtlessly did flee the plague as did many others, but the last line is not especially illuminating.

Rating: 8.5

Though the Seer's theory of divine retribution may be a little suspect, we have to be impressed that he correctly calls the sequence of the king's execution and the subsequent plague.

Quatrain IX-16: Civil War Erupts in Spain

> From Castile Franco will lead the assemblage. The ambassador, not happy, will cause a schism: Those of Ribiere (Rivera) will be in the squabble, and they will refuse entry to the great gulf.

> *De Castel Franco sortira l'assemblee,*
> *L'ambassadeur non plaisant fera schisme:*
> *Ceux de Ribiere seront en melee,*
> *Et au grand gouffre denieront l'entree.*

The word *Franco* has led commentators in the right direction though the interpretations have been somewhat cursory. Franco did lead his Falangist assemblage from western Castile while eastern Spain (Catalonia) held out for the republicans. "Those of Rivera" were in the fray as most of former dictator Rivera's followers—and his son—joined Franco. The "gulf" is the great Gulf of Valencia, which Franco blockaded to cut foreign aid to the Loyalists. The knotty second line must refer to ex-foreign minister Lerroux, who headed a centrist government from 1933–36. His effort to reach out to conservatives spawned a violent leftist uprising ("schism") in late 1934.

Rating: 10

The naming of Franco and the designation of Rivera completely over-whelm any trivial imperfections in this astonishing quatrain.

Quatrain IX-17: The Ovens of Auschwitz

> The third premier does worse than Nero. How much
> human blood to flow; valiant, be gone. He will cause
> the furnace to be rebuilt; Golden Age dead, new king,
> great scandal.

> *Le tiers premier pis que ne fit Neron,*
> *Videz vaillant que sang humain répandre:*
> *R'edifier fera le forneron,*
> *Siècle d'or mort, nouveau Roi grand esclandre.*

The "third premier" is a reference to the premier of the Third Reich, Adolph Hitler, who did in fact do worse than Nero. "The valiant" are those who opposed the Nazis and paid the price in the concentration camp furnaces ("great scandal"). The "new king" is Hitler himself. From the Seer's point of view, since he was a confirmed royalist, the "Golden Age" would be the age of monarchy, which was dead in Germany and most of Europe after World War I.

Rating: 9

Le Pelletier saw this one as a presage of the doings of the Third Estate during the French Revolution, which almost works except for line three. He equates the furnace with the Tuileries, once the site of tile kilns. But the Tuileries palace was built more than two centuries before the Revolution. Of course, Le Pelletier knew nothing of Hitler.

Quatrain IX-18: Montmorency Gets the Ax

> The lily of the Dauphin will reach into Nancy, as far as
> Flanders the Elector of the Empire: New confinement
> for the great Montmorency, outside proven places
> delivered to celebrated punishment.

Le lis Dauffois portera dans Nansi,
Jusqu'en Flandres Electeur de l'Empire:
Neuve obturee au grand Montmorency,
Hors lieux prouves delivre à clere peine.

This is a quatrain of wide renown because it specifies its principal subject by name. In 1632 the Duc de Montmorency, after much honorable service, joined a rebellion against King Louis XIII, was defeated, and then confined at a newly built prison in Toulouse ("outside proven places") where he was beheaded. His punishment was "celebrated" indeed since it was the talk of the entire nation. The next year Louis, a former Dauphin whose emblem was the fleur-de-lis, did enter Nancy, and, in 1635, the Elector of Triers was arrested by the Spanish and taken to Flanders.

Rating: 10

It is possible to nitpick minor aspects of this prophecy, but it is extraordinarily specific and quite accurate.

Quatrain IX-20: The Flight to Varennes (1791)

By night will come through the forest of Reines, two
couples by roundabout route, Queen of the white
stone. The monk king in gray in Varennes: Elected
Capet causes tempest, fire, blood, slice.

De nuit viendra par la foret de Reines,
Deux pars voltorte Herne la pierre blanche,
Le moine noir en gris dedans Varennes:
Elu cap. cause tempete, feu, sang, tranche.

One of the Seer's most celebrated successes, this verse depicts the circuitous flight through wooded country to Varennes by Louis XVI and Marie Antoinette, accompanied by Madame de Tourzel and Count Ferson. The king was dressed in a plain gray suit and a broad brimmed hat, looking like a Carmelite monk. The "white stone" alludes to the notorious Affair of the Diamond Necklace, which undermined the

Queen's popular support. Louis, a Capet, was "elected" in the sense that he had been confirmed as king by the national assembly. The French Revolution is described in the last line, with its ominous finale, "slice," foreshadowing the demise of the royal couple by guillotine.

Rating: 9.5

A difficulty with the verse has been the "forest of Reines." Since there is no such forest, *Reines* may be an anagram, perhaps for Aisne R[iver] (one letter changed as per custom). The forest in question is adjacent to that river.

Quatrain IX-34: Saulce and the King

> The partner alone, vexed, will be mitered, return, con-
> flict to pass over the tile: by five hundred. One who
> betrays will be titled. Narbonne and Saulce, we will
> have oil for the knives.

> *Le part soluz mary sera mitré,*
> *Retour conflit passera sur la tuile:*
> *Par cinq cents un trahir sera titré*
> *Narbonne et Saulce par couteaux avons d'huile.*

France's ill-fated King Louis XVI shows up again in this famed quatrain. He was "mitred" by being forced to don the red hat of a revolutionary upon his return from Varennes where he was intercepted in his flight by the town procureur named Saulce (or Sauce). The "tile" is the Tuileries palace, built on a tile kiln site, which was overrun by a revolutionary mob. Louis' Minister of War, Count Narbonne, was a man of dubious loyalties. Saulce was a merchant of oil (*d'huile*). "Knives" obviously suggest the guillotine.

Rating: 9

While the inclusion of the names Narbonne and Saulce is startling, the verse is unusually choppy and the characterization of Narbonne as a betrayer may be a tad overdrawn. The count was a typical political gamesman, but little worse than most.

Quatrain IX-35: King Ferdinand of Bulgaria

> And fair Ferdinand will be detached, to abandon the
> flower, to follow the Macedon: In the great pinch his
> course will fail; and he will march against the Myrmi-
> dons (Greeks).

> *Et Ferdinand blonde sera descorte,*
> *Quitter la fleur, suivre le Macedon:*
> *Au grand besoin defaillira sa route,*
> *Et marchera contre le Myrmidon.*

This is a thoroughly brilliant quatrain—though not fully appreciated—centering on the career of King Ferdinand of Bulgaria, who
assumed the throne in 1887. Ferdinand was a north German and certainly "fair" by Bulgarian standards. He had done notable work in
botany before abandoning that field ("the flower") to take the throne
of Bulgaria. "Macedon" is a credible designation for Bulgaria since the
Bulgars long occupied much of Macedonia. Further, in 1913, Ferdinand did get into a war over Macedonia with the Greeks and their
allies, which he lost (failed course).

Rating: 10
The verse is clear, highly specific, and entirely accurate. The Myrmi-
dons were the tribe of the Greek Achilles.

Quatrain IX-42: The Turks Trounced at Sea

> From Barcelona, from Genoa and Venice, from pesti-
> lent Sicily, Monaco joined: They will take their aim
> against the Barbarian fleet; Barbarian driven well back
> as far as Tunis.

> *De Barcelonne, de Gennes et Venise,*
> *De la Secille peste Monet unis:*
> *Contre Barbare classe prendront la vise,*
> *Barbare pousse bien loin jusqu'à Thunis.*

The epic Battle of Lepanto in 1571 was a disastrous defeat for the Turkish fleet. The victors were Spain, Venice, and the papacy. (Genoa and Monaco were Spanish satellites.) Two years later, the leader at Lepanto, Don Juan of Austria, captured Tunis from the Turks. The "Barbarians" are, as usual, the Muslims, though the Turkish fleet actually included many ships from the Barbary Coast.

Rating: 9
The pestilence in Sicily (line two) is hard to pinpoint since health records at the time were extremely haphazard. The Seer may just be referring to Sicily as a generally pestilent place, which was no doubt true in those days.

Quatrain IX-44: The Specter of World War II

> Leave, leave Geneva every single one. Saturn will be
> converted from gold to iron. RAYPOZ will exterminate
> all opposition; before the coming the sky will show
> signs.

> *Migrez, migrez de Geneue trestous,*
> *Saturne d'or en fer se changera,*
> *Le contre RAYPOZ exterminera tous,*
> *Avant l'avent le ciel signes fera.*

In the opening line the Seer seems to be telling those of the League of Nations in Geneva to give it up and go home because World War II is surely fated. The transmutation from gold to iron symbolizes the change from peace to war. "RAYPOZ" remains unsolved, but with the customary change of one letter ("p" to "n") it can transmute to NAZROY (Nazi King), i.e., Hitler. The changes in the sky could mean something astrological or it might refer to the Luftwaffe's air strikes, which always preceded the great offensive onslaughts of the Nazi armies.

Rating: 8
The prediction is a shade too general and the anagram may be less than 100 percent satisfactory; still, the quatrain is one of the more intriguing.

Quatrain IX-49: An Ax for the King

> Ghent and Brussels will work against Antwerp. The
> Senate of London will put their king to death: Salt
> and wine will overthrow him. To have (it) for them-
> selves the realm turned upside down.

> *Gand et Bruceles marcheront contre Anuers,*
> *Senat de Londres mettront à mort leur Roi:*
> *Le sel et vin lui seront à l'envers,*
> *Pour eux avoir le regne en desarroi.*

The second line clearly depicts the execution of England's Charles I
in 1649, an event initiated by Parliament ("Senate") that certainly
turned the realm "upside down." "Salt" most likely refers to tax revenues, a particularly thorny issue during Charles' reign. The "wine"
must allude to the mass. Charles' other big problem was religious; he
was sympathetic to Catholicism. The two issues together were enough
to cause his overthrow. In 1648, Philip IV, ruler of Ghent and Brussels,
signed a treaty with the Dutch closing the Scheldt River, thereby ruining the city of Antwerp.

Rating: 9

The second line is brilliant. While the rest is a little murky, the net
impact of the verse remains quite strong.

Quatrain IX-50: Henry IV Wins Out

> Mendosus will soon come to his high realm, eclipsing
> the Lorrainers: the pale red one, the male in the inter-
> regnum, the fearful youth and the foreign terror.

> *MENDOSVS tôt viendra à son haut regne,*
> *Mettant arrieve un peu les Norlaris:*
> *Le rouge bleme, le male à l'interregne,*
> *Le jeune crainte et frayeur Barbaris.*

"Mendosus" is an anagram for Vendosme, the Bourbon branch of Henry IV who beat out four rivals for the throne of France in the 1590s. *Norlaris* is an anagram for Lorraine. Henry's competitors, three from the Guise family, are well drawn: the "pale red one" is the old Cardinal of Bourbon; the "interregnum" male is the Duke of Mayenne; the "fearful youth" is the young Duke de Guise, son of Balafre; while the "foreign terror" is Philip II of Spain. The Guise family, perhaps the most illustrious in France, was from Lorraine.

Rating: 10

The anagrams are quite satisfactory and the quatrain is marvelously descriptive—so much so that some have found it hard to believe. There is no question though in this commentator's mind about its validity.

Quatrain IX-51: The Specter of Communism

> Against the red ones sects will conspire; fire, water,
> steel, cord through peace will weaken: On the point of
> dying (are) those who will plot, except one who above
> all will ruin the world.

> *Contre les rouges sectes se banderont,*
> *Feu, eau, fer, corde par paix se minera:*
> *Au point mourir ceux qui machineront,*
> *Fors un que monde surtout ruinera.*

Even Leoni, who is not easily convinced, admits that this verse is descriptive of the reaction against Soviet Communism after the Russian Revolution. Fascism, Nazism, and the Anti-Comintern[8] were all "sects" whose main thrust was vehemently anti-Red. Fire and steel were used against the Reds by intervenors, and the "cord" is the Cordon Sanitaire designed to isolate the USSR. The Cordon did "weaken" somewhat as Russia calmed and gained a measure of acceptance and

---

8. Pact of avowedly anti-Communist nations formed in 1936.

recognition. The leaders who were most alarmed by the Red menace were for the most part elderly, except Hitler, who certainly fulfilled the last line.

Rating: 9

This is a good quatrain, but not quite specific enough for top marks.

Quatrain IX-52: Religious Wars in France

> Peace is nigh on one side, and war, never was the pursuit of it so great: Men and women to bemoan innocent blood on the land; and this will be throughout all France.

> *La paix s'approche d'un coté, et la guerre,*
> *Onc ne fut la poursuite si grande:*
> *Plaindre homme, femme sang innocent par terre,*
> *Et ce sera de France à toute bande.*

As peace approached with Spain in 1559, France was on the verge of a series of religious wars between Catholics and Calvinists. The relentless struggles raged for decades, spilling the blood of thousands of innocents. It was only with the eventual victory of Henry IV in the late sixteenth century that some semblance of order returned to France.

Rating: 8.5

This is not an especially specific quatrain, but one that works nicely. The interpretation is usually credited to Jaubert (seventeenth century).

Quatrain IX-55: World War I and Influenza

> The horrible war that is being prepared in the West,
> the following year will come the pestilence so very
> horrible that young, old, nor beast (escape). Blood,
> fire, Mercury, Mars, Jupiter in France.

> *L'horrible guerre qu'en l'Occident s'apprete,*
> *L'an ensuivant viendra la pestilence*
> *Si fort horrible que jeune, vieux, ni bete,*
> *Sang, feu Mercure, Mars, Iupiter en France.*

The most "horrible war" in the West was doubtless World War I, when four years of trench warfare in France took a ghastly toll of human life. Hard on the heels of this calamity came another: a severe influenza epidemic that spread over much of Europe and the world, claiming more millions. Thus, this prediction was fulfilled all too well.

Rating: 9
The only drawback with the verse is the astrological references in the last line, which seems quite obscure.

Quatrain IX-57: A "King" is Dead

> At the place of Dreux a King will rest, and will look
> for a law changing Anathema. While the sky will
> thunder so very loudly, a new entry, the King will kill
> himself.

> *Au lieu de DRUX un Roi reposera,*
> *Et cherchera loi changeant d'Anatheme:*
> *Pendant le ciel si tres fort tonnera,*
> *Portee neuve Roi tuera soi-meme.*

A king killing himself is such an extraordinary event that it brings to mind Adolph Hitler, and the thunder in the sky suggests another twentieth-century circumstance: aerial warfare. Dreux was in the old province of Ile de France, which included the capital city of Paris, so "the place of Dreux," especially since the whole word is capitalized, means Ile de France. Hitler's armies did rest for many months after the conquest of Paris (1940) before invading the Balkans and then Russia. Hitler killed himself with the "entry" of Russian troops into Berlin to the "thunder" of bombs, rockets, and artillery. The change in "Anathema" no doubt has to do with the increasing persecution of the Jews.

Rating: 8.5
While the Jews had already been declared anathema and their property confiscated by 1940, Hitler was still contemplating his "final solution" to the "Jewish problem." (A previously unsolved verse.)

Quatrain IX-65: The Space Program

> He will come to go into the corner of Luna where he
> will be taken and put in a strange land: The unripe
> fruits will be a great scandal, great blame, to one great
> praise.

> *Dedans le coin de Luna viendra rendre,*
> *Ou sera pris et mis en terre étrange:*
> *Les fruits immurs seront à grand esclandre,*
> *Grand vitupere, à l'un grande louange.*

The first half of the verse is plain enough; it describes the first Apollo mission to the Moon, certainly a "strange land." The rest of the quatrain is a good description of the uproar created when Russia's Sputnik jolted Americans, who assumed they would be the first into space. The "unripe fruits" are figures of the American satellites, which were not ready in time to beat the Soviets into orbit. The American space effort was severely criticized at the time while Russia reaped a propaganda bonanza ("great praise").

Rating: 9
The verse is impressive since the idea of man on the moon in Nostradamus' time would have seemed entirely preposterous. Yet this is clearly what the Seer predicted.

Quatrain IX-66: The Reconstruction Era

> There will be peace, union, and change—estates and
> offices, low high and high very low: To prepare a trip,
> the first fruits torment. War to cease, civil process,
> debates.

> *Paix, union sera et changement,*
> *Etats, offices, bas haut, et haut bien bas:*
> *Dresser voyage, le fruit premier tourment,*
> *Guerre cesser, civil proces, debats.*

Quite clearly this previously unsolved verse depicts the American
South during the Reconstruction. The victory of the Union is cited in
the first line followed by a description of the fall of the southern aristocracy and the elevation of many former slaves to public office ("high
low, low high"). There is an obvious reference to the carpetbaggers who
journeyed south to "torment" Dixie in the wake of the Civil War. The
question of how to deal with the defeated Confederacy generated endless debates and civil processes.

Rating: 9

The verse has been criticized as too general, but it really includes
numerous facets, all of which apply perfectly to the Reconstruction
and not nearly as well to any other episode.

Quatrain IX-74: San Francisco Area (1978–89)

> In the city of Fertsod (Rich Sodom) homicide, deed,
> and deed, many oxen plowing (but) no sacrifice.
> Return again to the honors of Artemis, and to Vulcan,
> bodies of dead ones to bury.

> *Dans la cité de Fertsod homicide,*
> *Fait, et fait multe boeuf arant ne macter:*
> *Retour encore aux honneurs d'Artemide,*
> *Et à Vulcan corps morts sepulturer.*

"Rich Sodom" is an excellent designation for San Francisco, which has one of the highest per capita incomes in the country and is also the unofficial capital of America's homosexual population. The homicide "deed and deed" must refer to the double assassination of Mayor Moscone and supervisor Harvey Milk in 1978. The Seer warns the Bay City to return to the honors of Artemis and Vulcan or there will be many bodies to bury. Artemis was the goddess of chastity while the mention of Vulcan clearly implies a punishing earthquake. The area was, of course, hit by a great quake in October of 1989, which killed sixty-seven people and injured thousands.

Rating: 8.5

The oxen plowing with no sacrifice seems to imply a failure to give thanks for prosperity. The verse may be a shade too metaphorical but has some very strong aspects.

Quatrain IX-76: A Bruising for Saddam

> With the rapacious and bloodthirsty king issued from
> the pallet of the inhuman Nero: Between two rivers,
> an inept military hand. He will be bruised by the
> shaven youth.

> *Avec le noir Rapax et sanguinaire,*
> *Issu du peaultre de l'inhumain Neron:*
> *Emmy deux fleuves main gauche militaire,*
> *Sera meurtri par Jeune chaulveron.*

The first part of the verse is a peerless description of Saddam Hussein, the reference to Nero suggesting an Antichrist or at least an anti-Christian. Iraq (Mesopotamia) is specified by the phrase "between two rivers" (the Tigris and Euphrates). Certainly, Saddam's conduct in the Persian Gulf War was militarily inept, and he was badly bruised by the shaven, young Allied soldiers.

Rating: 9
The one dubious aspect here is the intended meaning of *chaulveron*, which is uncertain because it is one of the Seer's coined words. (A previously unsolved verse.)

Quatrain IX-77: Marie Antoinette

> The realm taken, the King will conspire; the lady
> taken to death by ones sworn by lot: They will deny
> life to the Queen and son, and the mistress at the
> fortress of the wife.

> *Le regne pris le Roi conjurera,*
> *La dame prise à mort jures à sort:*
> *La vie à Reine fils on deniera,*
> *Et la pellix au fort de la consort.*

The lady of the verse is Marie Antoinette, who was in fact condemned by a jury chosen by lot—a very unusual procedure. Her young son, Louis, was not actually executed but died, perhaps by design, while a prisoner of the French revolutionaries. The opening line is accurate: King Louis XVI continually conspired against the revolution even after he was named as constitutional king. The reference to the "mistress" has been something of a problem. Most likely, it means Madame du Barry, who was still at court for a time after Marie married Louis and who was also executed by a revolutionary tribunal.

Rating: 8.5
If "fortress of the wife" can be taken to mean the French court, then the du Barry identification works well enough.

Quatrain IX-80: Mussolini Mucks It Up

> The Duke will contrive to exterminate his followers;
> he will send the strongest ones to strange places:
> through tyranny to ruin Pisa and Lucca. Then the
> Barbarians will gather the grapes without the wine.

Le Duc voudra les siens exterminer,
Envoyera les plus forts lieux etranges:
Par tyrannie Bize et Luc ruiner,
Puis les Barbares sans vin feront vendanges.

"The Duke" is Il Duce whose bumbling efforts to emulate the Caesars led to the death of hundreds of thousands of his followers. Mussolini sent his hapless troops to such strange places as Ethiopia and the eastern front in Russia. "Pisa and Lucca" are merely synecdoche for Italy, which was ruined by the Fascist tyranny. The last line is a figure of the Fascists' failure; their wine of conquest never came to fruition despite their strenuous labors.

Rating: 8.5

The first line is ironically phrased, which tends to fog up the meaning somewhat. But the use of "the Duke" for Il Duce is a strong plus for this previously unsolved verse.

Quatrain IX-89: Louis Philippe of France

For seven years fortune will favor Philip. He will beat down again the exertions of the Arabs: Then at his noon a perplexing contrary affair, young Ogmios will ruin his stronghold.

Sept ans sera Philipp. fortune prospere,
Rebaissera des Arabes l'effort:
Puis son midi perplexe rebours affaire,
Jeune ogmion abimera son fort.

For his first seven years in office Louis Philippe enjoyed high popularity with his subjects, but about the middle ("noon") of his reign, ca. 1840, his inept handling of the controversial Eastern Question began the erosion of his popular support. Though he gained Algeria for France (beating down the Arabs), his increasing tendency to put dynastic considerations ahead of the people's interest led to his ouster in the 1848 revolt. Ogmios, the Celtic Hercules, seems to be a figure of the youngish radicals who engineered the downfall of the monarchy.

Rating: 9.5

The bulk of the quatrain is straightforward and accurate, and even the Ogmios metaphor is not hard to accept.

Quatrain IX-90: The Iron Chancellor

A captain of Great Germany will come to deliver, through feigned assistance, to the King of Kings the support of Pannonia, but its revolt will cause a great flow of blood.

Un capitaine de la Grande Germanie
Se viendra rendre par simulé secours
Au Roi des Rois aide de Pannonie,
Que sa revolte fera de sang grand cours.

Since Otto Von Bismarck was the architect of the modern German state, he is aptly called a captain of Great Germany. He did secure in 1882 an alliance with Austria-Hungary ("Pannonia") under the guise of protecting Austria from Russia ("feigned assistance"). Otto's true purpose was to short-circuit any chance of an Austrian alliance with France. "The King of Kings" suits Kaiser Wilhelm I since Bismarck's machinations made him grand monarch over the many petty king-doms that composed the fragmented old Germany. It was unrest among the subject Slavic people of Austria-Hungary that triggered World War I and its "great flow of blood."

Rating: 9.5

The prevalent efforts to apply this verse to Hitler are patently strained, whereas Bismarck fits it precisely.

Quatrain IX-92: Victor Emmanuel and Garibaldi

The King will want to enter the new city. Through its enemies they will come to subdue it: Captive free to speak and act deceptively. King to be outside, he will keep far from the enemy.

Le Roi voudra en cité neuve entrer,
Par ennemies expugner l'on viendra:
Captif libre faux dire et perpetrer,
Roi dehors etre, loin d'ennemis tiendra.

The "new city," as usual, is Naples (Neapolis), which was the prime objective of Garibaldi's revolutionary army driving north from Sicily in 1860. Garibaldi's arms-length ally, King Victor Emmanuel II, steered clear of involvement in the Naples campaign until the last minute ("King to be outside"), but then met Garibaldi there to personally take possession of the conquered territory for Italy from the hands of Garibaldi himself. A genius at revolutionary warfare, Garibaldi, as the verse indicates, made effective use of intrigue and deception. He was taken "captive" and confined more than once during his Risorgimento campaigns.

Rating: 9.5

There is not much to quibble about here; this is a very strong quatrain. The background politics are fairly complex, but essentially Garibaldi and the king were cooperating, without being too obvious about it, on the reunification of Italy. (A previously unsolved verse.)

Quatrain IX-94: Czechoslovakia

Weak galleys will be joined together, fraudulent enemies the strongest on the rampart: Weak ones assailed;
Bratislava trembles. Lubeck and Meissen will take the
barbarian side.

Faibles galeres seront unies ensemble,
Ennemis faux le plus fort en rempart:
Faibles assailies Vratislaue tremble,
Lubecq et Mysne tiendront barbare part.

"Bratislava" is the major city of central Czechoslovakia while the "weak galleys" probably symbolize Slovakia and Bohemia-Moravia, joined in 1918 to comprise the Czechoslovak state. The verse, then, deals with the partition of that country in 1938. The strong and fraudulent

enemy is Hitler who claimed only to want the German-speaking Sude-
tenland but soon gobbled up the entire Czech nation. "Lubeck and
Meissen" are synecdoche for Nazi Germany, described here and elsewhere in the quatrains as "barbarian." The "weak ones" are the Czechs
and, perhaps, their equivocal British and French allies.

Rating: 7.5

The galleys metaphor seems a little too abstract though it might be justified as an oblique reference to "ships of state."

Quatrain IX-100: The Battle of the Atlantic

> Naval battle, night will be overcome, fire in the ships,
> in the West ruin. New trick, the great ship colored,
> anger to the vanquished and victory in a drizzle.

> *Navale pugne nuit sera superee,*
> *Le feu aux naves à l'Occident ruine:*
> *Rubriche neuve, la grande nef coloree,*
> *Ire à vaincu, et victoire en bruine.*

The most intriguing aspect of this verse is that it refers to night battles at sea, which were practically unknown until World War II. Radar
did "overcome" the night, and German subs often struck after dark, sil-
houetting their targets by moonlight. There is also an interesting reference to camouflage in the "great ship colored." Though German subs
and surface raiders took a massive toll on Allied shipping in the drizzly
North Atlantic, they were eventually frustrated by America's incredible
shipbuilding capacity and new sub-hunting techniques such as sonar.

Rating: 8

Since the Seer places the action "in the West," he is clearly talking about
the North Atlantic, but the verse suffers by its failure to identify the victor or the vanquished.

Quatrain X-4: The Adventures of Charles II

At midnight the leader of the army will save himself,
suddenly vanished: Seven years later, his repute
unblemished, to his return they will say not but yes.

Sur la minuit conducteur de l'armee
Se sauvera subit evanoui:
Sept ans après la fame non blamee,
A son retour ne dira onc oui.

A century ago Charles Ward saw this verse referring to the career of England's Charles II, an interpretation that holds quite well. The king was defeated by Cromwell at Worcester in September of 1651 and forced to flee. After some harrowing escapades, Charles made his way safely to France. Exactly seven years later the death of Cromwell made the restoration of the monarchy the only feasible course for England. After many months of maneuvering and negotiations Charles assumed the throne.

Rating: 8
The last line of the verse is awkwardly phrased, but the intent seems clear enough.

Quatrain X-10: A Portrait of Stalin

Stained with murder and enormous adulteries, great
enemy of the entire human race: One who will be
worse than his grandfathers, uncles or fathers, in steel,
fire, waters, bloody and inhuman.

Tache de meurte, enormes adulteres,
Grand ennemi de tout le genre humain:
Que sera pire qu'aieuls, oncles ni peres,
En fer, feu, eaux, sanguin et inhumain.

There are three obvious candidates for the subject of this verse—Napoleon, Hitler, and Stalin—but the use of the word "steel" (line four) suggests Stalin, whose name means "steel" in Russian. Line three indicates a man of barbarous heritage, which fits the Russian Stalin better than the French Bonaparte or the Austrian Hitler. And Stalin, head of world Communism and wielder of a huge nuclear arsenal, was the one that most threatened the "entire human race."

Rating: 7.5
The description, while apt, is nevertheless too general to merit a top-notch ranking.

Quatrain X-16: A Fortunate King

> Happy in the realm of France, happy in life, ignorant
> of blood, death, fury, and rapine: For a flattering
> name he will be envied, a concealed king, too much
> faith in cuisine.

> *Heureux au regne de France, heureux de vie,*
> *Ignorant sang mort fureur et rapine:*
> *Par nom flatteurs sera mis envie*
> *Roi derobé, trop de foi en cuisine.*

This one seems to be a good description of Louis XVIII, a gourmand who enjoyed a generally placid and popular reign as king of France after the monarchy was restored in the wake of the Revolution. Unlike his brothers, Louis lived out the fullness of his years and died a natural death in 1824 while still on the throne. He was given the flattering surname of Le Desire. The term "concealed king" may refer to the fact that Louis had to take refuge in Ghent during the Hundred Days of 1815.

Rating: 8
Since he lived through the French Revolution, albeit in exile, the second line of the quatrain seems something of an overstatement, but it is valid enough if applied only to Louis' reign as king.

Quatrain X-17: The Travails of Madame Royale

> The convict Queen seeing her daughter pale because
> of a sorrow locked in her breast: Lamentable cries will
> come then from Angouleme, and the marriage to the
> first cousin impeded.

> *Le Reine Ergaste voyant sa fille bleme,*
> *Par un regret dans l'estomac enclos:*
> *Cris lamentables seront lors d'Angolesme,*
> *Et au germain mariage forclos.*

Because it is so specific, this is one of the more striking of the Seer's quatrains. The "convict queen" is Marie Antoinette, held prisoner in the Temple during the Revolution. Her daughter, Madame Royale, is grieved over the misfortunes of the royal family. Royale was in fact engaged to her cousin, the Duke of Angouleme, at the time but was unable to marry him until years later (1799) due to the political tumult. Doubtless the duke lamented the situation.

Rating: 10
The verse is clear and descriptive, and the specific inclusion of Angouleme is uncanny.

Quatrain X-18: The Rise of the House of Vendome

> The house of Lorraine will make way for Vendome,
> the high put low, and the low put high: The son of
> Mammon will be elected in Rome, and the two great
> ones will be put at a loss.

> *Le rang Lorrain fera place à Vendosme,*
> *Le haut mis bas, et le bas mis en haut:*
> *Le fils de Mamon sera elu dans Rome,*
> *Et les deux grands seront mis en defaut.*

All this happened exactly as predicted. Henry de Navarre, Duke of Vendome, beat out the Duke of Guise and his brother Mayenne, scions of the prestigious House of Lorraine, for the throne of France. Henry, scorned as *le petit Bearnais,* had been a heretic Huguenot ("son of Mammon") but made a quick conversion to Catholicism in 1594 to gain papal backing ("Paris is well worth a mass"). Henry became one of the greatest kings of France while Guise and Mayenne were left to oblivion.

Rating: 10

Even the cautious Leoni categorizes this verse as "completely and indisputably successful."

Quatrain X-20: The End of the Fascists

> All the friends who will have belonged to the party,
> through the rude in letters put to death and plun-
> dered: Property up for sale at fixed price, the great
> one annihilated. Never were the Roman people so
> outraged.

> *Tous les amis qu'auront tenu parti,*
> *Pour rude en lettres mis mort et saccagé:*
> *Biens publies par fixe grand neanty,*
> *Onc Romain peuple ne fut tant outragé.*

The quatrain describes the fall of the Italian Fascist party and the outrage of ordinary Italians ("the rude in letters") when they realized Mussolini had led them to destruction. The "great one annihilated" is, of course, Mussolini himself, who was killed by his own people. Many of his cohorts lost their lives and/or their property when Il Duce's regime collapsed.

Rating: 8.5

A reasonably specific verse that nicely summarizes the situation in Italy as the Fascists fell.

Quatrain X-22: The Abdication of Edward

> On account of not wishing to consent to the divorce,
> which thereafter will be perceived as unjustified, the
> King of the Isles will be driven out by force; in his
> place put one who will have no mark of a king.

> *Pour ne vouloir consentir au divorce,*
> *Qui puis après sera connu indigne:*
> *Le Roi des Îles sera chassé par force,*
> *Mis à son lieu qui de roi n'aura signe.*

The "King of the Isles" is almost certainly the king of Britain so the verse pertains to the abdication of Edward VIII in 1936 due to the uproar over his marriage to Mrs. Simpson, a divorcee. Edward was succeeded by George VI who, though conscientious, did not cut a kingly figure as he suffered from a speech impediment. Line two suggests that it was not just Mrs. Simpson's divorce that was the problem, but the fact that it was seen as somewhat frivolous in nature, that is, lacking grounds of sufficient gravity.

Rating: 8

While the quatrain can be seen as quite correct, the first half has some vagueness about it.

Quatrain X-24: The Escape from Elba

> The captive prince conquered in Italy will pass Genoa
> by sea as far as Marseilles: through great effort over-
> come by the foreigners, safe from gunshot, barrel of
> bee's liquor.

> *Le captif prince aux Itales vaincu*
> *Passera Gennes par mer jusqu'à Marseille:*
> *Par grand effort des forens survaincu,*
> *Sauf coup de feu, baril liqueur d'abeille.*

In 1815 Napoleon escaped from the Italian island of Elba, crossed the gulf of Genoa, and landed at Cannes in southern France—actually about eighty miles east of Marseilles. He made it to Paris safely but was defeated by the great efforts of the British and the Prussians ("foreigners") at Waterloo. Noteworthy here is the fact that Napoleon adopted bees as his emblem and that the Seer makes use of this fact in another Napoleon quatrain (see IV-26, page 148). The spilling of the "bee's liquor" may represent the blood shed by Napoleon's troops at Waterloo.

Rating: 9

Despite the slight geographic imprecision, this verse has some striking aspects. It might be noted that the Latin name for Elba was Aethalia, close to the word "Italy."

Quatrain X-31: Events Around 1990

> The good Empire will come to Germany. The Ishmaelites will find open places: The asses will also want Carmania, the supporters all covered by earth.

> *Le saint Empire viendra en Germanie,*
> *Ismaelites trouveront lieux ouverts:*
> *Anes voudront aussi la Carmanie,*
> *Les soutenants de terre tous couverts.*

This is a remarkable quatrain that covers German reunification and the Iraqi wars, circa 1990. The first line describes the takeover of the Communist East German state by Christian democratic West Germany. The rest centers on contemporaneous events in the Persian Gulf area. "Ishmaelites" means Arabs—in this case the Iraqis—who found an opening into Kuwait, only to be soon disappointed. Iraq also wanted Carmania, the Iranian region at the head of the Gulf that was the scene of a lengthy war ending only in 1988. The last line is most striking. Many Iraqi soldiers were indeed "covered by earth" when the Allies employed huge bulldozing machines in their Gulf War offensive.

Rating: 9.5

Previously unsolved, this is one of the superior quatrains, quite specific and completely accurate, suffering only from some geographic scatter.

Quatrain X-34: Murat's Double-Cross

> The Gaul who will hold the empire through war, he
> will be betrayed by his minor brother-in-law: He will
> be drawn by a brash, prancing horse. The brother (in-
> law) will be hated for the deed for a long time.

> *Gaulois qu'empire par guerre occupera,*
> *Par son beau-frere mineur sera trahi:*
> *Pour cheval rude voltigeant trainera,*
> *Du fait le frere longtemps sera haï.*

A half century ago Stewart Robb noted that this verse fits the career of Joachim Murat, the most dashing cavalry officer of the Napoleonic era (hence, the "prancing horse"). "The Gaul who holds the empire through war" is plainly Napoleon himself who made Murat king of Naples. But Joachim, who had married Napoleon's sister, betrayed the emperor in 1814 in an act that Bonaparte condemned as "infamous." Though Murat did his best to make amends later, Napoleon never forgave him.

Rating: 9.5

This is a convincing quatrain except for the somewhat odd word "minor," unless the term is used in the sense of denoting subsidiary rank (Napoleon).

Quatrain X-36: Winston's Comeback

> Upon the King of the stump speaking of wars, the
> United Isle will hold him in contempt: For a good sev-
> eral years one gnawing and pillaging, though tyranny
> esteem changing in the isle.

> *Apres le Roi du souche guerres parlant,*
> *L'Ile Harmotique le tiendra à mepris:*
> *Quelques ans bons rongeant un et pillant,*
> *Par tyrannnie à l'ile changeant pris.*

The "King of the stump" has long stumped commentators, but it must refer to Winston Churchill, the greatest "stump speaker" of the twentieth century. The rest of the verse fits perfectly. Churchill, discredited in World War I, was held in widespread contempt while he railed against the Nazi menace as Hitler continued for several years to build his power and snatch neighboring territories ("gnawing and pillaging"). Britain at last realized that Churchill was right all along ("esteem changing") and elevated him to prime minister.

Rating: 9.5
Once the "King of the stump" is rightly identified, this becomes an extremely strong—indeed, virtually flawless—quatrain.

Quatrain X-39: Francis and Mary

> First son, widow, unfortunate marriage without any
> children, two Isles in discord: before eighteen, incom-
> petent age. For the other one the betrothal will take
> place while younger.

> *Premier fils veuve malheureux mariage,*
> *Sans nuls enfants deux Îles en discord:*
> *Avant dix-huit incompetant age,*
> *De l'autre près plus bas sera l'accord.*

Francis II of France, a first son, died at the age of seventeen in 1570 after an unfortunate and childless marriage to Mary Stuart, which lasted less than two years. His death and Mary's subsequent return to Britain did lead to great discord in England and Scotland (the "two Isles"). Charles IX ("the other one"), younger brother of Francis, was engaged at an even earlier age, eleven, to Elizabeth of Austria.

Rating: 9.5

This quatrain was not in print until about two years before the death of Francis. That fact and its amazing accuracy have aroused the suspicions of some critics. But it is recorded that the verse was quoted by the Venetian ambassador at the time of Francis' death.

Quatrain X-40: Richard Cromwell

> The young heir to the British realm, whom his dying
> father will have recommended: the latter dead,
> LONOLE will dispute with him and from the son the
> realm demanded.

> *Le jeune ne au regne Britannique,*
> *Qu'aura le pere mourant recommandé:*
> *Icelui mort LONOLE donnera topique,*
> *Et à son fils le regne demandé.*

On his deathbed, Oliver Cromwell nominated his son Richard to be his successor, the new Lord Protector of England. But the son lacked the track record of the father and could not command the loyalty of the army, which soon reached an agreement with parliament to restore the Stuart monarchy. Richard did not resist. "LONOLE" has not been satisfactorily solved, but it may simply mean Old London (Ole Lon.), referring to the old-guard conservatives of the English capital who favored the monarchy's return.

Rating: 8

Most analysts see this verse involving James I, his son Charles I, and Oliver Cromwell, but that interpretation gets difficult on a couple of counts. It also requires a time span of half a century for fulfillment.

Quatrain X-42: The Pax Britannica

The humane realm of Anglican offspring, it will cause
its realm to hold to peace and union: War half-captive
in its enclosure, it will cause them to long maintain
the peace.

Le regne humain d'Anglique geniture,
Fera son regne paix union tenir:
Captive guerre demi de sa cloture,
Longtemps la paix leur fera maintenir.

The century of relative peace and order following Napoleon's defeat
(1815) is noted in this quatrain. The period is associated with Britain's
era of world hegemony and hence is often called the "Pax Britannica."
It was not utopia but it was probably as close to it as the world has been
so far.

Rating: 9

With the emergence of the United States as the last superpower, there
is an intriguing chance here for a double fulfillment. If there should be
an extended period of peace under American dominance, a Pax Amer-
icana, it would also be covered by this quatrain since the United States
could be considered "Anglican offspring."

Quatrain X-43: Louis XVI

Too much good times, too much of royal goodness,
ones made and unmade, quick, sudden, neglectful:
Lightly will he believe falsely of his loyal wife; he (is)
put to death through his benevolence.

Le trop bon temps, trop de bonté royale,
Faits et defaits prompt, subit, negligence:
Leger croira faux d'epouse loyale,
Lui mis à mort par sa benevolence.

Commentators generally see this verse as a well-drawn picture of the ill-starred French king, Louis XVI. Louis at heart was an amiable character, but weak, irresolute, and neglectful. He readily believed scandalous rumors about his queen, and he was, of course, the most notable victim of the French revolutionary terror.

Rating: 8.5

This is a neat characterization that is weakened only by the lack of a geographic context.

Quatrain X-51: The Struggle for Lorraine

> Some of the lowest places of the land of Lorraine will
> be united with the Low Germans (Prussians).
> Through those of the siege (World War I), Picards,
> Normans, those of Maine, they will be rejoined to the
> cantons.

> *Des lieux plus bas du pays de Lorraine*
> *Seront des basses Allemagnes unis:*
> *Par ceux de siege Picards, Normans, du Maisne,*
> *Et aux cantons se seront reunis.*

Quite plainly, the verse is an account of France losing, then regaining, parts of Lorraine. Such a sequence did, of course, occur; France lost a segment of Lorraine to the Prussians in 1871, then retrieved the area after World War I. The word "cantons," which brings Switzerland to mind, has befuddled commentators, but cantons are also a French political subdivision—most likely the meaning here. "Picards, Normans, those of Maine" is just poesy for Frenchmen in general, i.e., those who fought in World War I.

Rating: 9

The word "siege" seems slightly curious at first, but the western front of World War I could easily be seen as a siege of France.

Quatrain X-55: A Marriage Not Made in Heaven

The unfortunate nuptials will be celebrated in great
joy, but the end unhappy. And the mother will slight
the daughter-in-law, Mary—the Phybe dead and the
daughter-in-law more pitiful.

Les malheureuses noces celebreront
En grande joie mais la fin malheureuse,
Mari et mere nore dedaigneront,
Le Phybe mort et nore plus piteuse.

Like Quatrain X-39, page 284, this appears to be a commentary on
the marriage or Francis II of France and Mary Stuart in 1558. Francis
died a couple of years later and there were no children. It is a fact that
there was considerable chafing between Mary and her mother-in-law,
Catherine de Médici. "Phybe" requires some interpretative ingenuity. It
has been suggested that "Phy" (Phi) could stand for the "F" in Francis,
and "be" means the second letter of the alphabet, ergo, "Francis II."

Rating: 8

This is a fair-to-middlin' quatrain, but the solution requires a little too
much massaging.

Quatrain X-56: The Bishop and the Admiral

The royal prelate, his bowing unduly low, a great flow
of blood will come out of his mouth: The Anglican
realm a realm pulled out of danger. One long dead as
a stump lively (again) in Tunis.

Prelat royal son baissant trop tiré,
Grand flux de sang sortira par sa bouche:
Le regne Angelique par regne respiré,
Longtemps mort vif en Tunis comme souche.

This is an unsolved quatrain which, however, can be applied well
enough to two midseventeenth-century Englishmen: Archbishop of

Canterbury Laud and the great Admiral Robert Blake. Laud was a controversial religious leader closely tied to King Charles I. Parliament had Laud beheaded in 1645. (Beheading causes blood to flow from the mouth.) "Bowing too low" may reference the fact that Laud had to beg for the ax rather than a torturous death. Shortly, Britain experienced virtual civil war but managed to soon recover ("out of danger"). Admiral Blake was severely wounded in action in 1653 and retired, but two years later Cromwell's request brought him back to shell Tunis to punish its pirates.

Rating: 8.5
It might be noted that stumps are not always as dead as they appear but occasionally sprout anew.

Quatrain X-58: France and Spain in the Thirty Years' War

In the time of mourning the feline monarch will
make war on the young Aemathien. Gaul to shake,
the bark to be in jeopardy. Marseilles to be tried, in
the West a talk.

Au temps du deuil que le felin monarque
Guerroyera le jeune Aemathien:
Gaule branler, pericliter la barque,
Tenter Phossens au Ponant entretien.

In 1635, the armies of Louis XIII pounced on Spain's Philip IV ("Aemathien"), then barely thirty years old. The French declaration of war followed by one year the murder of the great Wallenstein ("mourning") who was trying for a peaceful settlement of central Europe's Thirty Years' War. The conflict with Spain dragged on for almost a quarter of a century during which France was shaken by the Fronde revolts and the papal bark was rocked by the Jansenist heresy. France finally won a decisive victory in 1658, and peace was concluded by Louis XIV at the Isle of the Conference at the western extremity of the Franco-Spanish border. Soon after, Louis breached the walls of Marseilles and entered that city.

Rating: 9

Le Pelletier was close on this one though he saw Louis XIV as the Aemathien. Aemathia was an ancient name for Macedonia whose great king was named Philip. In the quatrains (as Leoni insisted), Aemathien always seems tied to Spain, more particularly to the Philips of Spain.

Quatrain X-65: Il Duce's Bloody Reign

> O vast Rome, thy ruin approaches, not of thy walls, of
> thy blood and substance: The one harsh in letters will
> make a very horrible notch, pointed steel driven into
> all up to the hilt.

> *O vaste Rome ta ruine s'approche,*
> *Non de tes murs, de ton sang et substancce:*
> *L'apre par lettres fera si horrible coche,*
> *Fer pointu mis à tous jusqu'au manche.*

The key to this unsolved quatrain is "harsh in letters." Mussolini's profession was journalism and he wielded an acid pen towards any that disagreed with his Fascist philosophy—before and after he took power. He eventually led Italy to ruin and cost the lives of hundreds of thousands of his countrymen, as poetically depicted in the last line. Notably, Rome suffered little physical damage in World War II ("not of thy walls") since it was declared an open city.

Rating: 8.5

It is curious how many of the Mussolini quatrains have been overlooked. Most, such as this one, are fairly obvious.

Quatrain X-66: The Alliance Against Hitler

> The chief of London through the realm of America, the
> Isle of Scotland will be tried by frost: King and Reb will
> face an Antichrist most false which will put them in the
> conflict together.

Le chef de Londres par regne l'Americh,
L'Ile d'Escosse tempiera par gelee:
Roi Reb auront un si faux Antechrist,
Que les mettra trestous dans la melee.

Previously unsolved, the essence of this fascinating quatrain lies in the third line that states that the leader of England and "Reb" (rebels—the United States) will team to confront an Antichrist. This was exactly the situation in the struggle against Hitler in World War II. The "chief of London" here is clearly Churchill whose mother was an American. Scotland, as the most northerly sector of Britain, is the area most "tried by frost," but especially during the fuel shortages of World War II.

Rating: 9.5

This is a nicely balanced verse, slightly abstract but not overly so, and entirely accurate.

Quatrain X-71: Portrait of the United States of America

The earth and air will freeze a very great water when they will come to venerate Thursday: That which will be never was it so fair. From the four parts they will come to honor it.

La terre et l'air geleront si grand eau,
Lorsqu'on viendra pour Jeudi vénérer:
Ce qui sera jamais ne fut si beau,
Des quatres parts le viendront honorer.

Analysts have guessed the subject of this clever verse though they have not entirely worked it out. The United States is the country that venerates Thanksgiving Thursday late in November, when the Great Lakes ("great water") begin to freeze over. The last two lines merely say that the United States will become the fairest of nations and will draw honor (and immigrants) from the four corners of the world.

Rating: 9

The verse is not terribly complex, but in as much as it was written over 400 years ago it still borders on brilliance.

Quatrain X-76: Nixon Gets the Gate

> The great Senate will ordain the triumph of one who
> afterwards will be vanquished, driven out. At the
> sound of the trumpet the wares of his adherents will
> be made public; the enemies expelled.

> *Le grand Senat decernera la pompe,*
> *A l'un qu'après sera vaincu, chassé:*
> *Des adherents seront à son de trompe,*
> *Biens publies, ennemis dechassez.*

The "great Senate" clearly indicates the United States Senate, and the verse well describes the case of President Richard Nixon. Nixon's 1972 election triumph was one of the greatest landslides in American history. Yet a couple of years later he was driven from office. The electoral votes are counted by the president of the Senate before the full Congress ("Senate will ordain"). The "wares made public" may specifically allude to the Nixon administration's records and files on the Watergate scandal, or, more broadly, it may be the Seer's way of saying that the public finally realizes the real nature of the Nixon administration. In the end "the enemies" (of the people) are expelled.

Rating: 8

The first two lines are quite lucid; the rest is somewhat less so. The trumpet sound would represent the media pronouncements that brought Watergate to public attention. (A previously unsolved verse.)

Quatrain X-78: A New Capital for Italy

> Sudden joy in sudden sadness, it will occur at Rome for
> the graces embraced: grief, tears, weeping, blood, excel-
> lent mirth; contrary troops surprised and trussed up.

> *Subite joie en subite tristesse,*
> *Sera à Rome aux graces embrassees:*
> *Deuil, cris, pleurs, larm. sang, excellent liesse,*
> *Contraires bandes surprises et troussees.*

This one has been a puzzler but is less murky than it first appears. It's a good account of the takeover of Papal Rome by Italy's King Victor Emmanuel in 1870. The seizure of the city was a feverishly emotional event for Italians who wanted Rome for the national capital. At the same time, Victor's "embrace" of the "graces" (churchmen) was fiercely opposed by the papal government of Pius IX. The contrary troops would be the pope's. They must have been "surprised" that the Italians would actually send forces against the Holy City. After a brief resistance, the papal troops surrendered and were taken prisoner ("trussed up").

Rating: 9
Pius IX never got over Victor's "bloody sacrilege" and railed against it to the end of his days.

Quatrain X-88: Pacification of Marseilles

> Foot(men) and Horse(men) at the second watch, they
> will make an entry, ruining everything per the sea:
> Within the port of Marseilles he will enter—tears,
> cries, and blood, never times so bitter.

> *Pieds et Cheval à la seconde veille,*
> *Feront entrée vastient tout par la mer:*
> *Dedans le poil entrera de Marseille,*
> *Pleurs, cris, et sang, onc nul temps si amer.*

This is a nicely descriptive prediction that has escaped the analysts. It describes the suppression of the Marseilles revolt against the Paris Convention during the French Revolution. In 1793 the Convention dispatched an army under Jean Carteaux to suppress the rebellion, an action that threw the citizenry of Marseilles into factional strife, bloodshed, and general disarray ("never times so bitter"). The chaos made it easy for Carteaux to seize control of the city. The maritime ruin of line two pertains to the fact that Marseilles' prosperous sea trade was devastated by the French Revolution; it took the city decades to recover.

Rating: 8.5

The phrase *vastient tout par la mer* seems less than crystal clear, but with the interpretation used here, the verse conforms well with the historical facts.

Quatrain X-89: High Tide for the Bourbons

> The walls will be converted from brick to marble,
> seven and fifty pacific years: Joy to mortals, the aque-
> duct renewed—health, abundance of fruits, joy, and
> mellifluous times.

> *De brique en marbre seront les murs reduicts,*
> *Sept et cinquante annees pacifiques:*
> *Joie aux humains, renoué l'aqueduict,*
> *Sante, grands fruits, joie et temps melifique.*

The closest fulfillment of this one is to be found in the first fifty-seven years of the reign of France's Louis XIV. These were the glory years of the monarchy when a prosperous France became the great state of Europe, culturally as well as politically. Unfortunately, Louis ruined the whole thing by getting into the disastrous War of the Spanish Succession in 1701, fifty-eight years after he became king (at the age of five). The questionable aspect in the quatrain is the word "pacific." Louis was involved before 1701 in some of the "chessboard wars" of that era, though the argument can be made that these had a negligible impact on the French people.

Rating: 8

Certainly the overall tone of the verse does reflect the times of the Grand Monarch. The *pacifique/melifique* rhyme may have been a factor here.

Quatrain X-90: The Terrible End of Ivan the Terrible

> A hundred times will the inhuman tyrant die, in his
> place put one wise and moderate. The entire Senate will
> be under his hand. He will be vexed by a rash scoundrel.

> *Cent fois mourra le tyran inhumain,*
> *Mis à son lieu savant et debonnaire,*
> *Tour le Senat sera dessous sa main,*
> *Faché sera par malin temeraire.*

Commentators have hatched a couple of not-too-convincing scenarios for this verse. In actuality, it fits Ivan the Terrible, who died a hundred deaths after he killed his own favorite son (Ivan) in a fit of rage. The deed threw the czar into a sink of remorse and despair, and he died three years later (1584), a hermit monk. He was succeeded by Boris Godunov, whose rule was remarkably enlightened and moderate. Godunov was plagued in his last year by a pretender to the throne, a thorough scoundrel who claimed to be Ivan's dead son, Demetrius. The "Senate" is most likely the Russian Duma, entirely dominated by Godunov.

Rating: 9.5
The "Senate" might also be taken as the national assembly that elected Godunov as czar by a unanimous vote.

Quatrain X-91: A Pain in the Papacy

> In the year 1609, Roman clergy, early in the year you
> will hold an election: Of one gray and black issued
> from Campagna, never was there one so wicked as he.

> *Clergé Romain l'an mil six cents et neuf,*
> *Au chef de l'an feras election:*
> *D'un gris et noir de la Compagne issu,*
> *Qui onc ne fut si malin.*

This is a dated verse, rejected as a failure, that really has considerable merit. There actually was a conspicuously bad pope elected near the designated year, and he was born in the Roman Campagna. Arrogant, stubborn, and impractical, Paul V provoked severe disputes with England, France, and the Italian states that cost the Church much support. He also funneled huge sums of money to his relatives on the side. "Gray and black" may just refer to his hair color and his character. Though elected four years earlier than predicted here, it is remarkable that most scholars believe Christ's birth was actually in 4 or 5 B.C.—which puts Paul's election at just about A.D. 1609 in real terms.

Rating: 7.5

The phrase "early in the year" would be correct if Nostradamus is referring to the zodiacal year, which starts March 21, so this is likely enough. Paul was elected in early May.

Quatrain X-100: The British Empire

> The great empire will be for England, the all-powerful
> one, for more than three hundred years: Great forces will
> pass by sea and land; the Lusitanians (Portuguese) will
> not be satisfied.

> *Le grand empire sera par Angleterre,*
> *Le pempotam des an plus de trois cents;*
> *Grandes copies passer par mer et terre,*
> *Les Lusitains n'en seront pas contents.*

An unusually plain verse, this one predicts a great empire for England lasting over three centuries—right on the mark. Britain's empire-building era began in the early 1600s and peaked in the wake of World War I, i.e, the 1920s. It disintegrated following World War II, but in the Empire's heyday—roughly the century after Waterloo—it constituted the only real superpower (*pempotam*), moving great forces by land and sea. The unfathomed last line is actually very good. The Portuguese were the great rivals of Britain in India and the Far East but were routed by the British in a series of naval battles in the Indian Ocean in the early 1600s.

Rating: 9.5

Nostradamus ends his work appropriately with a beautifully successful verse that could arguably rate a 10.

Chapter 4

COMMENTARY ON THE FUTURE

T he great conundrum in prophecy is the same as that involved in the hypothesis of time travel; both concepts inevitably seem to lead into paradoxes. In the case of prophecy, if a seer predicts some catastrophe and the prediction is taken as a warning, which then diverts the very event predicted, was the seer right or not? There can really be no answer, because there can be no certainty about what might have happened if the prediction had never been made.

Ironically, it seems the success of prophets often depends to an extent on their predictions being ignored. Indeed, this consideration may have dawned on Nostradamus himself and could be one reason he went to some lengths to disguise his forecasts. Fortunately for the batting averages of most prophets, including the biblical ones, their auguries usually fell on deaf ears.

Another facet in the prophetic diamond: If there is a deep, wide-spread, even religious kind of faith in the words of a prophecy, that very belief may make it more likely to happen. The Muslim conviction regarding the advent of the mahdi is a case in point. Several pretenders to the mantle of the mahdi capitalized on this faith to launch their careers. If one day a successful revitalizer of Islam does arise, he will owe much of his triumph to the mahdi prophecy. Would the prophecy then be authentic, or merely self-fulfilling?

There is no overwhelming religious faith in the forecasts of Nostradamus, and his esoteric phraseology has largely prevented the key players in history from anticipating his forecasts. However, in the case of the predicted Mediterranean War, the Seer's words are uncommonly clear, detailed, and unequivocal. So much so, that if world leaders heeded Nostradamus they might well be able to devise means and methods to avoid the realization of most of these predictions, either by policy decisions or judicious use of their assorted intelligence and military agencies. It seems that the Mediterranean War is something of a special case that the Prophet evidently considered to be of some particular importance.

Clearly enough, events are now moving in the direction foreseen by Nostradamus. Militant Islam is snowballing down the slopes of history, heading for an eventual collision with the West. This does not mean the conflict is inevitable, as the Seer himself would attest. But, assuredly, it does mean that a shrewd perception of events and the right responses, overt or covert, at the right time will be needed to avoid the ravages of yet another major war.

Like the prophets of old Israel, Nostradamus would seem to prefer that his warnings be taken to heart even if at some expense to his own prophetic prestige. Indeed, it is an interesting speculation whether the prime purpose of the *Centuries* might have been to admonish the world of the dangers of a final confrontation between the Islamic and Western societies. Otherwise, why are these particular quatrains so manifestly clear while most others are purposely shrouded?

Is there something uniquely portentous about the prospective Mediterranean War to rate this specialized treatment?

Perhaps, there is.

A particularly arresting aspect of the future quatrains is that they seem to set the stage for the end-time prophecies of the Bible. The famous forecasts of Ezekiel 38 are popularly interpreted to mean a future Russian invasion of the Middle East and Palestine itself. Nostradamus does not say anything about an attack on Israel, but he sees Russia defeating or helping to defeat Turkey, Iran, and Iraq in the Mediterranean War. These successes would obviously establish Russia as a major player in the Middle East. In fact, the Russian entry into the war would likely be motivated by the prospect of extending Russia's sphere of influence to the Indian Ocean, a long-cherished national dream. The very fact that Russia becomes a Middle Eastern presence clearly increases the chances of Israeli-Russian conflict and fulfillment of Ezekiel 38.

But the probabilities do not seem to favor a Russian-Israeli collision growing directly out of the Mediterranean War. For one thing, a motive for a Russian assault on Israel does not spring readily to mind. It is feasible, then, to view the events of Ezekiel 38 as being farther down the time line, maybe even by centuries.

Still, improbable things have a way of happening in the turbulent wakes of wars. Who thought the Treaty of Versailles would be the midwife of Nazism? Who foresaw the British Empire falling apart after its great victory in World War II?

What if the Israelis, seeing the surrounding Arab states flattened in the Mediterranean War, read the situation as a golden opportunity to expand Israel's rule over all the lands granted to the Jews by scripture? By then the Russians would have replaced the radical Muslim governments of Turkey, Iran, and Iraq with "friendly" regimes and might decide to cement their new power in the Middle East (and gain prestige throughout the Muslim world) by beating back the Israelis. This scenario, while not the most likely, is far from being out of the question.

Russia would probably be joined by troops from its new satellites of Iran, Turkey, and Iraq in the combat against Israel. These nations are specifically mentioned as accompanying tribes from north of the Black Sea (the Russians) in Ezekiel 38: "Persia" is, of course, Iran, while "Kush" was a name sometimes applied to Iraq, and "Magog" has affinities to Asia Minor (Turkey).

In short, there is some prospect, though it is far from certain, that the Mediterranean War leads straight into Ezekiel's end-time prophecies. And even if it does not do so directly, the war's outcome sets up the basic parameters for some more distant Middle Eastern Armageddon—if, in fact, Armageddon is what Ezekiel is talking about. (Biblical prophecy is murky enough that we cannot be sure Armageddon and Gog's invasion of Palestine are the same event.)

The Ten Nations of the Antichrist

A second portentous aspect of the Mediterranean War is that it could well be the fulfillment of Revelation 17. This widely known and oft-quoted chapter predicts the rise of a ten-nation anti-Christian coalition that will be led by the final Antichrist himself (the beast), a sort of reincarnated Nero. The prophecy is obviously related to the popular ancient belief that the dead Emperor Nero would one day return to retake Rome. Significantly, he was supposed to come with his armies out of the East—Parthia (Iran) to be exact. Iran has already emerged as the leading force of the new Islamic militance. According to this chapter of Revelation, the ten nations will war against the Lamb (Christ, Christendom) and will attack and burn Rome. As we have seen, this is just what Nostradamus predicts the militant Muslims will do in the Mediterranean War.

Also, there will be about ten Muslim nations engaged in the Mediterranean conflict: Iran, Iraq, Turkey, Egypt, Tunis, Algeria, Morocco, and Albania. They are specifically indicated in the quatrains along with the new Bosnian Islamic nation. Azerbaijan is strongly hinted at. Some Bible interpreters see the ten nations of Revelation 17 as the members of the European Union, but this does not work well since there are already twelve nations (1994) in the Union and soon there will be sixteen. Beyond that, it is hard to imagine the nations of western Europe sacking and burning Rome. Even in the fury of World War II, Rome was declared an open city and escaped the havoc almost unscathed.

The last great Antichrist is probably not a west European at all, as posited by popular interpreters (on rather flimsy evidence); rather, he is one of the leaders of the future Islamic coalition. The new mahdi of Future Quatrain X-75, page 31, or the mighty warrior of Future Quatrain V-55, page 25, are the two obvious prospects.

It is noteworthy that chapter 13 of Revelation portrays the Antichrist in dualistic terms, a secular leader accompanied by a false prophet or false religion. This symbolism is accurate for the Antichrist Nero where the false religion is emperor worship. It would also be accurate for the modern antichrists such as Hitler and Stalin, the false prophets being Mussolini, originator of fascism, and Marx, the prophet of statist Communism.

A parallel can be drawn, too, in the case of early Islam with Mohammed as the prophet and the conquering Caliph Walid I as the secular Antichrist. It might be expected that the familiar pattern will hold into the future, i.e., the mighty Arab of Future Quatrain V-55, is to be the new sword of Islam and the new Mahdi its trumpet.

———

It should be evident soon after the turn of the new millennium whether events are following the Seer's script. Meanwhile, it should be remembered that Nostradamus did not regard the future as immutable, which in itself implies that he could not have been infallibly accurate.

In fact, we see in the specifically dated quatrains clear evidence of an element of indeterminance. While most of the exact dates in the *Centuries* are on the mark or very close to it, there are exceptions. In Quatrain X-91, page 295, the Seer appears to miss the election of Pope Paul V by four years. In Quatrain VIII-71, page 250, he is six years too early on the date of the heresy declaration against Copernican theory. Though these errors are relatively minor, they do demonstrate an irreducible element of uncertainty in the prophecies. The dated verses, then, as well as many undated ones, indicate that the future foreseen by Nostradamus has worked out approximately, but not exactly, according to prediction.

This variability could be due to unclear perceptions by the Seer or to the function of the free will factor over time—or both. In the end, then, even the best of prophets perceives the future only by a flickering light.

There is yet another consideration on a more cosmological level. If scripture is correct in its portrayal of man's relationship with the Divine, then our fate is almost never etched in granite. Various biblical books, notably Job and Jonah (both obviously Midrashic), plainly preach that God may sometimes alter his intention in response to changes in human conduct. If so, there is little that can be classed as absolutely inevitable.

———————

Even with all these factors considered, the future quatrains of Nostradamus leave us with a strong impression that human history is on the verge of some fateful turn. The omens and portents are that something apocalyptic comes our way. We may be engulfed by it, but there seems a chance to avert it—depending, perhaps, on how much attention we give to the words of the world's preeminent seer.

BIBLIOGRAPHY

Aubrey, Octave. *The Second Empire*. Philadelphia & New York: J. B. Lippincott Co., 1940.

Cheetham, Erika. *The Prophecies of Nostradamus*. New York, NY: Berkley Books, 1981.

Collins, Larry, and Dominique LaPieffe. *Is Paris Burning?* New York, NY: Simon & Schuster, 1965.

Conquest, Robert. *Stalin: Breaker of Nations*. New York, NY: Viking Penquin, 1991.

Deakin, F. W. *The Brutal Friendship: Mussolini. Hitler and the fall of Italian Fascism.* New York, NY: Harper & Row, 1962.

de Jonge, Alex. *The Life and Times of Grigorii Rasputin*. New York, NY: Coward, McCann & Geoghegan, 1982.

Dupuy, Trevor N., and R. Ernest. *The Harper Encyclopedia of Military History.* New York, NY: Harper Collins, 1993.

Garrison, Omar V. *The Encyclopedia of Prophecy*. Secaucus, NJ: Citadel Press, 1979.

Hitler, Adolph. *Mein Kampf.* Boston, MA: Houghton Mifflin Co., 1971.

Kitchen, Martin. *The Cambridge Illustrated History of Germany.* Cambridge University Press, 1996.

Kronk, Gary. *Comets and Meteor Showers.* American Meteor Society sponsored Web Site, AMSmeteors.org. 1999.

Leoni, Edgar. *Nostradamus and His Prophecies.* New York, NY: Bell Publishing Co., 1982.

Mahoney, Irene. *Madame Catherine.* New York, NY: Coward, McCann & Geoghegan, Inc., 1975.

Moore, Patrick. *Atlas of the Universe.* New York, NY: Cambridge University Press, 1998.

Noorbergen, Rene. *Nostradamus Predicts the End of the World.* New York, NY: Pinnacle Books, Inc., 1982.

Plaidy, Jean. *Mary, Queen of Scots.* London: Robert Hale & Co., 1975.

Prieditis, Arthur. *The Fate of Nations.* St. Paul, MN: Llewellyn Publications, 1974.

Robb, Stewart. *Nostradarnus and the End of Evils Begun.* Stamford, CT: Longmeadow Press, 1991.

————. *Nostradamus on Napoleon, Hitler and the Present Crisis.* New York, NY, 1942.

Salisbury, Harrison. *The 900 Days: the Siege of Lenningrad.* New York, NY: Harper & Row, 1969.

Shepherd, William R. *Shepherd's Historical Atlas.* New York, NY: Barnes & Noble, 1976.

Thompson, James W. *The Wars of Religion in France 1559-76.* Chicago, IL: University of Chicago Press, 1907.

Thorne, J. O., and T. C. Collocott, ed. *Chambers Biographical Dictionary.* London & New York: Cambridge University Press, 1974.

Ward, Charles A. *Oracles of Nostradamus.* New York, NY: Charles Scribner's Sons, 1940.

Watt. "Diplomatic History 1930-39." In *New Cambridge Modern History, Vol. XII: The Shifting Balance of World Forces.* London & New York: Cambridge University Press, 1968.

Woolfolk, Joanna Martine. *The Only Astrology Book You'll Ever Need.* Lanham, MD: Scarborough House, 1990.

Young, Peter Brig., ed. *Atlas of the Second World War.* New York, NY: G.P. Putnam Sons, 1974.

INDEX

Index

☾ REACH FOR THE MOON

Llewellyn publishes hundreds of books on your favorite subjects! To get these exciting books, including the ones on the following pages, check your local bookstore or order them directly from Llewellyn.

ORDER BY PHONE
- Call toll-free within the U.S. and Canada, 1-800-THE MOON
- In Minnesota, call (651) 291-1970
- We accept VISA, MasterCard, and American Express

ORDER BY MAIL
- Send the full price of your order (MN residents add 7% sales tax) in U.S. funds, plus postage & handling to:

    Llewellyn Worldwide
    P.O. Box 64383, Dept. 1-56718-816-7
    St. Paul, MN 55164–0383, U.S.A.

POSTAGE & HANDLING
(For the U.S., Canada, and Mexico)
- $4.00 for orders $15.00 and under
- $5.00 for orders over $15.00
- No charge for orders over $100.00

We ship UPS in the continental United States. We ship standard mail to P.O. boxes. Orders shipped to Alaska, Hawaii, The Virgin Islands, and Puerto Rico are sent first-class mail. Orders shipped to Canada and Mexico are sent surface mail.

International orders: Airmail—add freight equal to price of each book to the total price of order, plus $5.00 for each non-book item (audio tapes, etc.).

Surface mail—Add $1.00 per item.

Allow 2 weeks for delivery on all orders.
Postage and handling rates subject to change.

DISCOUNTS
We offer a 20% discount to group leaders or agents. You must order a minimum of 5 copies of the same book to get our special quantity price.

FREE CATALOG

Get a free copy of our color catalog, *New Worlds of Mind and Spirit*. Subscribe for just $10.00 in the United States and Canada ($30.00 overseas, airmail). Many bookstores carry *New Worlds*—ask for it!

Visit our website at www.llewellyn.com for more information.

Violent Weather
Predictions 2000–2001

Countdown to Cataclysm

JENNIFER LAWSON

Worried about Y2K? Well, listen to this: the year 2000 is also expected to bring severe weather patterns that will affect many countries. *Violent Weather Predictions 2000–2001* is the first and only book to predict weather and seismic forecasts for the entire planet, using the scientifically based theory of Astrometeorology.

Weather charts foretell fierce weather, powerful earthquakes, and possible volcanic eruptions during the months of April, May, August, and October. As the new century approaches, more focus will be on the planetary alignment of May 5, 2000, when six planets will form a straight line for the first time in 6,000 years. This grand alignment will occur at a time of sunspot maxima—the perfect combination to trigger a violent earthquake. The predicted location? Charts point to northern California, near the city of San Francisco.

1-56718-414-6
192 pp., 5³⁄₁₆ x 8 $9.95

To order, call 1-800-THE MOON
Prices subject to change without notice